Mixed Blood

Reconciling My Colonial Family's History in the Dutch East Indies

Astrid Berg, PhD

Cover design by Astrid Berg

Printed in the United States of America

First printing: July 2021

ISBN: 9798526701525

Dedication

For my son and grandchildren, nieces and nephews, and the generations to come. And for my ancestors—I hope that bringing to light your hardships will integrate the intergenerational wounds towards healing.

Also by Astrid Berg:

Imaginal As Cradle of the Divine: Engaging the Imaginal in Non-Traditional Spiritual Practices

Finding the Work You Love: A Career Guide for Women

Finding the Work You Love: Audio Tape of Guided Imagery for Finding Life Purpose and Balance

Fishing for Values: Values Clarification Game

Creatavision: Exercises for Counselors

Career Metamorphosis: Career Development through Self-Understanding

Table of Contents

SECTION I – SHADOW OF THE INDIES   1

INTRODCUTION – BEING INDISCH   3

CHAPTER ONE – MY FATHER IS SHRINKING   9

CHAPTER TWO – OUR FATHER THE HERO   15

CHAPTER THREE – MY FATHER'S DAEAMONS   21

SECTION II – WEST MEETS EAST   29

CHAPTER FOUR – FROM MESTIZO TO INDISCH   31

CHAPTER FIVE – FRANSZ JOSEPH – THE DUELIST   39

CHAPTER SIX – HELENA FALCK AND THE WHITE GLOVE   51

CHAPTER SEVEN – SARINA AT THE WARUNG   65

CHAPTER EIGHT – FRANSZ MEETS HELENA   71

CHAPTER NINE – A CULMINATION OF EVENTS   83

CHAPTER TEN – LINTANG FROM SOERABAJA   93

CHAPTER ELEVEN – FURLOUGH AND AFTERMATH   105

SECTION III – INDISCH COMMUNITY   113

CHAPTER TWELVE – FAMILY LIFE WITH CHRISTINA   115

CHAPTER THIRTEEN – JOHAN JACOB -

SALUTE THE FLAG IN THE NAME OF OUR KING   121

CHAPTER FOURTEEN – JOSEPHINE SUSANA PAULINA ABELS –

AN ENIGMA   127

Chapter fifteen – Adele Ravenswaaij – The Orphan   141

Chapter sixteen – Adele and Adriaan –

The Unlikely Couple   151

SECTION IV – MY GRANDPARENTS

AND FATHER'S GENERATIONS   163

Chapter seventeen – Fritz and Sok – Opposites Attract   165

Chapter eighteen – Anton – From Loner to Leader   177

Chapter nineteen – World War II – Prisoners and Spies   191

Chapter Twenty – Ton and Anne –

Restless and Adventurous   211

SECTION V – INTEGRATION TOWARDS HEALING   229

Chapter Twenty-one – Unleashing the Dark Side   231

Addendum – Indonesian History, Georgraphy and culture   247

Afterword   259

Glossary   265

Berg Geneology   271

References   277

Images   285

Section I – Shadow of the Indies

With wajang, or shadow-puppet theater, there is a lingering connection with ancestors, life cycles, and with the boundary between the seen and unseen world.

Introduction

Being Indisch

    A couple of years ago my mother made a comment about my disposition, "I never realized before, but you're more *Indisch* than your brother." *Indisch* and *Indo* are terms used for persons of Dutch (or other European) and Indonesian heritage. The genetic mix between the Dutch and people of the Indonesian archipelago is a result of the 350 years of occupation by the Netherlands. Both Indo and Indisch can be applied by anyone referring to those of mixed heritage, whereas Indo—with the same meaning—tends to be an expression favored by other Indos to describe themselves or others of mixed heritage. I will use Indisch and Indo interchangeably.

    While my mother did not mean to criticize, I felt a pang of discomfort. It was shame. I wanted to deny it, argue with her. In calling me Indisch, my mother was not intending to be critical. However, in my upbringing the term implied being less than or being *other*—referring to the hot tempered, slow, passive, and (too) easy-going nature of my Dutch-Indonesian relatives. These were the characteristics my mother used

---

[1] Astrid, age 3.

3

inadvertently in judgment of the Dutch-Indonesian family she married into. As children do without parents realizing, I overheard these comments.

In many ways, my mother is accepting, empathic, and open minded. Yet, she came from a generation and a place in which class and racial discrimination was common. It's not that long ago that science 'proved' how people of non-white races had smaller brains, hence were less intelligent and had weaker morals. The overlay of Christian prejudices regarding those of other beliefs also had a strong hold on culture. Being a person of her times, my mother discriminated, however subtly. It was implied that I was better off than my older half-siblings because I had less Indonesian blood and because I looked Caucasian.

My Indisch father, whose external behavior was quite western, showed mixed preferences. He told us many stories portraying the cultural differences between Dutch and Indisch and/or Indonesians. One of these referred to the difference in habits of hospitality. He reflected: *At our home, or any Indisch home, there would always be a guest at the dinner table, or someone stopping by. There was plenty of food prepared assuming others might join. However, if you come to a Dutch person's home at dinnertime, the polite will ask you to wait in the parlor while they have their dinner, and others will send you home.*

I'll add that it would have been considered rude in the Netherlands to visit at dinnertime unannounced.

Indos (Dutch-Indonesians)

My father, with Javanese, Dutch, German, and French heritage, was born and lived on Java in what was then Dutch East Indies (*Nederlands-Indië*) until his mid thirties. The place and circumstances familiar to my mixed blood, Dutch-Indonesian relatives can never be revisited except through story, image, and imagination. "The Java we knew no longer exists," my Indo elders would say. My father, along with many other Indos, repatriated to the Netherlands after the *Bersiap* period (1945-1949)—the Indonesian independence movement from the Dutch that occurred after World War II. Many of the Dutch-Indonesians were neither completely at home with the European culture in which they were raised, nor with their indigenous ancestry. While they were educated alongside full-blooded European classmates, learning western history, philosophy, European languages, they were not equal

4

to their Caucasian contemporaries. The *totoks* were those with only European ancestry or Dutch born and who lived in the Dutch East Indies for numerous years. Another term also used was *belanda* or *blanda*, referring to blonde or light. The totoks, and less so the Indisch along with the wealthy Javanese, ruled most of the indigenous peasant population. The three groups: the locals (*inlander, inlandse*), the mixed Indonesian and European group (*Indisch or Indos*), and the Europeans (*totoks* or *blandas*) each had their own society. The Indonesian aristocrats and wealthy landowners carried out what is similar to a feudal system, and the remaining Indonesians, or lower classes, were treated as such. There was also the category of *Vreemde Oosterlingen* (Other Easterners), which included Chinese and Arabs. They often were merchants. Each group had their own legal system. In the colonial communities, Indos most often dated other Indos. A *blonde* (blonde, light-skinned, or Caucasian-looking) Indo might get away with dating a totok.[2] Parents insisted that their children marry within their sub-cultures—that is, dark-skinned with dark-skinned, light skinned with other light-skinned, etc. There was also the difference in religion. The Europeans were Christian and the Indonesians were Moslems. However, as you will see, not everything unfolds as the traditions prescribed.

My father, a career military officer (required of first born male sons in his family), was a pilot for the *Koninklijk Nederlands-Indies Leger, KNIL* (Royal East Indies Army). He was a prisoner in Fukuoka, Japan for three and a half years during World War II. With 65,000 members of Dutch, Indonesian, and Dutch-Indonesian heritage, the KNIL was disbanded in 1950 after Indonesia officially became independent. The Indonesians and Dutch-Indonesians in the KNIL were given the option of joining the Indonesian military or to be transferred to the Dutch military. As it became clear that their Indisch lifestyle would radically change, most of the colonials (Dutch and Indisch) left Indonesia, some to North[3] and South American continents, Australia, and other places. Most went to the Netherlands, a place many had not seen except in pictures or paintings, to repatriate. The exodus had begun in the late 1940s and continued into the 1970s.

---

[2] All these terms will be expounded upon as the stories ensue.
[3] 18.5 percent departed for the United States; an estimated 60,000 immigrated to the United States in the 1960s.

They departed with the reality that they would never return to what they considered home. Nearly nine years of war and three to four years in internment or prison of war camps had traumatized these refugees. Most lost their homes and family belongings once during Japanese occupation and then again upon leaving Indonesia. Many lost family members through disease, starvation, or murder while they were imprisoned in the camps by the Japanese or during the Bersiap period.

The first generation offspring (like myself) living in the Netherlands or in other places where they emigrated may have heard some of this story, but many of the refugees did not want to speak of their experiences of war, abuse, losses, and confinement. There was little opportunity to grieve, and the focus was on looking ahead and forgetting the horrific past. They accepted life in their new homes and quietly assimilated.

Like many refugees, most Indisch took on new professions and jobs that were less advanced than their education and prior work experience. The Indisch experienced the racism common in those times. In addition, the Netherlands was recovering from five years of German occupation and faced a serious lack of housing. All in all, the experience the Eurasian colonists had of their 'fatherland' was dismal and inhospitable. The children, whether born in Indonesia or later in the Netherlands, suffered as a consequence of the unprocessed and repressed pain and suffering of their parents and grandparents.

Upon arrival in the Netherlands, the Indisch came to realize that the Dutch had not been educated about their colonial conquests (as history often neglects the ugly feats of those writing the history). For instance, the Dutch were amazed that these so-called 'Indonesians' had Dutch heritage and education. Many were unaware that the refugees (with Dutch nationality but often with dark skin, eyes, and hair) spoke fluent Dutch, had 'civilized' manners, and had obtained a better western education than the average Dutch in the Netherlands. Many of the Indisch had some connection to their Indonesian roots; however, most identified themselves as Euro- or Dutch-Indonesian or with the colonial rulers.

On a humorous note, a booklet comparing Dutch and Indisch etiquette[4] was developed and handed out to the Indisch women who came to Holland[5] in the early 1960s so that they could adapt to the customs of their new country. For instance, it suggested:

How do I receive guests?

In the Indies, not between 2 and 4 o'clock. In some circles it is not uncommon to receive visitors in clean pajamas. This is influenced by the climate. After a fresh bath wearing clean, neatly ironed pajamas, it is best to receive (not officially).

In the Netherlands, it's socially desirable to visit between 3 and 5 o'clock. Receiving guest in pajamas is not known here. Pajamas are to sleep in and luxury pajamas can be worn in the house, but one prefers not to receive visitors in them.

Here is another:

In the Indies: Cookies are usually presented in a small container (because of the heat they easily become soft and attract ants). Tasty, cozy sweets, such as dried plums, manisans and quince, and homemade cookies are very much appreciated and offered in large quantities. This is also related to our hospitality and our easy way of life.

In the Netherlands, the cookies are usually arranged on a dish, sometimes with chocolates or other delicacies. The small amounts offered may come across as stingy, but this is not how it should be interpreted.

My father repatriated in the Netherlands with his wife, Louise, and two children, Virginia and Danny. Luckier than many, he was able to continue

---

[4] *Fragmenten uit: Djangan Loepah! Huishoudelijke wenken voor gerepartrieerden.* (Jan. 1960-Dec.1961). Den Haag, The Netherlands: Comite van Kerkelijk en Particulier initiatief voor Sociale Zorg t.b.v. gerepatrieerden (C.C.K.P.).
[5] Term used during this historical period in the Dutch East Indies. Now correct use is the Netherlands.

his career with the Dutch military where he served as a test pilot for equipment received from the US and later with a NATO assignment in Fontainebleau, France working in intelligence. Sadly, Louise soon died after an operation. This left their three-year-old daughter and four-year-old son without a mother.

My relationship with my father was difficult. It took many years of therapy to untangle and even more years trying to connect to him. I understood that some of his inability to be intimate came out of his past, effects of colonialism, experiences in prison camp, and the aftermath of having to leave his home. And, as in all families, there is the legacy, the 'sins of the father,' or the unconscious shadow that is passed from generation to generation. Part of my healing process is to tell the stories of my ancestors that were an integral part of the colonial period in the Dutch-East Indies. My father was a storyteller. I have five hours of narratives of him sharing his experiences growing up in *Nederlands-Indië* as well as his experiences as a POW in Japan, during the Bersiap period, and repatriating to the Netherlands.

My curiosity about my Javanese roots did not appear until I was in my forties. It took visiting Indonesia and seeing the faces of my denied ancestry for that curiosity to grow into an ache. Who were these unknown relatives? I began my genealogical research in the Netherlands. Thus far, no names of *inlanders* (indigenous to Indonesia) appear in any records. In my quest, I read many historical books, fiction and non-fiction, and psychosocial commentaries about the colonial period and the Indisch and the Indonesian cultures. These offered not only facts but also the ambiance of the colonial lifestyle and that of the indigenous peoples. In addition, I have transcribed and translated my father's stories and thirty pages in letters written by my Aunt Mildred, his sister, about the family. These are integrated into the stories of their and their parents' generations. My siblings, cousins, and my mother have helped fill in some of the blanks. The stories about my great-great-grandparents and great-grandparents are partially fictionalized based on what typically occurred in the Dutch East Indies during the historical periods between 1830 and 1950s. And, as what often occurs with the imagination, eventually the characters took over and guided the writing.

Chapter One

My Father Is Shrinking

I had a dream that my father was shrinking. I was in a wingback chair with him sitting on my lap when he slowly reduced to the size of a six-month old baby. Six months later, we learned that my father had Alzheimer's. I made several visits that ensuing year to where he and my mother lived in Las Vegas. He was eighty-eight and I was fifty years old.

The experiences of being with my father as he faded were bittersweet. In the mornings, he was docile and grateful. In the afternoons, he would become agitated, sometimes angry about being treated like an invalid. At breakfast, still groggy, I'd put the spoon of oatmeal to his mouth. With eyes closed, he accepted the mouthful, chewing slowly. He used to tell us when we were kids that we must chew thirty-two times. I scraped off the bit of oatmeal left on his lips and chin with the spoon. Once he swallowed, I offered another bite.

---

[6] Papa (Anton) about 85 years old

He slept most of the morning in his white leather recliner. In the afternoon, we looked at old photos that I had scanned onto my computer of KNIL (Royal East Indies Army) buddies, classmates, or high school girl friends. Or we would line up pictures of five or more generations of family members to spot the resemblances. We could zoom-in close and look at those faded black and whites to see the faces of *Opa en Oma* (grandpa and grandma). We could see more clearly those in the group school pictures or at his cousin's wedding. And there he was with Emmy Tibot, his high school sweetheart. I know all the stories well, yet I am glad to have them on cassette-tape, now digitized.

After his afternoon nap, *Pap* (or *Papa,* Dutch for dad) asked for his Mercedes. He always liked automobiles: the Edsel was totaled when he ran into a train; the old Peugeot became Danny's (my brother) first car; the blue Mercedes, my favorite; the BMW he had shipped from Europe to the States; the silver Toronado, too big to park on the streets of The Hague; and his all-time favorite was the souped-up Cougar, which he later had painted orange. The recently acquired wheelchair had been christened 'the Mercedes.' I'd tease by asking him if it wasn't a BMW. "No. A Mercedes." His response was firm.

We played the Thielman Brothers, a Dutch-Indonesian rock and roll band, on the CD player. He listened with his eyes closed, sometimes singing along. I sat in the chair opposite, and he told some of the stories about his encounters with Andy Thielman.

"You know, Andy was never accepted in Holland," he mused. "But they became very popular in Germany. They were number one at many song festivals in Germany, Belgium, and Denmark."

I nodded; I knew the story well.

"I understand how Andy felt. It was the same for me." My father related to Andy, this very talented and misunderstood Indisch man.

Getting Dressed

It's interesting to see what remains important at the end of one's life. At eighty-eight, barely able to walk, in adult diapers, body withering away, Pap remained fastidious about his wardrobe. One day, when preparing to visit a

10

notary, *Mam* (or *Mama*, Dutch for Mom) had picked out his clothes and put them on the bed, but he ignored her and headed for his closet to pick out something himself. Hardly able to stand and walk on his own, he stood in front of his closet unhurriedly looking through his slacks and sweaters.

"I'll wear this," he asserted while handing me a red sweater and tan slacks.

Mam entered from the other room all in a tizzy and flustered that we might be late. After witnessing his pace, I already knew and had surrendered. Mam was at another closet pulling out shirts for his approval.

"No, that doesn't match. Yes, that one," he commanded.

I stood next to him for fear that he might fall. It would be the red button-down shirt with red sweater and tan slacks. Then Mam looked for a belt.

I flashed back twenty-five years to an image of dressing my son. I'd bunch the pant legs or sleeves to make it easier to get the legs and arms through, slowly one limb at a time. I'd be careful with his stiff arm. As his feet were quite swollen from diabetes, we located the largest pair of shoes. "Okay, foot in, now push. Push again. There we go. Again, push down." Man size feet instead of a toddler's. I helped him stand. I had learned to allow him to arrange his shirt and the diaper so it was comfortable and not bunched up. It had to be just so. He then reached for his belt that he buckled himself. I pictured my son as a toddler vying for autonomy. Meanwhile, Mam hovered in hope that she could speed things up. I helped pull down the sweater over his slacks.

"Are you ready? Is it comfortable? You look pretty sharp." I meant it.

He offered a grin, but he wasn't ready. He shuffled to the bathroom. Even though he looked fine, he methodically combed his hair as he looked at himself in the mirror. That was my Papa.

11

April 24, 2006

Dear Papa,

On my last day in Vegas, I had an errand to do on my way to visit you in the nursing home. I got slightly off course on the way and was disappointed that I had lost time with you. When I finally reached the nursing home, walking down its halls, I wanted to run.

When I got to your wing and found the room number, your bed was stripped. 'Where are you?' I thought, worried. I rushed to inquire at the nursing station. The nurse, too casual for my liking, told me to look in the activity room. But you weren't there. I didn't think so. You weren't one for doing activities. I rushed back. 'Where are you?' The hallways were like a maze. I hurried to the other end of the hall to enquire at the other nursing station. And then I saw from the corner of my eyes, your hands. Those Indisch hands, now old and permanently discolored because your skin is so thin.

"Papa!" I called with relief.

They had you propped in a lounge chair with wheels. Your eyes were closed. Your hands were cold, and one was hanging lifelessly.

"Hallo, Papa. Ik ben er. (I am here.) Astrid." I spoke in Dutch, more familiar and intimate.

You woke and smiled, the smile of a baby—happy in the moment. This part of you was always there, but I had a hard time noticing. Then you fell asleep. I lifted your hand that was hanging, put it in your lap, and covered it with a blanket. It felt so cold. I asked one of the staff to move you back to your room so we'd have privacy.

"You've had a bath today. You look so nice, and smell so good. Your hair looks great combed."

You went in and out of consciousness for much of the morning. Yesterday, you dozed between mouthfuls of food. I hope you'd be more alert today. Where do you go when you sleep, Papa? You no longer speak. This was a switch, as you have been quite the talker. I think that's why I became a teacher, Pap. I was the quiet one, and teaching became my outlet. Why did you have so much to say? Did you finally get it all out? Are you done? Do you now feel at peace? You look as if you do.

Playing music and looking at old photos have been our new mode for interacting. On this visit you were less interested in the photos. You still recognized some: you and your brother as children, you and Mama. Did you recognize me at eight years old? Or was it the defiant expression I had that made you smile?

They brought your lunch. Who would have thought it would be such a pleasure to feed you? You ate so heartily. On the menu was pureed sweet and sour pork, cream of rice, pureed green beans, and . . . ice cream! Remember the last time we went to get ice cream? You had the sugarless, and I had coffee flavor. You went to the bathroom twice, once before and once after we got our ice creams. How long ago was that, Pap? A year?

"How did the sweet and sour pork taste? I promised to make and bring you saté (pronounced satay, marinated pork, chicken or lamb on skewers cooked on a fire) my next visit."

You looked up when I said, "Saté."

"Okay, all done. Wasn't the ice cream good?"

You've livened up a bit, more in this world than your own. Thank you, Pap. I wanted this last opportunity just to be with you. I just wanted to hold your hand as I long as I still could. I wanted to feel the warmth of your aliveness. I rested my hand on your chest and felt it move up and down. You're so thin. Had you been in bed, I would have held you in my arms and taken in your smell. Just like in my dream about you shrinking. You sat on my lap like a child and I just held you.

I love you, Astrid

Sorting Through Pap's Office – July 4, 2006

I'm sitting here in his office. At his computer with Internet connection using the telephone line is very slow, I have time to look around. On the desk are the monitor, scanner, and printer that no longer are in working order. It had served its purpose. To the right along the same wall is a bookcase with the *Great Books of the Western World.* He sold this 51-volume set filled with Western knowledge when he first came to this country. I don't know how much of it he has read. I remember him mentioning people like Marx and Freud. The bookcase also contains a couple of my old paintings, reams of paper, a mini-cassette player, very old books in French and German, aged binders, maps, and a container with US copper pennies. There's a brass trophy of a man holding a briefcase. The emblem is missing. Is it an Agent of the Year award? And there sits one of Danny's drawings of a train, sketched when he was in the sanatorium in Holland. On the top three shelves are photos of us kids, his grandchildren and great-grandchildren. Against the other wall are several filing cabinets decorated with framed photos of Oma and Opa's sixtieth wedding anniversary, the Berg *wapen* (coat of arms), Pap's military intelligence diploma, a model airplane, a picture of him in uniform (the one that Danny made a painting of). Pasted onto the metal filing cabinets are various letters of recognition. And below that is a table covered in brown, batik cloth on which lay a brass-colored doorknocker with Berg engraved on it. I think that was from our house in Santa Ana. There's also a shoe *lepel* (horn) with a castle design on the handle, a Spanish sword that tourists could buy I think from Toledo (we used to get smaller versions of those in our steaks at a restaurant in Madrid), and an eight by eight box with his military metals and badges. The wall opposite the computer desk holds two more six-feet bookcases containing books mostly about economics, politics, history; dictionaries in various languages; and law books from the time he thought he would take a law degree through correspondence. And there are some on health and medicine. Once he learned he had diabetes, he began to research it thoroughly.

Now, as I sit here and look around, *lieve* (dear) Pap, you're still present, and I'm afraid of losing that in the busyness that often comes with life. I want to hold onto those precious moments we had these last months without the barriers of defenses built over the years.

Chapter Two

Our Father the Hero

Papa was the hero-idol, admired by us children, and respected by the wider family. He was wise, confident, disciplined, persistent, and grand. He had integrity and strong beliefs, and was always right. A pilot during World War II and a POW camp survivor who later worked in intelligence for NATO, he had charisma and was a natural leader. He was also a great dancer.

Adoring Him

Before I was old enough to attend school, I shadowed my father as he got ready for work. My mother would be asleep after her night shift as a nurse. Meticulous, my Papa took his time grooming. While in the shower, we'd sing songs from the radio by Bing Crosby, Nat King Cole, Perry Como, and others. One I remember in particular is by the Mills Brothers:

"I'm going to buy a paper doll that I call my own

A doll that other fellas cannot steal."

---

[7] Captain Berg, early 1950s

I would sing along from my place on the lid of the toilet. Or we would sing soldier songs. I can still recite them, but won't. I didn't understand much of the meaning and luckily it was all in Dutch so I couldn't get in trouble for repeating these bawdy lyrics. However, just like my grandchildren today, to say words like, 'butt' and 'poop,' while singing these songs felt daring.

As Papa was shaving, I'd tell him stories about Jeannieland, my imaginary world.

"Jeannie has black hair, just like yours, Papa, and it's really long like Vivi's. She lives in a castle. Not a *real* castle, but a house that looks like a castle. And her room is round."

His "ahum" let me know I could continue.

"And she's MAGIC! When she goes like this," and I'd wave my hand in front of me like I was wiping a mirror, "and she says 'Jeanie shield, Jeanie shield,' then she's invisible."

While shaving, he explained to me each step of the process.

"It can't be too thick or too thin," he'd say as he mixed the shaving cream with a brush in a cup. "Then you spread it evenly." He'd demonstrate lathering his face with the creamy substance, making small peaks like the snowdrifts in cartoons. "The razor is very sharp. Don't *ever* touch it! I hold it at this angle so it won't cut into my skin. See?"

He'd glide up, and do it again, and then rinse the razor. He'd move in a slow and consistent pace. Once done, he'd splash his face with water, dry it with a hand towel, and then slap on aftershave. And then he'd let me feel his smooth face. I liked getting up close and touching his face. After shaving, he'd reach in the cabinet and pull out his brush and a comb. He then vigorously groomed over his wavy but short hair with the brush and his free hand in rhythm until the hairs laid flat. He switched to the comb to make a part on the left and moved each side to rest in place.

I'd follow him up the wide staircase to the master bedroom and sit on the edge of the bed with my elbows on my knees and my chin in my hands, watching. Each day he'd follow a similar routine. While still cooling from the hot shower, he'd take out the shoe-polish kit from the bottom dresser drawer and choose a pair of black or brown Oxfords, pull out the shoetrees, and begin by spreading the polish with a rag. Leaving the shoe polish to set in, he'd pick out a shirt, tie, slacks, and belt from the closet that he'd lay neatly on the bed. He'd then pull out the shoe brush from the kit and brush swiftly as the Oxfords slowly transformed to a brilliant shine. Moving each shoe in a circular manner, he'd inspect, making sure they were even on all sides.

"We polished our boots everyday in the military," he'd say, more to himself than to me.

He'd put on his socks, shirt (placing the tails between his legs), and pants. After fastening all seven buttons (which I'd silently count) in the front and two at the cuffs, he'd lift the collar and put on a tie. My favorite was the blue one with small white dots that made a diamond pattern. While watching

Rosicrucian pendant

himself in my mother's dresser mirror, he'd wrap the long end around twice and then over and through the loop to make a knot. I wanted to try, but knew I was too young. Even Papa had to redo it until it was just right. Then came his belt, which matched his shoes. Before putting on the pants and jacket, he brushed off the lint. Then we were ready to go back downstairs to the kitchen where he'd make breakfast. Or sometimes my mom had already made it. I liked it better when she hadn't because then I'd get to watch him do that too.

Once I entered the first grade, I lost this time with my father. As he was a late riser, I was already in school by the time his routine began. By then I abandoned Jeannieland, and my father and I had more mature exchanges. He'd tell me about karma, or what he called "the natural consequences of behavior." He explained how one must live harmoniously within one's community. He also expounded on how we should not pride ourselves with personal accomplishments or material things. I'd listen with fascination, perhaps understanding or perhaps not. My father was interested in what we now call spirituality. During his youth, he had explored the major religions. He later relayed to me the story about questioning the local Catholic priest and the Protestant minister in Malang (Java, Indonesia) when he was eleven so as to understand the difference in their beliefs. He then questioned the local Islamic Imam. When he lived in the Netherlands, he had been involved with the Rosicrucians, originally a community of mystics who claimed to possess knowledge that was concealed from the average man (my father would have liked that), offering insight into physical nature and the spiritual realm. He had given my mother a gold pendant that had been given to him from someone in the order. The ball opened into a black cross with gold symbols engraved in it. As a child, I loved to open it and look at the symbols. Three decades later, he gave me his books by Madame Blavatsky,[8] which he had studied in those early years he lived in the Netherlands. He had also shared with me some of the animistic beliefs of Java. His connection to these ways had thinned over the years. As I began this writing venture, I reread a prized book he had given to me on Javanese mysticism that had the following inscription:

Dear Astrid,

Just a small token of my love for you and my appreciation for deep interest in what is labeled the Orient.

Let this book be your first step in your search. When the time is ripe and your understanding of the real East has reached maturity, my writings may be helpful to fill certain gaps.

July 10th, 1981

Love, Papa

Unfortunately, we never had those exchanges I so longed to experience. Instead, there would be monologues to endure.

Another favored topic of his was the honor and nobility of the Berg family. Papa had given my mother a ring in which the Berg coat of arms was engraved. (He didn't wear rings.) Impressionable, these stories invoked in me the incentive to behave with integrity and with principles. It also inspired a sense of self-importance and the idea that we were better than the average.

---

[8] https://en.wikipedia.org/wiki/Helena_Blavatsky. He later gave me a two-volume set of books called *The Secret Doctrine: The Synthesis of Science, Religion and Philosophy.*

Move to Hawai'i

Prompted by a new job selling property on the Big Island, my father became fascinated with Hawai'i. The climate and culture, similar to that of Indonesia, was an opportunity to recapture what he had lost. My father brought home Hawaiian records that now replaced the music that we had listened to previously on the radio. He organized luaus featuring Hawaiian foods and entertainment. Enchanted, he decided to move us there. My mother's sister and bother-in-law (also in the real estate business) were already living in Hilo on the Big Island. At the end of third grade, I had to fit all the toys I wanted to take in an eighteen-inch cube box to be shipped to Hawai'i. This meant I would have to leave behind my rock collection. My parents left behind all the furniture and their car.

I can understand the draw to these islands, with its slower pace and softer culture, the tropical beauty, and hospitality. I was, however, horrified by the enormous spiders and the geckos that lived on the walls, indoors no less. Mosquitoes were ubiquitous. One day having forgotten to put on repellent, I came home with dozens of bites after staying overnight at a house that had no screens. The most alarming experience occurred when I went to shower and discovered a two-inch, upside-down cockroach with all its legs wiggling back and forth. I screamed bloody murder.

We stayed with my aunt and uncle in Hilo for several weeks and then moved to Kailua on the far side of Honolulu on Oahu. Our sojourn to these islands was brief, and we barely returned in time for the new school year back in California. My mother was relieved. Hawai'i was not her kind of place. I vacillated between my father and mother's partialities. I had become interested in Hawaiian and Tahitian dancing (to replace tap dancing), which would be part of my life for the next five years. As he continued to sell Hawaiian real estate in California and later to the Indisch people in Holland, I performed at those luaus. This was a new way to connect with my father.

Chapter Three

9

My Father's Daemons

Fiery Eyes

I was in the fifth grade. We lived in a house across from the orange grove in what was appropriately called the City of Orange. I remember the feast from picking bags and bags of oranges that my mother would squeeze with a hand juicer. We had fresh orange juice for weeks. After our first winter, they bulldozed the grove to build a high school for the influx of baby boomers. I'd missed a couple of months of school because we had been visiting family in Holland—from August through November. I had a bit of catching up to do at school, socially and academically. The year before, due to the surge of families with kids moving into the new neighborhoods, I had been bussed to another part of Orange while the new school in my neighborhood was being built.

---

[9] Painting of Captain Berg by Danny Berg

About mid year, we had an assignment to write a report about one US state to include its history, geography, cultural heritage, and current economic resources. I had been very keen the year before learning how to use encyclopedias and had written several short reports on topics such as dolls, dogs, and horses. For this year's report, I had chosen three instead of just one state: California, where we lived; Hawai'i, because my father loved it; and Alaska, perhaps for a sense of symmetry. I came home from school donning an A+ on each colored-cardstock cover bound with three staples on the sides—green for Hawai'i, yellow for California, and blue for Alaska. Mama, who no longer needed to work, was home and had a pot of tea and home-baked butter cookies waiting for my younger brother, Carl, and I.

On this day, my father happened to be home. His salesman job required that he be at work mostly in the afternoons and evenings. As a consequence, we didn't see him that often. Full of exuberance, I showed him my good work. I anticipated with delight as he read through the report on Hawai'i.

"Where did you get your information?" he finally said.

I told him I had learned to use encyclopedias and how to find books in the library.

"This story about King Kamehameha is not true," he said pointing to the spot on the page and then forcefully flipped the pages. "And this about Hawaiian culture is incorrect." The muscles in his face tightened, and his eyes narrowed with that fiery look we all feared. "You've done a sloppy job," he continued, throwing the paper on the white Formica dining room table. "You need to get your facts straight and don't assume the information you get from an Encyclopedia is correct. I know. I know because I've been to Hawai'i and worked with officials there." As he continued, those fiery eyes looked beyond me, and the demon took over.

My eager anticipation for recognition deflated to disappointment and the lecture went on and on about being sloppy, lazy, making assumptions, believing everything one reads. I would end up in prison if this kind of behavior continued. My initial joy regressed to shame and humiliation. At first, I listened with respect, as I had been taught, but after the minutes turned beyond an hour, I imagined different outcomes and then wished I had not shown him the reports. I longed to hide, escape, be forgotten and unnoticed.

My older sister and brother, too, endured these lectures. Decades later they'd laughingly tell stories about sitting on the stairs at the Big White House (the Victorian where we had lived before Hawai'i) during these lectures. They'd elbow each other at the anticipated often repeated lines, like "If so and so is going to jump in the lake, are you going to jump in the lake?" Both would try hard not to laugh, but finally one would burst, and then they'd both giggle. That would, of course, infuriate him more. It may have been funny in the telling, but not to experience, particularly when you didn't have another to bear it with you.

I learned to keep a low profile around my father and was a good and quiet girl. On occasion I'd still do something that would set him off. During teenage years, I'd internally roll my eyes. Yet, sitting there on a chair with him above pointing his finger at me in such distress, I felt invisible, powerless, and wanted to hide under a rock. Twenty-five years later I discovered in therapy that I had adopted that same voice and tone in my head criticizing myself.

In contrast to my father's judgments, that had been my best academic year thus far. I continued receiving 'A' grades and, to my astonishment had straight A's on my final report card. It was also the first year we had the new math, which was much more interesting than the timetables and rote of years before. We were encouraged by the teacher to write and think and did creative projects, like skits of historical events. However, I was not able to complete the fifth grade because right after Easter vacation we moved to the Netherlands. My mother imparted the news a couple of weeks before the actual move. My older siblings would remain in California. Vivi was already living with *Tante* (aunt) Maggie

Flat on the Groot Hertoginnenlaan, 2016.

in LA to finish high school where she had been attending until we moved to Hawai'i. After graduating, Vivi joined us in Holland to work as a secretary for an international company in The Hague. Danny, also a senior soon to graduate and legally an adult, would remain in the house in Orange.

Pap had sublet a furnished apartment in a section of The Hague near the Peace Palace. I enjoyed an extra long summer vacation—four months. The remainder of that spring and into the summer, I frequented the small, local library kitty-corner to our house, reading all the age appropriate books written in English—like *Nancy Drew* and *The Black Stallion* series. Never bored, I filled a notebook with my own stories and drawings and listened to Beatle records. We had an apricot toy poodle—a good companion. I often took her to the local park. On the way, we passed a series of three-story row houses made of blood-red brick with white trim and shiny, green doors. They were actually three and a half stories, as there were stairs leading down to a cellar that, in earlier times, housed servants. The park formed a J-shape. It continued along our street—*Groot Hertoginnelaan* (Grand Duchess Lane) and then curved following a canal back and around into the street behind ours with single-family dwellings, most of which were homes of diplomats, including the American ambassador and his family.

While small, the park was an escape into nature. An enormous weeping willow hung over the pond-like canal. I'd hang out mesmerized by the reflection of this grand tree in the water. I also fed the ducks. In those days I did not know that bread was not good for them. It was an exceptionally sunny summer, or perhaps my fond memories have made it so. I remember taking my six by eight notebook and a pencil to the park and writing the

Favorite spot on the Groot Hertoginnenlaan, 2019.

adventures of Charlotte and Renee, two young teenagers traveling in England in search of the Beatles. Or, I'd sketch the weeping willow with its elegant branches reflecting in the green water. Now, more than fifty years later, the tree still stands bringing me back to the best time of my youth.

As a family, we would visit Pap's friend and colleague from the KNIL and later NATO, Paul Jolly and his wife Bea. They had three sons who were much older than me: Humphrey, Willie, and Renee. We would have great Indisch dinners with *saté* (satay). Willie had several Beatle albums and we'd listen together.

Not uncommon in those years in Holland, with its housing shortage, we shared the apartment with an elderly couple, each family having their own floor. We nicknamed the place 'The Barn.' Not sure why except perhaps because of the high ceilings and wide open rooms that felt large and looming. However, as many have experienced, when Carl and I went back forty years later and were invited inside, it was no longer huge, not even large.

Pride and Shame

Like many immigrants, my father was grateful and proud to be an American, and so were my American-born, younger brother, Carl and I. During the turbulent and expanding sixties, there were signs all around The Hague that said, "Get out of Vietnam," or "Americans go home!" In seeing them, my father would fume.

At that time, Carl and I attended a Dutch school. I was in the sixth grade and he was in the first. While we spoke it at home, I had never learned to read Dutch. My sixth-grade teacher had a creative solution. On his trip to the US the summer before, he had bought American science and history text books, which he let me use rather than the Dutch ones my classmates had. While the class did sixth grade Dutch grammar, I learned to read in Dutch. Math was relatively the same in both languages and my best subject.

About mid-year, Mr. Schouten asked if I would share my thoughts about and experiences with riots and the civil rights movement. This was most likely prompted by something in the news. I was into the Beatles and hip clothing, but I was quite naïve regarding any civil or political situations. We had lived in a Hispanic neighborhood in East LA, but I had little experience with African-Americans. The only Black person I'd known was my third grade teacher. Never fast on my feet, I fumbled for a response. Whatever it was, it didn't satisfy my teacher. So Mr. Schouten then told the story of *his* experience visiting the South that preceding summer. This was 1966, and what he described was most likely a genuine experience. All the same, I was extremely embarrassed to be so insensitively put right by a teacher I admired. Distraught, I told the story to my parents.

"Those #%&*! liberal Dutch. Who does he think he is? What does he know?" my father responded. "Look at us! Look how we were treated!" And so he continued for more than an hour telling me how good it really was in the US of A.

Hoping for sympathy, instead Papa was enraged as if my experience with the teacher was a personal affront on him. To prove this arrogant, liberal teacher wrong, Papa prepared a slideshow conveying the prosperity of the US—of the places we lived, including our homes, his cars, and his airplane. The trouble was, they were not our actual homes or cars. And we didn't own an airplane. I knew there was no way that I could get out of doing the slide show. Oh, the shame.

Hidden Pain

As I relive these memories now in writing them down, I feel compassion for my father, Anton Berg, born in 1917 in *Soerabaja* (now Surabaya). These over reactions, I did not understand at the time, were due to a litany of circumstances beginning with colonization and its racism and classism and nine years of war, with nearly four years in a POW camp, and thrice losing one's home, possessions, and identity.

For decades I listened to his stories, and since his passing (14 years ago) I have researched Indonesian history and our genealogy. More so, I continue to integrate and heal this inheritance, the sins of the fathers, or the collective and intergenerational trauma. It's not just my father who was unconscious and delusional with overwhelming feelings of loss, fear, pride, shame, and rage. I now understand that the pain I feel is not only from my or his life experiences. Thomas Hübl, who works with intergenerational and collective trauma, writes:

Whether we refer to a person as victim or victimizer, oppressor or oppressed, it appears that no one, given time, remains untouched by collective suffering. Historical traumas impart their consequences indiscriminately upon child and family, institution and society, custom and culture, value and belief. Collective traumas distort social narratives, rupture national identities, and hinder the development of institutions, communities, and cultures, just as personally experienced trauma has the power to disrupt the psychological development of a growing child. [10]

It is estimated that 64,000 children of Dutch colonial prison camp veterans in the Netherlands have serious psychological complaints.[11] Research on the Indisch population of refugees and their children addresses many concerns. Many of these children feel isolated and have to make up for what their parents lost and experienced during the war and aftermath. The message is: "be brave," "don't feel what you feel," "do it yourself," "you don't need anyone," "don't trust anyone," "keep at it until you drop," "adjust," "fit in," and "don't be noticed." The children live with their parents' silence and learn to hide their pain "achter hun glimlach" (behind their smile).[12]

Harpe and Dolman write, "Wie het verleden verzwijgt, blokkeert de toekomst" [13] which loosely translates as "whomever doesn't speak about the past blocks the future." They and others have researched *Indische na-oorlogse generatie* (post war Dutch-Indonesian generation) for psychotrauma.[14] The traumas not acknowledged or dealt with by those who lived through POW and internment camps are passed on to the generations that follow. Sometimes these symptoms become more severe with ensuing generations. The consequence of colonization, such as racism and violence, has traumatic effects on the Indisch community and the indigenous people. This trauma affects future generations, even those who did not directly experience trauma of, for instance, internment camps, or those who did not grow up in the Dutch East Indies, like myself.

---

[10] Thomas Hübl. (2020). Healing collective trauma: A process for integrating our intergenerational and cultural wounds. Boulder, CO: Sounds True, pp. 78-9

[11] Tanja Harper and Wilmar Dolman. (2002). *Achter mijn glimlach: Vanuit het donker naar het licht.* Diemen, The Netherlands: KKJJB '40-'49.

[12] Tanja Harper *and* Wilmar Dolman. (2002). *Achter mijn glimlach: Vanuit het donker naar het licht.* Diemen, The Netherlands: KKJJB '40-'49, p. 10.

[13] IBID.

[14] http://www.stichtinginog.nl/

Recent research on epi-genetics (changes made to gene expression by nongenetic factors) shows that the effects of trauma are passed on from generation-to-generation through one's DNA.[15] In biblical terms, this is referred to as sins of the father. The children of those who sin (in psychological terms, those who are traumatized) inherit the seed of sin (effects of trauma), which can have intergenerational consequences, such as abuse, alcoholism, and other sins of personal assault. This collective, ancestral trauma regenerates the psycho-spiritual problems that we are born into (inherit) affecting our health, behavior, work, relationships, and how we relate to the world.

Indisch Monument, The Hague
8 Dec 1941 – 15 Aug 1945   Spirit Conquers
Photo taken in 2021

---

[15] Isabelle Mansuyat the Brain Research Institute, University of Zurich examines the mechanisms of epigenetic inheritance and the influence of life experiences on mental and physical health across generations. The research focuses on adverse experiences in early life and their link with psychiatric and metabolic disorders. Retrieved November 3, 2020 from: https://www.hifo.uzh.ch/en/research/mansuy.html

Section II – West Meets East

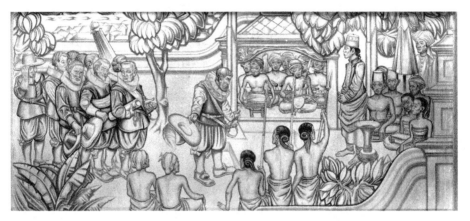

Wall painting 'The reception of Cornelis de Houtman in Java in 1595'
by Paulides in the Dutch Pavilion at the Colonial World Exhibition in Paris

Chapter Four

16

From Mestizo to Indisch

Fourteen thousand islands spread 3500 miles along the equator dissecting the Indian Ocean from the Pacific Ocean. Volcanoes, some remaining active, formed the tropical islands. The warm and humid climate engendered a rich diversity of plants and animals that evolved during hundreds of thousands of years. In early times when physical needs were easily met, the island people developed complex cultures before they began to travel beyond their own regions. Their diversity, my father would proudly

---

16 A beautiful example of John Cary's 1801 Map of the East Indies that includes Singapore, the Philippines, Borneo, Sumatra, Java, the Celebes, and parts of Papua New Guinea. Retrieved June 9, 2021:
https://commons.wikimedia.org/wiki/File:1801_Cary_Map_of_the_East_Indies_and_South east_Asia_(_Singapore,_Borneo,_Sumatra,_Java,_Philippines)_-_Geographicus_-_EastIndies-cary-1801.jpg

proclaim, is more pronounced than that of Europeans. The five main islands are Sumatra, Java, Kalimantan (Borneo), Sulawesi (Celebes), and Irian Jaya (New Guinea). The islands, historically, were independent, with 300 population groups and 250 languages. Each island has distinct cultures with architecture, arts and crafts, music, behavioral codes, spiritual traditions, as well as their own languages. Malay (from Malaysia just east of the archipelago) was the common trade language used since the fifteenth century.

Java is where my father was born and lived—except during wartime—for his first thirty-two years. It is nearly 1,000 kilometers (600 miles) long, and depending on where you measure, 100 to 200 kilometers (60 to 120 miles) wide. It has thirty-eight volcanic mountains, some rising from 3,000 to 3,600 meters (10,000 to 12,000 thousand feet.) Due to the tropical heat and moisture, lush vegetation, and forests, and an enormous variation of birds, insects, and animals evolved, some of which are not seen anywhere else on the planet. Following is a description of the Javanese by Eliza Ruhamah Scidmore, an American who visited the island in the late nineteenth century:

> The Javanese are the finer flowers of the Malay race—a people possessed of civilization, arts, and literature in that golden period before the Mohammedan and European conquests. They have gentle voices, gentle manners, fine and expressive features…. Their language is soft and musical—"the Italian of the tropics"; their ideas are poetic; and their love of flowers and perfume, of music and the dance, of heroic plays and every emotional form of art, proves them as innately esthetic as their distant cousins, the Japanese.[17]

Portuguese explorers seeking spices arrived in the archipelago in 1509. Along with Malay, the Portuguese language remained the official languages (particularly for trade) until the early 1800s. The Dutch followed the Portuguese with better guns, organization, and financial backing, and were able to establish a foothold in Java.[18] They established the *Vereenigde Oostindische Compagnie, VOC* (Dutch East India Company) in 1602. From that time until the mid-twentieth century, the VOC controlled much of Indonesia

---

[17] Eliza Ruhamah Scidmore. (1899). "The Kampongs," *Java, the garden of the East.* New York: The Century Company, p. 41.
[18] IBID., p 26.

and, as a result, a sub-culture of mixed European, Indonesians, and other ethnicities made these islands their home. [19]

The social order of the colony was based on racial and social structures with the Dutch living separate from, but linked to, indigenous aristocracy and their subjects. Early on, the Dutch strategically made alliances with the ruling Indonesians by marrying their daughters, and a society particular to the Indisch was established by the mid 1600s. The high-ranking governor-general, company directors, and residents formed the upper class of Europeans. Medium- and low-ranking VOC employees initially were Dutch, but in later years would include those of mixed heritage with the better jobs left for the Europeans even if less qualified.

Few women came to the Indies, in part, because it was difficult for them to survive in the tropics. Women born in the tropics were accustomed to heat and more immune to diseases, and their children could more readily survive. European women would more likely aspire to return to Holland after fortunes were made, and the children

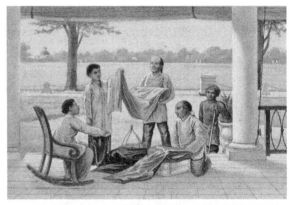

Chinese selling fabric, litho from the watercolor by Rappard

(mainly sons) were sent home to be educated. This would necessitate a constant need for newcomers to be trained and acclimated. Hence, it made more economic and practical sense to make ties with local women. Most men took on Asian (local, Chinese, and Japanese) *njais* (translated as concubines but were actually housekeepers who also shared sexual relations with her employer) and concubines, and had children with them or with their slaves. Whether the mothers were slaves, njais, concubines, or wives, their children were raised in the manner that Asian women raised their children and they spoke Javanese or Malay. This created the Mestizo culture.

---

[19] See Addendum: Indonesia: History, Geography, and Culture for more in depth history.

The Indonesian and other Asian wives had very different habits from the sober, Calvinist, upper-class Dutch. They were, for instance, more extravagant, indolent, surrounded by many servants and/or slaves, chewed betel (tobacco), and bathed several times a day, even in public bathhouses, which was frowned upon by their European counterparts. Women followed the status of their husbands. Hence, no matter their ethnicity, the Asian spouses and their children would be considered European. They also dressed as Europeans. This, along with other things, would change later. The male children of these liaisons were often sent to Europe to be educated, and the females were married for financial alliances. Over time, European immigrant men would acquire positions by marrying into established families that usually were of mixed heritage (Mestizos), and they followed matrilineal lines.

'View of the Tijgersgracht on Batavia:' In the mid-17th century, the Tijgersgracht was deemed the most attractive of the fifteen city center canals in Batavia. The canal was lined with the houses and buildings of the city's most prominent families

In researching for this book and learning about the social habits and the workings of the early Mestizo culture, I wondered if some of my Indonesian ancestry came from these early alliances, njai, concubine, or even slaves. I was not able to find this information.

Unlike the English that separated races and half-castes, the racially mixed group of Eurasians, later *Indos* or *Indisch*, was allowed to assimilate into the European stratosphere of the colonial hierarchy in the Dutch East Indies.

However, the Dutch shared similar racist values and beliefs based on proto-social Darwinism, placing the white Caucasian race at the top of society and naturally in charge of dominating and civilizing non-white populations. It was simply Dutch pragmatism that accounted for the social structure in the Indies.[20]

Hence, a hyper-class consciousness developed (both racial and class) with its brutality, entitlement, vanity, and condescension. The colonists believed in their own superiority, which justified their behavior towards the 'other.' The Dutch privileged, social-middle and lower classes consisted of soldiers, administrators, managers, teachers, and pioneers. They lived together with the 'natives,' but at the top of a rigid social and racial caste system.

British Influence

While brief, the presence of British rule in the early nineteenth century in the Indies induced a shift in the European and Mestizo societies. The British ruling class, made up of younger sons or lesser branches of English families or commissioned officers that were educated in Britain, was offended by the mixed racial heritage of Dutch officials. They could not condone women of European status dressing in adapted local clothing that looked like petticoats and chemises, spoke Malay rather than Dutch or other European languages, and consumed Asian foods. In addition, the British found a "poverty of education, as they saw it, which resulted in there being no common language through which they might communicate." [21] The languages spoken in Java by the Mestizo was Javanese, Malay, or Madurees, not Dutch.

A new social structure initiated by the British was continued by the Dutch after the British left. New immigrants taking high-ranking offices were no longer migrating for economic reasons, but came without debt and planned to retire in Holland. This broke the matrilineal character of the Mestizo culture. The Dutch men received their posts on the basis of their birth and educational qualifications and were united by a nationalism directed toward the homeland and not the Batavian upper class society as had been in

---

[20] "Indos in Colonial History," *Wikipedia*. Retrieved April 23, 2019 from: https://en.wikipedia.org/wiki/Indos_in_colonial_history
[21] Jean Gelman Taylor. (2009). *The social world of Batavia*. Madison, WI: The University of Wisconsin Press, p. 97.

the past.[22] New constitutional laws excluded Mestizo/Indisch families from politically influencing posts in government, as the positions went to those entirely educated in Europe and who passed an examination. The Delft Academy was opened in Holland for the education of career officers in the colonies.

In spite of the influx of European women, the Mestizo culture continued within the colonial caste system along with its unique customs. However, those who followed indigenous (*inlandse/inlander*) customs were degraded, while upper class Europeans and, to some degree, Javanese aristocracy were admired. The feudal style of living made possible for wealthy Europeans to exploit the inlander, and a social division between Europeans and Indonesians continued.[23]

Some factors that contributed to the social separation between Europeans and Indisch were that the Indisch culture relied more on oral language and visual arts and they spoke in Malay and Javanese rather than Dutch. With less access to European doctors and the church with its social functions, they followed the values, sayings, and used local magical or herbal remedies. They also preferred the cooler Indonesian clothing and food more appropriate for the climate. The European men continued to hide and/or not marry their Indonesian mistresses.[24] Yet, many of the children were *erkent* (recognized) and received European last names so they would know their heritage.

---

[22] IBID., p.115.

[23] There were about 4,000 people with European status when the British took over Java in 1806. The overall population of the city of Batavia was 47,000 and Soerabaja had 24,500. By 1852, the number of Europeans increased to more than 17,000 in Java and close to 5,000 scattered on the other islands. One fifth of the European population would die each year from malaria, dysentery, and small pox. In the 1870s, there were more opportunities for private entrepreneurs who immigrated to the Indies and the European population was up to 36,467, and it was 58,806 two decades later throughout the islands. Most of this increase in European population was due to immigration and mainly on Java. By this time, not only men immigrated. The majority of women that came were wives and daughters, but some came to the Indies to earn a living. In the span of the nineteenth century there were between four and six million people indigenous to Java.

[24] IBID., p. 132.

It was into this social world that my paternal great-great-grandfather, Fransz Joseph, arrived in 1830.

[25] Image of *pasar* (market) at the time Fransz Joseph arrived in the Dutch East Indies by Steven Adriaan Buddingh (1811-1869). Retrieved June 9, 2021 from: https://commons.wikimedia.org/wiki/File:Bazar_te_Buitenzorg.jpg

Chapter Five

26

Fransz Joseph Berg – The Duelist

Dietz, Germany, July 22, 1829

Fransz stared at the dark stain spreading across the fabric of his rival's shirt. Not hearing his friend call out, Fransz stood frozen as images of the past twenty-four hours appeared in the pool of blood. It wasn't suppose to have gone this way. After impulsively accepting the challenge to dual, Fransz was sure, Johan, his silver-tongued friend and second would be able to resolve the dispute.

"Fransz! Fransz!" Johan had been crying out. "Please. You must leave. Now!" he said as he pulled his friend away from the body of the duke's nephew.

---

26 *The Code Of Honor—A Duel in the Bois De Boulogne, Near Paris*, wood-engraving after Godefroy Durand, *Harper's Weekly* (January 1875). Retrieved May 23, 2019 from: https://commons.wikimedia.org/w/index.php?curid=2947200

His mother, Trudie, and sister, Carolina, sat huddled holding each other, as his grandmother recounted the plan to Fransz. Trudie wasn't sure that she could bear the pain in her heart. She would lose her son forever. Carolina, responding to her mother's anxiousness, showed her fear and grief by crouching in fetal a position and rocking herself. *Oma* (grandma) Augusta was the force that held the family together, even when her own son, Pieter, had died in an accident. And now this . . . how could it come to this?

Augusta spoke calmly, yet forcefully, as Fransz listened to the plan to flee to Holland. Unequivocally terrified, he stood erect with his shoulders squared attempting to show a brave front. His shoulders then fell and stomach tightened with shame seeing that his mother was weeping quietly. Somehow he would make this right.

Fransz was to leave after dusk. Until then, he remained with the women in the three-story narrow home of his birth. For their own sanity and due to potential curious onlookers, the women carried on with their work as if it were a normal day. The atmosphere was heavy. Johan stopped by briefly to say farewell. The friends were wretched, as they knew they would never see each other again.

As per plan, Fransz enlisted in the ground forces of the Koninklijk Nederlands-Indies Leger (KNIL) on August 16, 1829 and was given 10.50 guilders spending money. Fransz had committed to the standard six years of service, and, in a few months, he would sail to the Dutch East Indies.

This is the story of how my great-great-grandfather, Fransz Joseph Berg left Dietz, Germany for Holland and then sailed to the Dutch East Indies. On October 21, 1829, he embarked the *Antonij* for the long journey down the Atlantic, around the southern tip of Africa to Madagascar, and then across the Indian Ocean to finally disembark at Batavia on Java. The lower deck, where the newly-enlisted soldiers spent the ensuing months, had assigned hammocks. This was his first of many years living in close quarters with other men and their habits. While there were German-speaking men on the ship and others seemingly friendly enough, a sense of needing to look over his shoulder and remain incognito persisted throughout the four-and-a-half month voyage. Fransz kept to himself during the journey, writing letters to his mother and grandmother, which he posted at each port. He also read and reread the one treasured book, *Hymnen an die Nacht* (Hymns to the Night) that he was given by his father before he had passed away.

The long journey offered time to reflect on the events of the past several months. He cringed at the impulsiveness of his actions and the ensuing consequences, not only for himself but his dear family. During these months of sailing, so internal and solitary, Fransz resolved to bring honor back to the family. As the island of Java grew closer, Fransz could anticipate the opportunities ahead, a clean slate to begin life in this mysterious land. It was February 28, 1830 when Fransz disembarked, nearly two months before his eighteenth birthday. In spite of the oppressiveness of the thick muggy air of the city port, Fransz felt hopeful.

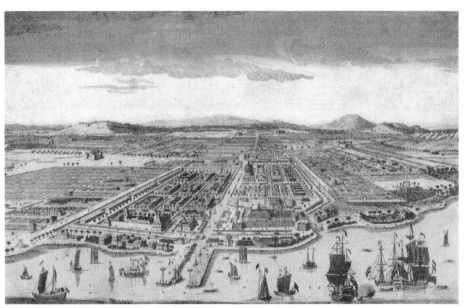

City of Batavia circa 1780

Batavia, 1830

The five-year Java War had just ending when the Antonij arrived ay Batavia in the Indies. Pangeran Dipo Negoro, who believed that the Goddess of the Southern Ocean would help him become king, had led a revolt that was supported by half the leaders of Yogyakarta in

Nicolaas Pieneman –The Submission of Prince Dipo Negoro to General De Kock, Painting at Rijksmuseum

central Java. By the end, more than 200,000 Javanese people died and the population of Yogyakarta, an ancient city that had housed many Hindu and later Islamic royal families, was reduced by half. In addition, 7,000 Javanese soldiers and 8,000 Europeans fighting for the Dutch had died, and five million guilders were spent on the war.[27]

The new governor-general, Johannes van den Bosch, arrived the same year as Fransz. He implemented the *cultuurstelsel* that required each village to use one-fifth, and eventually one-third, of its land to produce export crops for the colonial government. More than two-thirds of the *inlanders* worked to produce mostly coffee, sugar, and indigo, which kept them from cultivating much needed food for themselves.

When writing home, he did not tell his mother and grandmother about the debaucherous lifestyle of the soldiers. His peers were not always of the best caliber. Poverty was a major incentive to join the military. For others, it was adventure, warfare, or, like Fransz, the need to flee from something or someone.

---

[27]"Diponegoro," *Wikipedia*. March 20, 2019 from https://en.wikipedia.org/wiki/Diponegoro

Batavia
4 April 1830

My Dear Oma and Mama,

I am now at the barracks of the 18th division of the infantry in Batavia. While living circumstances are very crowded, I now can walk more than the short length of the ship. My words will scantly describe the exotic beauty of Java. I think of you when I take in its lush and vibrant colors. Some leaves are the size of a small man, and the waringin (banyan) trees grow roots from their branches to a circumference as wide as 5 meters. Everything bombards the senses, both pleasantly and unpleasantly so. The relentless heat and humidity leaves one with a constant layer of perspiration.

I am still in training. Daily routine is organized so as to avoid heat. We rise at five, and at six we begin the day with physical exercise, weapon training, and theory classes. We then eat and nap (due to heat) and resume with work duties until noon, and with a midday break until four. Then we work until dinner, which is at eight. They try to make canteen meals like the food at home but use substitutions, as not everything from home grows here. We also eat local foods such as rice, pickled vegetables, and heavily spiced meats that I have trouble digesting.

In the barracks, I live and work with men speaking Dutch, French, German, and English. There are separate barracks for the Hindus and Arabs and the local (inlander) soldiers. There are more inlander than there are European soldiers. Most come from the island of Ambon. We also have zwartjes (blacks) from the island of Guinea.

The European men in my company may have more drive and intelligence, but they are not always better soldiers than the inlanders, who are more adapted to the tropics. They have many superstitions, and the Ambon's practice magic. Not I, but many of my peers are fearful of their so-called powers.

As for your grandson, so far away from you and home, I will bring honor to the name Berg. You taught me how to live and everyday I thank you.

Your faithful son and grandson,

Fransz

As Holland was a small country, it was difficult to recruit for the colonial army from its own population. In part, this was because the mortality rates on board the ships and in the Indies was high. The service was onerous and the military discipline was difficult. Climate, disease, and warfare took its toll. At the beginning of the nineteenth century, only forty-eight percent of the recruits under the age of thirty-six remained alive in their six years tour of duty. Most of the foreign recruits were Germans, but there also were many Belgians, French, Swiss, and Eastern Europeans. They came from many walks of life. Some were actors, bakers, chemists, gas fitters, glove makers, coachmen, musicians, teachers, wigmakers, writers, rope makers, veterinarians, and winegrowers. Most of those who survived returned to Europe. About twenty percent of the non-Dutch European remained, with

many making it to sergeant. If the non-commissioned officers were literate, they later moved on to colonial civil service jobs, married, and became part of the Dutch culture.[28] In addition, many soldiers were of Indonesian heritage.

Indigenous, Indisch, and European soldiers. Photo taken at Bronbeek Museum, Arnhem, 2018

It was a custom in the barracks to use a large amount of alcohol, particularly gin. The government provided Dutch Genever, as it was discovered that a certain amount of strong drink delayed the passage of food in the intestinal tract; hence, the soldiers were saturated for longer periods, which was important for the very long marches.

---

[28] Vijf Eeuwen Migratie. Retrieved October 25, 2018 from: http://www.vijfeeuwenmigratie.nl/term/Europese%20KNIL-soldaten/volledige-tekst/ ; http://www.vijfeeuwenmigratie.nl/land/Duitsland#521-inhetkort/

Batavia
2 November 1830

Dearest Oma and Mama,

At home, the oak and birch are changing to golds, yellows, and rust, covering the ground. By now there may even be snow lacing the pines and rooftops. You'll be stoking the fires and wearing your woolen coats and boots. This I envision as I march through the wet fields of rice or through dense jungle in the heat and humidity. Will I ever get used to it? In training we learned to recognize poisonous flora and fauna and eat garlic to minimize mosquito bites. Several of my peers have been sick with malaria and other diseases of the jungle. We must be careful with wounds that so quickly fester and take long to heal.

I've had more opportunity to see Batavia. It is a vibrant, but swampy city—a tropical version of Amsterdam, including the canals and bridges. The white-washed houses and buildings with red-tiled roofs have large verandas, and many of the more affluent ones include gardens with fish ponds. The old town is near the strand with a wharf, town house, and other government and commercial buildings. The new town, that is higher in altitude, is where many of the Europeans have their homes.

The Javanese have flat features, meager limbs, and dark skin. Oma, you would not approve of their scanty clothes—a cotton cloth wrapped into a skirt and with their chests bare (both the men and some women). Many other foreigners live here. The Chinese work in trade or have shops called tokos, selling wares from many parts of the world. As do the Arabs. The Chinese are most industrious. Europeans not part of the military, primarily work for VOC and in the country may own or work at the plantations. Most natives do menial work—house servants, assistants to the Chinese, or are laborers. In the country they work the lands of their nobles called Regents. From what I've seen, they are idle, have a circuitous nature, and are incurable gamblers. There are also many slaves of every color and from all over the world.

I so miss you both and my loving sister.

Your faithful and affectionate son and grandson,

Fransz

Fransz could barely tolerate his bunk neighbor, Wim, who was the epitome of some of the riff raff that made up this company. This was not the honorable profession he had imagined from his father's experiences in the service and fighting against Napoleon. Fransz envisioned bringing forth and upholding civilized law and culture to this land of superstitious and indolent people.

Wim returned earlier than usual, which meant that he had lost at the cockfights.

"Writing your mother again?" Wim said, mockingly.

Fransz didn't respond.

"I think those letters are to a maiden. No man can have this much to say to his mother. Are you saving yourself for the maiden? Are you sure she is doing so for you?" the other goaded.

Franz felt the blood rise to his face and his fists clenched, but he took a breath to keep his cool.

Wim then fell into his bed still in uniform, followed by a cacophony of muttering, snoring, and farting as he slept. Franz, in spite of the heat, kept his uniform clean and tidy, his boots polished to the shine of a mirror, and weapons free of rust. Clothing was always folded neatly and put on a shelf before he went to sleep. When possible, he picked up the habit of bathing often, as the locals did—one of their customs he condoned.

Wim never received mail. Franz was not sure if his bunk neighbor could read. When Wim would come upon Fransz reading his mail, he would say, "What news from home?" While Holland was not home to Fransz, the differences between neighboring countries narrowed. They all longed for home and a kinship grew.

Even a brief comment would encourage Wim, who would ask longingly, "Are the canals frozen?" Or, "Are we still independent?"

While Franz would be civil, he did not want to encourage, for Wim would stick to him like a puppy—the untrained, biting kind. Was the man that thick skinned or did he simply ignore the cues? Over time, Fransz became well acquainted with the habits and proclivities of his peers in the barracks.

By 1860, there were fewer than 1,000 European females to the 22,000 European males in the Indies. Consequently, many European men had relations with native women, or *njai* (pronounced nyai, a housekeeper who also shared the bed with her employer; sometimes referred to as a

Barracks. Photo taken at Museum Bronbeek, Arnhem, 2018

concubine). Their offspring was considered Indo-European and, if acknowledged by the father, belonged to the European legal class in the colony.[29] Even if there had been European women to wed, the enlisted men were not allowed to marry. As an alternative, those who could afford them had permission to live with their njais in a specially designated part of the barracks. This custom was condoned because the men were better cared for, hence, more reliable. It was found that those who learned to eat the spicy food cooked by the inlandse remained healthier. In addition, men with njais were much less likely to contact venereal diseases, which was a huge problem.[30]

---

[29] Ulbe Bosma and Remco Raben. (2008). "The Baggage of Colonialism," *Being "Dutch" in the Indies*. Reggie Baay. (2008). "Blanke Heren en Inheemse Bedienden," De Njai: *Het Concubinaat in Nederlands- Indië*.

[30] "It wasn't until the late nineteenth and early twentieth century that more Dutch women came to live in the Indies. The Colonial School for Girls and Women in The Hague had manuals to prepare them for life in the Indies, imparting their duties which was to civilise the untamed colonial community... uphold the values of white morality and prestige and prevent a loosening of their husband's sexual standards. They had an obligation at home to educate not only their children, but their servants as well, and they had an important role in the development or uplifting (*opheffing*) of the indigenous population in their surrounding." Elsbeth Locher-Scholten. *Women and the Colonial State: Essays on Modernity and Gender in the Netherlands Indies 1900-1942*. Amsterdam University Press, p. 125

The barracks were separated between those who had families and those who didn't. The space provided measured roughly two by two and a half meters (six feet by eight feet) and contained a bunk bed, a trunk for storage, and some pegs and shelves to hang or put things. The soldiers with families lived in even tighter quarters, having the same amount of space with only slightly a broader area between beds. The children used the lower bunk beds and would play in the area between the beds. The spaces were separated by cloth, obviously offering little privacy. In the (relative) cool of the evenings, inlander soldiers would sit hours squatting and telling stories about their villages, evil spirits, or about the fighting they had experienced. The Indisch might join inlander circles or the European soldiers, who also shared stories of their villages afar, of battles, and while not of evil spirits, of evil doings.

Fransz could not imagine lowering himself to a liaison with an njai. He was raised with a strong sense of honor, pride, and ethics. And this just seemed wrong. However, even had he wanted a 'housekeeper,' it would be many years before he would be able to support an njai.

Fransz came from a long line of military officers. His father, Pieter, served under Duke Friederich, fought against Napoleon, and was killed in an accident when Fransz was thirteen. Fransz remembered stories his father told in admiration of the Duke. In 1806, Friederich had joined the Confederation of the Rhine in order to prevent Napoleon from annexing the principality of Nassau. A liberal ruler, he established the elimination of tax privileges for the nobility and introduced freedom of press. After his death in 1816, his cousin Wilhelm took over as the Prince of Nassau.

Perhaps not surprisingly, Fransz was a natural to military life. He liked shooting, physical training, obstacle courses, learning about tactics and strategies, and even the long marches. In addition to enjoying the physical exertion and self-discipline, he was most skilled with weapons. He was well acquainted with fencing and was capable of killing with a pistol. Fransz soon became practiced at using a rifle and lance and how to fight in combat. He practiced for perfection and came to be a Master of Three Weapons—the rifle, sword, and kris.

From early on, much of his efforts were at curbing his impulsiveness and hotheadedness. He learned to channel this energy in other activities like vigorous exercise and by mastering what he needed to learn. He possessed a practical intelligence. All these characteristics made him a good leader. His courage, mastery, and temperament brought him respect, and instead of being challenged, newcomers or even bullies sought to befriend him. This, along with bravery and wit, brought him successive promotions—sergeant in 1833, sergeant-major in 1834, second lieutenant in 1836, first lieutenant in 1839, and captain in 1845.

Chapter Six

Helena Falck and the White Glove

Nijmegen, The Netherlands, 1839

Between the crack of the heavy drapes, the sunlight shining through the beech tree danced on her bedroom wall. Helena pulled the covers up to her chin. Early spring is cold and damp in Holland, and central heating had not yet been invented. Nevertheless, it would be a glorious spring day. From the position of the sunlight, Helena guessed that it was eight. While she'd normally be up, washed, and dressed to have breakfast with her family, this morning Helena allowing herself to linger. One of her birthday requests was to sleep in and take breakfast when she was hungry.

She rose and washed her face with the warm water brought in a pitcher. Then the twenty-two year old looked into the mirror. She understood that she was not considered pretty. Her chin stuck out and hair was too thick and bushy. But she had a glint in her lively, hazel eyes with their olive green specks.

Helena heard Mieke, the maid, in the hallway preparing for the guests. Aunts, uncles, and cousins would arrive for coffee at ten thirty in the morning or for tea at three in the afternoon. Those few who lived in the countryside or in distant villages were invited to join for supper at the Falck house.

The parlor was rectangular in shape, with high windows on one end and sliding doors with leaded glass on the other. For today's celebration, the doors were open to the dining area. Light from the back French doors cheered the dark rooms of deeply embossed paper with flower imprints adorned by paintings with thick gold frames. The tables were of dark, sturdy wood covered in red-brown Persian or Flemish wool rugs, and the chairs were upholstered in brocades in hues of brown, red, and tan. The guests formed a circle in the parlor, some facing each other in conversation, while others focusing on the consumption of coffee with *mokkataart* (yellow cake with butter-mocha icing). Helena's oldest aunt on her mother's side was discussing Sunday's sermon. Tante Nell liked to hear herself talk. Helena's eyes scanned the room for an opportunity to escape. When the doorbell rang, she politely excused herself and upon entering the hallway let out a sigh of relief.

In the hallway she heard *Oom* (Uncle) Carl. *Who could he be talking to? Had he brought a friend?* She opened the front door to her uncle's back. He was having an animated conversation with the neighbor across the street. Helena waved at Mrs. Evers as her uncle turned to greet her.

"Look at you," he said. His smile showed the dimple in his left cheek.

"Oom Carl! You're here in time for my birthday!" she cried happily.

Carl had been living in the Dutch East Indies since she was a young girl. Helena greatly missed him, especially since her father had passed away. In unison they kissed the other's cheek, and he handed her a bouquet of orange flowers with red veins.

"Oh, how I love tulips!" she burst.

He then pulled out of his raincoat pocket a small, wrapped gift. "And this is from Java."

As she reached to take his coat, he said, "I'll hang it up. Open the gift here. You know how the others are."

Helena looked in the direction of the parlor filled with relatives. Their comments would spoil the joy of the connection between her and her unconventional uncle. She carefully untied the ribbon and unwrapped the very thin, rough paper. Inside was a small, wooden, hand-carved box.

"Oooh," she cooed as she looked closely at the carvings.

"Open it."

Inside was a tiny wooden figurine of an ornately clad woman in a dance pose.

"Oh," she gasped and touched the piece with her fingertips. "It's . . . so . . . fragile." Helena looked up at her uncle. "Thank you so very much."

"Happy birthday, Helena."

As her uncle waited, she quickly brought the gift to her room.

"Who is here? And who have I missed?" he asked when she returned.

In ancient Java and Bali, Dewi Sri was the goddess of rice, fertility, and agriculture. Her left hand is holding a rice plant.

Helena began to name the relatives as the two entered the parlor.

Helena had not taken a liking to any suitable young or old men. She simply was not interested in the benign conversation and the behavior expected of a young lady. Instead, she fantasized at the prospect of traveling to where her uncle lived.

Helena had overheard a conversation about *trouwen met een witte handschoen*—literal translation is marrying with a white glove. This term refers to a wedding in which one of the partners is unable to be present at the ceremony. In early days, a nobleman would send an ambassador to the future bride with a glove to represent him, the bridegroom. At the wedding ceremony, the glove was placed on the altar. These weddings by proxy occurred because there often was a long, unsafe journey that could delay the marriage. These types of wedding ceremonies were common in the Dutch East-Indies, where the men could not travel easily to Holland to meet, marry, and then take home their brides. Somewhat akin to an arranged marriage, friends or family members recommended a bride or groom to be married with a white glove.

This idea planted a seed in Helena's imagination that would not let her be. Apprehensive, as she feared being judged as too unabashedly bold, she thought of her Oom Carl. Consequently, Helena shyly approached him with the idea.

"Married with a white glove? Where did you get an idea like that?"

Blushing, she asserted herself, "I want to go to the Indies."

He recognized in her eyes the same desire for adventure, the feelings of restlessness, and the confinement of her life. He understood. But a young woman going to the Indies on her own? After pondering the idea, he realized that he knew of an unmarried man who could be a suitable match for his niece.

Padang, 1840

She felt the thickness of the air as she walked the gangplank onto the island of Sumatra. Several barefooted *koelies* (coolie, indentured worker) boarded the ship, carrying trunks and other goods on their shoulders. They did their work without hustling, patiently waiting their turns on the platform.

Helena entered a long, red-tiled hallway that meandered through shades of green fauna with exceptionally large leaves. She looked around for Hans and Rita, seeing neither. Trying to remain composed, she paced the arrival area. Moving seemed to be more comfortable than standing in the steamy heat. Perspiration had already drenched Helena's most summery white cottons. As she waited, she observed many of the local inhabitants. Over time she would learn to recognize the Chinese, Arabs, and *inlanders*. The women were dressed in gowns, more like a skirt wrapped around the waste and that hung about ankle-length and tied at one side of the waste. Some wore a white jacket-like blouse with lace over the petticoat. They had slippers over their bare feet. The hair was drawn back from the forehead and twisted into a knot at the back of the head. Men had a similar costume, some with jackets over the *sarongs* (supple cloth wrapped around the waste with a fold in front) and some bare-chested. She saw a few men wearing long, satin gowns, who had plaited tails, some reaching the back of their knees. European men wore white linen suits. All these colorful characters walked about the dock like butterflies flying in a wildflower field.

As she began to think of what to do if no one arrived, a small, dark-skinned, graying man in perfect Dutch said, "Helena, I am Widjan, the man servant of Tuan Hans and Ibu Rita. Tuan Hans was not able to come, but Ibu Rita awaits in the carriage."

Helena followed Widjan to the horse and carriage, where a stout woman was waving and walking towards them. Her soft, powder blue eyes had fine lines from too much sun exposure and that clearly showed when she smiled or laughed, which was often. She had an abundance of curly, light brown hair that she had trouble keeping tidy. In spite of short stature, she stood as if she was tall. As she met her future sister-in-law, Helena was surprised to find that she was nearly a head taller than the other.

"Ah, there you are, Helena. Welcome. Welcome." Rita greeted with a vigorous handshake and a sturdy hug. She then explained that Hans had urgent business. In spite of Rita's, "But do not worry, you will meet soon enough," Helena was disappointed. Rita looked Helena up and down.

After she managed the loading of Helena's trunks, they both entered the buggy and began the journey to the *Bukit Berkabut* (misty hill) plantation. As they approached the city of Padang, they passed through a commercial area with shacks filled to the brim, displaying clothes, foods, household wares, and furniture. Interspersed were vendors with carts serving colorful delicacies in enormous pots. Some carts had stools in front for sitting. They then passed through the *kampongs* (villages) that her Oom Carl had described. Large, rectangular houses stood on stilts with dramatic curved roofs made of thatch and multi-tiered gables. The windows had brightly painted floral carved

House on stilts with curved roofs made of thatch

shutters. Smaller, much less impressive houses surrounded the centrally-located larger structure.

Rita explained, "It's the women that own the homes and it goes from mother to daughter."

Helena barely heard, so awestruck by the buildings themselves. "The roofs are enormous and it's all so colorful!" she exclaimed.

"Some of this is for ornamentation, but there is also a practical aspect. West Sumatra is very wet. That is why the houses are raised from the ground. The pointed roofs help water to run off, and shutters stop the rain from entering," Rita shared.

Leaving the city, they passed clumps of bamboo growing thirty meters (100 feet) in the air with a graceful canopy of foliage. Slowly, the terrain became hilly. Coming from a very flat country, Helena was awestruck by the enormous mountains. Their blue-violet peaks appeared mirage-like. At each new bend, terraces were cut into the slopes holding shallow pools of water called paddies. Among the paddies were grass huts, raised from the ground on posts with straw-like roofs and three walls, as if the building was not yet complete. Everywhere she looked was the dense foliage of the jungle with ferns and flowers teasing one's nostrils with sweet scents that reminded her of the lavender *sering* (Syringa or Common Lilac) at home. Men and women donned the sarong, or some men had diaper-like cloth worn like short pants and most often bare-breasted and chested. The guilelessness of their nudity struck Helena.

Rita, in anticipating Helena's reaction, said, "The inlanders own very little and they don't want for much. They are poor because they don't have ambition. We encourage ours to work hard and with a sense of accomplishment. But a leopard can't change its spots." Rita continued to inform Helena as they

56

passed new settings. The latter mostly listened, occasionally asking questions and responding with "Ohs" and "Ahs."

Eventually they came to a driveway so long that Helena could not see the end. When they arrived at the villa, a line of servants was waiting at the front entrance. Rita introduced each with their names and duties, but, Helena, tired from the heat, journey, and impressions, only heard words like *kokkie* (cook), *djongo* (house boy), *baboe* (maid, nanny), and *kebon*

Plantation home in the Dutch East Indies

(gardener). They then walked up the stairs onto a fully furnished veranda supported by columns with three sides open to the garden. This covered veranda surrounded the whole building, protecting its inhabitants from the intense sunshine or from rain. Rita took Helena into the villa to what she called the front gallery—sort of an extension of the front veranda—with a door (always open in the day) that led to a hall. To each side of the hall were sleeping quarters. They then entered another large room where meals were taken and the hot hours of the day were spent. Behind the house was a garden surrounded by the servants' quarters, the bathing room, water closet, kitchen, storerooms, and stables.

Between Helena's oohing and awing, Rita explained, "It's all arranged in this manner to keep us cool. That's why we have either marble or tile floors and we rarely use the heavy rugs that you are accustomed to."

As she took it all in, Helena said, "It's lovely to live so close to the outdoors."

"Yes and no," Rita responded. "Yes for the obvious reasons, but those outdoor creatures come indoors uninvited!" She laughed.

Helena already liked her sister-in-law.

"You are overheated and need to freshen up, " Rita began. " You will want to bath and change your heavy clothing. What are those totoks in Holland thinking?"

Rita took Helena to her room containing a carved-mahogany bed with sheer drapes that hung from the ceiling to the floor. A matching dressing table and armoire were of the same dark teak wood. Rita pulled a cotton dress from the armoire and handed it to Helena. "You will want more of these. We shall have some made."

As she then took her to the bathing room, Helena said, The WC?"

"Of course," replied Rita. "Right here." Opening an adjacent door, she pointed to a slightly raised platform with a hole. Next to the hole, as Rita explained, were several bottles filled with water for washing and small towels on the hook for drying. *That would take getting used to,* thought Helena.

After using the toilet, she entered the bathroom. Oom Carl had told her about *mandies* and the bathing habits in the Indies. The entire room was tiled — the floor and half way up the wall—with a drain in the center. There was a tub-like container with a faucet that kept it filled nearly to the brim. The 'bathtub' was not for sitting but to hold the water. Next to it, hanging from a hook, was a *gajong* (metal dipping cup with a long handle) and a bench for sitting. The cup was used to scoop the water and poor over oneself.

As Helena slowly poured the lukewarm water over her back and shoulders, she sighed with pleasure. First she lathered and rinsed her hair, and then lathered her face, neck, each limb, her body, pouring water over each part. The contrast between the cool water against her skin, now with goose bumps, and the warmth of the air was invigorating. As she wiped away the excess water from her face and squinted, Helena saw from the corner of her eye, perched on the ledge of the large tub of water, a three-inch creature with a gray-brown, armor-like shell. From it's pink belly protruded several legs. Its long tentacles moved up and down and left and right as if reaching for something to grasp. Startled, Helena stopped all movement in fear and just stared. She gasped and said, "Please don't fly or move." She hastily patted herself dry and threw on the dress that refused to cooperate because her skin was still tacky. She then exited the room by backing away while still tugging at the dress. With a sigh and a shiver, she turned and headed for her new room and plopped down on the bed. Helena fell asleep immediately.[31]

The following morning, Helena found her way to the front veranda where she found Rita with a steaming cup of tea and a bowl of what appeared to be yellow rice.

"Good morning, Helena," Rita greeted and seeing her expression, said, "I see you looking at my *nasi goreng* (fried rice). There may be a day that you prefer an Indisch breakfast." She then called out, "Sulu, *sarapan* (breakfast)."

Voorgallery (veranda) of house in Dutch East Indies

The servant, moving unobtrusively, arrived with bread, cheese, jam, and tea. When Helena looked up to thank her, Sulu nodded and disappeared walking backwards.

"It'll take time getting used to all these servants. How many are there?"

"Ten in the house, and then those working on the plantation," she began, then seeing Helena's astonishment, continued with, "We are not as wealthy as it may seem. We have more servants for one job or different jobs than it would require in Holland because they work so slow."

"Where do they live?"

---

[31] Customary in the Indies, they would take a siesta after the midday meal and sleep until about four. Then, at five, tea was brought to the veranda. This custom was a method of avoiding the hottest part of the day.

"In the kampong. They usually arrive a couple of hours before sunrise and return to their home and family in the evening. Some go home for a midday meal. A couple live here," she replied, and then seeing that the tea had steeped, she poured Helena a glass.

"Tea in this heat?"

"You will soon learn that warm drinks cool you. It's the same with the food. That's why they add the hot *sambal* (pepper paste) to almost everything. It's in my nasi goreng."

"Really?" Helena was curious.

"They say it helps with digestion."

"You don't seem affected by the heat. Is that because you were born here?" Helena asked, still inexperienced regarding her new home.

"Perhaps, but watch the inlanders. They move slowly and they avoid the sun."

"I don't see you moving slowly," Helena challenged with humor.

"Yes," Rita chuckled. "Do as I say, not as I do."

There was a pregnant pause. Then Rita said, "As I said yesterday, Hans was suppose to return from a hunting trip a few days ago. I'm so sorry that my dear but undependable and overindulged brother could not hold to the schedule and be here to meet you. I don't know what to say, except to apologize for him."

Helena smiled weakly unsure how to respond. While deeply disappointed, she felt in good hands with this strong, yet kind woman.

After breakfast, Rita rose to attend to household matters, leaving Helena to linger on the veranda. The tropical air was heavy and thick and the foliage closed in on her. Lovely, sweet scents intermixed with the fecund taunted her nostrils. Sounds of scurrying life forms were ever-present but difficult to see.

60

The density created a claustrophobic feeling within. Helena gasped for the familiar cool, fresh air of her home.

She wasn't quite sure what she had expected marrying a man she had met only once in Holland. Incredibly, she had been more preoccupied with the move to the Indies than with her future husband. Had that been a dreadful mistake?

Helena's upbringing was typical of an upper-middle class young woman of her times. Behavior, in some ways, was more confined than for those with less privilege. She was expected to marry, and her education had been focused on good dinner conversation and managing a home. Helena had many questions about life and the way things were in the world. She knew that there was more to it than the explanations both her parents offered. In fact, she stopped asking questions of her parents when she was five or six, and teachers did not encourage the sort of queries Helena posed. Instead, they made her feel foolish for the asking. It was Oom Carl who encouraged her to dream, inquire, read, and imagine.

Weeks after her arrival, Hans came home with an entourage of koelies and a dozen buffalos pulling a cart with the spoils of his hunting expedition. Greeting Helena with a broad smile and full of enthusiasm, he picked her up and spun her around. The ensuing days were filled with fervent stories, evenings with lively company, and tender moments alone. He proudly gave her a tour of the plantation, describing in detail its cultivation and production.

Hans took her to a small, oddly furnished bungalow that she had not yet discovered. It was filled with an assortment of hunting trophies. A tiger skin was spread on the floor with open mouth baring teeth. There were two odd-looking tables made of mammoth turtle shells. As he enthusiastically showed his victories, Helena nodded, but said, "I'd have trouble living in a room like this." He laughed it off saying, "This is just for display or to meet with hunting buddies."

Hans appeared knowledgeable about the music and arts of the Indies. One evening at the house of a friend, gamelan was being played during dinner.

"You see, Helena," he began to explain. "With gamelan, the compositions vary according to whether it is used for a religious ceremony, feasts, or theater." He continued as he pointed to the instruments, offering both the Malay and Dutch names. "That is a *paleb*, much like Persian-Pali viol, which carries the melody. The *soeling* is a bamboo flute. Then there are drums, the smaller *kedang* and the larger *ketipoeng*. And next to that is the *tjelem poeng*, a zither. Those set of horizontal gongs are called the *bonang*. And finally there's the *gambang kajoe* or xylophone. All together they make an unusual, to our European ears, type of harmony." [32]

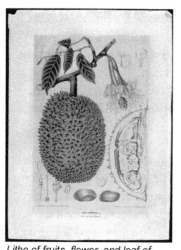

Litho of fruits, flower, and leaf of *Durio zibethinus L*

Helena found herself in a whirlwind of activity, conversation, and attention. Hans took her to Padang, where she was introduced to several of his friends and attended many gay parties. They went to the town *passer* (now spelled pasar, or bizarre, market-place) to enjoy the sights and to shop. She found local as well as imported cloths, combs from bone or hard wood, spangles and silver breastplates, household wares, a colorful assortment of fruit and other foods, and furniture.

The fruit came in a large assortment of shapes and colors. Helena bought the red *rambutans* with their round, feathery spines tinted a deep rose. The vendor pulled apart the juicy, translucent white pulp that surrounded a smooth pit. The *magosteens* were tied in bouquets looking like a bunch of grapes. They opened to a white flower-shaped pulp in a crimson-colored bowl that was the skin. The *duku* looked like large, green, individual grapes. The five-ribbed, yellow star fruit had the most interesting shape and lovely fragrance. The spiky durian had a smooth, solid pulp that is thick and creamy, less like fruit and more like

---

[32] Raden Adjeng Kartini, p. 22 from H. H. Bartlett.

62

buttery custard. Most delicious to eat, but had the most awful odor. Full of wonder like a kid in a candy store, Helena came home with many packages.

As suddenly as he arrived, Hans was gone. He would appear again a month later with no explanation, full of vivacity, and with little consideration for Helena's feelings. The story of Helena and Hans' marriage is brief. So brief, that after eight months, Helena was uncertain how she felt. Had she ever loved her husband, or had her enthusiasm for coming to the Indies predisposed him? Were those first moments of romantic bliss a fantasy on her part? That Hans had not come until weeks after she arrived should have been a sign, but his story made sense at the time, and she didn't want to think ill so early in their union. However, the excuses for his absences—plantation business, hunting—began to get stale. As time passed, she could no longer give him the benefit of the doubt and she had come to realize that she did not truly have a husband. It wasn't until a year later that she overheard women at the *SOS* (a social club for the colonials) talk about Han's njai. Hearing the words felt like a blow in the stomach. Her body froze, and her mind went rampant.

"Why didn't you tell me?" she asked Rita later.

"I was hoping that he would change after the wedding," Rita began.

Helena could not be angry with her sister-in-law, who she had come to love and trust.

"I'm sorry," Rita said sincerely. "I may have a lot of influence on the plantation, but none with my brother."

After weeks of dejection, depression, and anger, Helena confronted Hans by asking him directly. At first he wanted to deny and make excuses, but he could see in her eyes and from her stance that he may as well be truthful. The frankness of their conversation brought them closer in a certain way, and, in that moment of intimacy as he looked soulfully into her eyes with his face only inches a way, she almost succumbed to his charm. Instead, she said, "No!" quite loudly and more to herself. This gave her the strength to ask him to live somewhere else. He agreed. This was easy for him, as he preferred the city to country life. Hans moved to Padang. It was Rita and the plantation manager, not Hans, who actually ran things.

In spite of her failed marriage, Helena was fond of her new home in the Indies. In the months to come, she was more able to slow down in rhythm with the melody of the islands. Her sturdy and starched European cottons had given way to softer, more flowing fabrics. She could exist with abated activity. She learned to live with the constant layer of perspiration on her skin. Her eyes became able to distinguish between greens to subtle shades and deeper into the many other layers of existence. For slight moments, while sitting on the veranda, her favorite spot, she could feel the presence of other worldly beings in the density of the jungle—between notes of the birdsong, inside the scents, and amongst the greens.

Helena, along with the unusual example of her independent and competent sister-in-law, enjoyed uncommon freedom and self-sufficiency. Hans, her husband, was content with the arrangement. He had his freedom and, with the fact that he was married, prevented potential suitors not to expect too much. Helena eased into a life without Hans. She continued to live at the plantation with Rita. The two women remained close and found roles that suited their characters and proclivities. Rita ran the plantation and Helena managed the household and servants. The *baru* (person living in the Indies born in Holland) became like the Indisch, or a totok. Helena also took an interest in the arts, music, and literature. She learned Malay. The two sisters kept a busy social calendar with dinners and parties at their home. So the time went by in a harmonious and pleasant manner. She moved easily in the various circles and social strata of her life, something she would not have had an opportunity to do in her more restrictive, provincial life in Holland. This was in part due to the wealth she enjoyed in the Indies, but also because of her amicable and flexible temperament. The two sisters were well-liked in many circles.

Chapter Seven

Sarina at the Warung

Sarina was born in a village near Yogyakarta on Java. In the aftermath of the revolts against the Dutch, many of the people in her and surrounding villages went to Sumatra as koelies. Both her parents worked on a plantation, where her father passed away from exertion. Not wanting the same fate for her daughter, her mother sent Sarina to live with an aunt in Padang. Aunt Dewi was an njai to a Dutch sergeant and had bore him three children. The women's section in the barracks had their own hierarchy based on the rank of their men. Hence, as njai to a sergeant, Dewi was able to take in her niece. In turn, Sarina was able to help with the chores. Between six a.m. and noon, the women and children were in their own section of the barracks performing duties, such as cooking, sewing, and laundry. The children proudly referred to themselves as *Anak Kompanie* or child of the company (battalion). Often the sons would also become soldiers and daughters would become njais.

---

[33] Indigenous women and children gathering at a *warung* (food stand). Retrieved May 23, 2019 from: https://commons.wikimedia.org/wiki/File: COLLECTIE_TROPENMUSEUM_Een_groep_vrouwen_en_kinderen_staat_bij_een_kraampje_(warung)_met_gado-gado_en_nasi_langs_de_weg_tussen_Gegesik_en_Arjawinangun_West-Java_TMnr_10002711.jpg

Sumatra, 1840

Two men sitting at a warung (food stand).

Dewi had begun a side business of cooking for the soldiers who did not have their own housekeepers. Sarina, her adept helper, would leave the barracks to purchase goods for the day's cooking, set up cooking pots, and chop vegetables. Soldiers from the barracks or living in homes of their own could have their afternoon meals prepared by the aunt and niece.

"S*ate padang* (skewered beef with yellow curry sauce) and *goeleh toendjang* (meat with young bamboo shoots)," said a tall, thin man with eyes the color of the sky.

Sarina nodded slightly and lowered her eyes. Her aunt cooked various dishes on the three-foot wide skillet. The rice was boiled in a conical bag of plaited palm fiber. With a large spatula she mixed the curried meats and vegetables and then topped it with ground coconut. There too were dishes with hot peppered sauces on the side. The curry was placed atop of the rice on banana leaf—the cup, bowl, and spoon of the tropics. Sarina made a bowl out of the banana as her aunt prepared Fransz's meal.

Sarina had formed her impressions of blanda men. Aside from their large, heavy stature and light coloring, she could smell them from several meters away.

"They're from a place that is colder than the tip of Marapi. Too cold to bathe," Dewi said wisely. "You can smell what they've been eating."

Sarina turned towards her aunt, incredulous.

"And they don't believe in it," her aunt added, chuckling.

"That, I can tell," her niece responded with a smile.

The temperature in the Indies ranged between in the thirty to thirty-five Centigrade (85-95 Fahrenheit), with eighty percent humidity. The wise learn to wear light clothing and change and bathe often, not only for comfort but also cleanliness and health. The blue-eyed soldier, unlike most, had a subtle, pleasant scent Sarina did not recognize. Each time he came to eat, she and her aunt would discreetly get a whiff and take turns guessing.

"*Jahe* (ginger)," Dewi said as he left.

Sarina shook her head. "*Asam gelugar* (dried tamarind)?"

"*Cengkih* (cloves)?"

After exhausting their repertoire of herbs and spices, they began anew with flowers.

"But it isn't sweet like flowers."

"Maybe they have flowers that are less sweet, like the way their food is bland."

And then they guessed which fruit they smelled.

"Still too sweet. What about fruit that are not sweet?"

"Durian!" Sarina said.

They both burst out laughing. (Durian tastes like ice cream but smells like a sweaty sock.)

They never did guess the amber scent Fransz used, but it kept aunt and niece entertained and served as a way to sublimate Sarina's thoughts about the well-mannered, handsome, albeit stiff blanda.

During his now ten years in the Indies, Fransz had grown accustomed to the local food. In the early days, he found it too strong tasting and hot, as they used too many spices and sambal (hot sauce) on everything. He'd seen inlanders mix the thick-red paste with rice and nothing else. He'd been

67

introduced to their foods in the barracks by the njais of some of his peers, as cafeteria meals were sparse and monotonous.

Fransz sat on the stool under the woven roof used to shade customers from the sun or protect them from the rain. He watched the young inlandse fold banana leaves with a delicate economy of movement. He admired the graceful, nimble hands. Meanwhile, kokkie Dewi mixed goat meat with bamboo shoots on the skillet and turned the skewers on the grill over an open fire.

"Toewan Fransz," the young woman said, as she placed the meal in the banana bowl in front of him. (*Toewan* or *Tuan* was a word used in respect.) Before Fransz could acknowledge her, she was back behind her aunt.

Each afternoon Fransz would eat and watch the round-eyed girl with nimble hands. She never looked him in the eyes. And Fransz did not let on to himself that the graceful Sarina intrigued him.

With his promotion to sergeant, he had moved into a house. That was seven years ago. He was now a lieutenant. Not enticed by the extracurricular activities typical of the soldiers, Fransz focused on his work. When on expedition, he became alive with anticipation of combat and the exhilarated relief once it ended.

Near dusk while walking home, Fransz passed an outer building near the main road. Hearing a muffled cry, he entered a shack where he encountered a man in the shadows who had cornered a young, inlandse woman. Not showing fear, she had anger in her eyes. The fierceness in her look could not make up the difference in the size, as the soldier was nearly a foot and a half taller than this slender girl.

"Jan Piet!" the Lieutenant called out.

The soldier looked up, inebriated and reluctant to give-up his prize.

"Leave her be!" Fransz said.

The soldier acquiesced. If not for Fransz's rank, there may have been a scuffle. Jan Piet left with a sneer, and Fransz turned his attention towards the young woman. Her clothes were slightly disheveled with a rip in the kabaja. She was trembling.

He then recognized her. "Sarina? Are you hurt?"

She shook her head. "Terima kasih (thank you), toewan." And she promptly left.

When Fransz returned to Dewi's warung the following day, Sarina was not there. He asked, without indicating what he had witnessed the night before, where she was.

"She has returned to her kampong to attend her ill mother," Dewi lied.

Was this the truth? Is this something she told her aunt or did the two concoct it? Fransz wondered, but said, "Is she very ill?" This was his way of inquiring whether Sarina would be returning.

"Time will tell," was Dewi's vague response.

Not knowing whether he should inquire further, Fransz wished them well and then ordered his usual. He hardly noticed what he was eating, he was thinking of Sarina. Dewi saw the Lieutenant's concern and offered to keep him abreast. This seemed to cheer the man, and Dewi began to speculate.

While Fransz had discovered them before Sarina had been raped, the encounter with the blanda left her full of shame and fear. Living and working so close to the barracks, this could easily happen again. So she stayed in the kampong with another family from Yogya. Meanwhile, her aunt was brewing a plan.

A week later, Dewi went to visit Sarina, who was happily surprised to see her aunt.

"Blue Eyes has come by every day since you've been gone. He asked when would you return."

Sarina kept her eyes lowered and did not say anything.

Dewi had planted a seed. When she saw Blue Eyes again, she said, "Sarina will not return for she feels ashamed and that you may think less of her."

"But," he began, and then understood.

Dewi's plan was practical and simple. Sarina, in spite of her justifiable prejudices towards blanda soldiers, found Blue Eyes most agreeable. Dewi was merely fostering what may otherwise never unfold. Would not becoming an njai housekeeper for Blue Eyes be an advantage to her niece? She would have a good home and the ability to help her mother. Over a period of several weeks it came to pass that Sarina moved into Blue Eye's home to become his housekeeper.

I don't actually know the circumstances of the birth, family, and the upbringing of any of my ancestors that were indigenous to Indonesia. Since the brother of my great-grandfather was born in Padang, I have imagined this young inlandse woman, a taste of her early life and invented her relationship with Fransz Joseph. Her story is based on impressions from reading Reggie Baay's book *De Njai*. Sarina is not a direct ancestor, since my family does not come from her son, Joseph. However, I felt it important to clarify the lifestyle and typical experiences for both the colonial soldier and the mother of his children. Some of these soldiers married their njais or would remain faithful to them, as if they were husband and wife. While Fransz Joseph had honor and integrity, non-Western indigenous people were not valued or believed to be equal to the Westerner, hence not deserving honorable or even humane treatment. Hence, many njais were left behind, with or without their children, or passed on to another soldier.

Chapter Eight

Fransz Meets Helena

Helena was dressed in a white, cotton-lace skirt and blouse appropriate for visits to the home of the Assistant Resident, Willem Hesselink. Jenny, Willem's young wife, and Helena were second cousins. Helena disembarked from the coach, and Jenny warmly welcomed her with a kiss on the cheek. After refreshments, the two took the accustomed afternoon nap, and for the remainder of the day they were inseparable. In spite of the ten-year age difference, Jenny and Helena always got on well and had much to discuss.

---

[34] Intending to illustrate the couple Fransz and Helena, this image is from a few decades later than when they met. I chose this because it had the feel I sought. Retrieved May 23, 2019 from:
https://commons.wikimedia.org/wiki/File:COLLECTIE_TROPENMUSEUM_Studioportr etten_van_een_man_en_een_vrouw_Nederlands-Indi%C3%AB_TMnr_60026871.jpg

Dinner and the Ball

They were both in Helena's room where the baboe was helping her dress for dinner. Helena's hair had been braided and rolled into the usual chignon. But Jenny, taking over, fixed Helena's hair by taking it out and making several looplets held in place with an ivory comb. In the front she formed ringlets.

"Like this," Jenny said, looking at Helena. "It compliments your face." As Helena regarded herself in the mirror, she saw that her face, with its firm chin, was soften by the ringlets. She then stood up in front of the mirror appreciating how the dress with its low, pointed waist, and billowing skirt accentuated her well-shaped body.

Example of a resident's house. Litho of an original watercolor by Rappard, 'The Resident's House in Surabaya.'

Helena rode in the carriage with Jenny and Willem to the Resident's lavish home. On route, she took in familiar scents of tropical fauna, the ubiquitous chirping of birds and of monkeys screeching, and natives walking submissively or carrying goods to deliver or to sell. Upon entering the mansion, she was struck by the immediate shift—from luscious disorderliness to the stark, formality of the resident's home with its tidy opulence.

Dinner was served in the back gallery—a long hall supported by white pillars decorated with flowering shrubs. Three female servants entered and circled the table; one carrying a silver basin for pouring rose water, and the other had a silver bowl for washing hands. The last one followed with towels for drying one's hands. The meal was a Dutch version of Indonesian menu the colonials called *rijsttafel* (literal translation rice table), which was originally developed to impress visitors with the exotic abundance of the colony. A cone-shaped plate of rice was set at the center of the table (hence rice table), and then a line of servants brought out steaming bowls with fish, meat, and fricassees, a variety of curries, sauces, preserved fruit, pickles, fried bananas, and young palm shoots. The meal was eaten with a fork and spoon. It was not Helena's first rijsttafel, but the variety and splendor never ceased to astound her.

After dinner, the guests gradually advanced towards the ballroom, where an ensemble was playing Strauss. Men, dressed in black suits walked stately around the room. The women moved gracefully in their light-hued gowns with large sleeves and billowing skirts.

The men hovered around the lovely Jenny like hummingbirds at a flowering bush. Standing next to Jenny, Helena was situated in a perfect position across from the entrance to observe new arrivals. Entering the arched doorway, she spied a tall and erect man in blue military uniform. His head shifted from left to right scanning the scene. He had a square face with a mustache and dark, almost black, wavy hair. Helena continued to mingle, but her awareness remained with the officer.

As the Lieutenant entered the room, he continued considering the crowd, occasionally nodding to great someone. He then unexpectedly turned and gazed in Helena's direction. Then the blue eyes met the hazel ones.

"It's the customary elegant assembly," a gentleman next to Helena said. She nodded in response but did not shift her focus.

Jenny followed Helena's gaze and said with a broad smile, "Lieutenant Berg." Jenny knew everyone.

He came over, took and kissed Jenny's gloved hand. He then looked up with penetrating, yet playful blue eyes and an engaging smile, which contrasted with the correctness in his general attitude.

"Fransz, this is my cousin, Helena de Wit-Falck," Jenny said and then to Helena, "Lieutenant Fransz Berg."

He nodded with a deep bow, and she curtsied in return.

"Fransz is in the same unit as Willem's cousin, Eric." She then said with a glimmer in her eye, "He likes to entertain us with poetry."

73

"Indeed?" Helena's interest heightened. "Which poets? Or do you pen your own?"

"Not for public," he said, enigmatically. "I enjoy the Romantics, mostly the Germans."

"Which?" she asked, curiously.

"Goethe, Schiller, Pushkin," he said, as his eyes widened.

"I am more familiar with the English—Blake, Byron, Keats..."

"Tyger! Tyger! burning bright,

In the forests of the night,

What immortal hand or eye,

Could frame thy fearful symmetry?" he recited.

Helena followed with the next verse, and conversation between the two flowed easily. As the others moved away or to dance, Helena and Fransz found themselves alone.

"Would you care to dance?" he asked.

Helena affirmed, and they waltzed to Strauss and then danced a Schottische, the new rage in Europe. When they became heated, the couple stopped to seek refreshments.

It began as a comfortable friendship with sparks of attraction that, for each with a different, private reason, neither dared address. There was much to ardently discuss, like literature, philosophy, poetry, and music. Helena was surprised that Fransz showed knowledge of Indonesian culture and history. The two talked little about themselves. Aside from being an intelligent and witty conversationalist, she unexpectedly found him reflective and philosophic. She would later discover that he, in spite of his self-control,

74

could behave most impulsively. He did so with the kind of courageousness and trust that could make rash behavior look well thought out. When it was time for her to leave Padang for home, Fransz asked whether he could come to visit.

When in town, Helena and Fransz would meet at the resident's home or various gatherings in Padang. In due course, Fransz called on her at the plantation. Helena was concerned about Rita's reaction. However, her sister-in-law could plainly see the mutual attraction even before Helena acknowledged her own feelings. Helena had been open with Fransz about her white-glove marriage with Hans that had been a mistake. She told Fransz that she was not divorced and that they lived separately.

Over time the friends became lovers. When not in the company of others, their favorite activity was to lounge on the veranda reading to the other their favorite poets and novelists. Fransz had some Russian and Helena knew English, and they both read French. She read fragments of the English poets and quite enjoyed hearing him recite in his mother tongue.

On this evening, Fransz listened to Helena as she read out loud from *The Hunchback of Notre-Dam*:

'Do you know what friendship is' he asked.
'Yes,' replied the gypsy; 'it is to be brother and sister; two souls which touch without mingling, two fingers on one hand.'

'And love?' pursued Gringoire.
'Oh! love!' said she, and her voice trembled, and her eye beamed. 'That is to be two and to be but one. A man and a woman mingled into one angel. It is heaven'

They read and conversed deep into the night over a bottle or two of wine.

Fransz was in a quandary. He should have told Helena about his own circumstances when Helena had spoken of her failed marriage. And while he knew that these arrangements were common and accepted in the Indies, he could not fully concede to his current circumstances. He felt an urgency to tell Helena the truth and blamed himself for his cowardliness. Had he only met Helena sooner. Now with recent developments, he did not know how to broach the subject.

Determined, at their next meeting, he asked Helena to sit. "I have something important to tell you."

"You are so serious," she smiled, touching his face.

"I need to tell you . . . I need to tell you," he faltered, then started a new. "You know that many unmarried men have inlandse housekeepers?" He said this looking down at his hands. "I should have said something before…." He paused and then looked into her eyes. "I live with an njai, Lena. And she is with child."

The words pierced like a knife in her stomach. It was one thing to find out about Hans and his njai. She had not actually loved her husband, but now…. Not Fransz too! Feeling numb and unable to speak, yet obliged to say something, she muttered, "I see." She could not look at him.

Fransz wanted to tell her that the intimacy he shared with Sarina had ended, but these words sounded lame in his ears. The guilt from the events leading to having to flee Germany, that he had pushed away, now reemerged. Not able to endure the intensity of his thoughts and emotions, along with Helena's silence, Fransz rose, bowed, and left. Helena left alone and in shock, collapsed in anguish.

Hours later, Rita found Helena sitting on the veranda with red and swollen eyes staring into nothingness. When Rita asked what was the matter, Helena said, "I am such a fool." Then slowly the story came out.

After another good cry in Rita's arms, the sister-in-law said, "He's a thoughtless *lafaard* (coward). What is the man thinking? Fool!"

It felt good to hear Rita scourge Fransz. Yet…

After a time, Rita continued with, "As much of a bastard that he is, I know the man loves you."

"But, Rita, he has an njai with child," said Helena gloomily.

"I appreciate your principles, but do you want to hear what I think"

"I suppose…"

"You cannot use the same standards that you would in Holland. As honorable as Fransz is, he is a man. They will have their njais and, with or without children, very few remain with, let alone marry them. He isn't the type to remain with an inlandse. If it isn't you, Helena, one day it will be another totok he'll marry. I see that you love each other."

Padang Panjang, 1841

The midwife called him into the room and handed Fransz the baby boy. He was elated, as a son would continue the Berg lineage. He named the boy Joseph Carl Leonard (all family names). And yet his initial elation was overshadowed by his muddled feelings and behavior towards Helena. Fransz was conflicted between his joy and his shame and sadness.

Neither had attempted to contact the other. In spite of Rita's advice, Helena was caught by her convictions. Several weeks had passed when she realized that her courses had not come. *For how long? Three months?* After the initial feeling of joy, as she so longed for a child, Helena could not allow a romantic fantasy take control. She must write Fransz.

Dear Fransz,
It is most important I speak with you. Can we meet at the Club in Padang for tea
this coming Sunday?

Sincerely,
Helena

Relieved to hear from her, yet Fransz was troubled by the tone of her cryptic letter. Upon meeting, he detected distress in her kind eyes. Sitting across from each other, they both became shy. Then both spoke at once. Fransz gestured for Helena to begin.

"This would normally be good news, but I fear…" she faltered. Then gaining courage, she said. "I'm with child." She held his gaze, but Fransz's expression was blank. Slowly the corners of those blue eyes crinkled as his mouth lifted into a smile. This encouraged her to continue. "I am troubled, Fransz. You already have a woman and a child. But I thought that you should know."

"My dear, believe me, I am relieved that you want to see me and happy with your news," he began. "Please forgive me, Lena. I should not have run off like that."

It took some convincing to reconcile his personal state of affairs with her. While Helena did not want to share this man, even had she not been expecting, she had to admit she could not let him go. While swallowing her jealousy and principles, she put forward that Sarina remain in his home with their child, to continue as his housekeeper. In that way, both parents could be with the boy. As Rita predicted, Fransz would have dismissed his njai, but acquiesced, while admiring the integrity of Helena's proposal.

Fransz believed that his Oma would perhaps understand. While not 'officially' accepted in the colonial community, Fransz and Helena's marital arrangements were not uncommon. Helena would ask Hans for a divorce so she could marry Fransz.

Sarina modestly conveyed her competence as a mother. Due to her position as well as from her cultural background, she would be expected to defer to Fransz. In the Javanese community, *rukun,* to live in harmony, was an important value and lifestyle. Sarina did not express or show her feelings. That's how she lived with Fransz before Helena and so she continued. She engaged Fransz as she would her elders or superiors by being respectful, obedient, and with emotional distance. While in the beginning it was so with Helena, something about the blanda woman made it easier for Sarina to open up.

Sarina had not shared intimacy with Fransz for many months. When she realized the blanda was with child, Sarina became fearful. She did not fear for her son. Fransz wouldn't give him up, but he could take the child away from her. Knowing that she had no rights, she looked for signs of what she most feared. However, months passed and all continued as it had been before. Sarina learned that the blanda Helena was kind and sympathetic.

Sarina's private name for the boy was Yos, short for Yosef, which she only used when his father was not present. In spite of his instructions, when Yos' father was not home, which was often, she continued to allow him to sleep with her. Even though she was learning Dutch and instructed to speak it with her son, she continued to communicate in her own tongue. She did many other things that his father considered spoiling and pampering. Sarina raised Yosef as she had been raised. And when Fransz was present, she readily acquiesced to his ways.

At the same time, Sarina did her best to bring up her son so that he would have the advantages she saw of *nakinderen* (literal translation: after children, those from a European woman) versus *voorkinderen* (children before, or those from a njai). She also wanted to convey to him that there existed different perspectives to life. Sarina had no formal education, but she had an inner knowing that the circumstances in her world were not set by any natural law. One day things could change. She knew that there was much more that determined life circumstance and regimes, even more than what was presented as Adat.[35]

Sarina also could see the contradictions in Fransz's thoughts and beliefs. Fransz feared that Joseph would not be accepted in European society, but his fears came from his own prejudices. Could he accept a boy, so dark, and potentially possessing so many of the characteristics Fransz thought inferior? It mattered much less to Sarina what Fransz thought of her than his feelings for the child she loved and needed to protect. She wanted what was best for their son, and she was not convinced it was being part of the European community. This she only thought, but would never speak out loud, not even to Dewi.

Two months later, Helena awoke with cramps, feeling sticky wetness between her legs. *Oh no! It can't be*, she thought. *No, please, no!*

She called out for Sulu, who seeing Helena's distress, ran for Rita. The latter sent for help. The cramps and bleeding continued as they waited for the midwife. By the time she had arrived, Helena had already lost a lot of blood. The midwife examined the patient and then looked at Rita, shaking her head. "Even had I arrived sooner, this was not meant to be. I believe that the mother will recover." She treated Helena with some herbs to help stop the bleeding and others to quiet the suffering woman.

Two days later Fransz arrived. As Rita took him to Helena's room, he found her weak, pale, and sleeping. Both stood by Helena's bedside in silence, and then Rita left Fransz with his beloved.

"My dear, Lena. I am so sorry…" he trailed.

"I know that voice," Helena thought, but the pull of unconsciousness remained strong. As if it was a dream, she could hear in the distance someone

---

[35] The customary law of the indigenous peoples of Malaysia and Indonesia was an unwritten, traditional code governing all aspects of personal conduct.

weeping. It then reminded her of her own loss. As she stirred, mumbling with grief, "No," she could feel a hand gently taking her own. With effort she opened her hazel-green eyes looking straight into his sky blue ones.

"My love," he whispered.

It took quite some time for Helena to recover. Fransz visited frequently. When she was well enough, he spoke to her.

"Lena. I am so very sorry for all that has happened. I wish…I wish…." he trailed. "One day we shall have a child." Then with questioning eyes, "Is that what you want, too?"

"Yes," she replied weakly.

Chapter Nine

A Culmination of Events

In November of 1845 Fransz was promoted to captain. As life goes, one thing supervened another. Not long after the good news, he received a letter from Dietz that his grandmother had passed away. He knew when he left Dietz all those years ago that his goodbyes would most likely be final, but hearing of his Oma's passing hit him hard.

"My mother was not very resilient. She relied on my father's strength. And when he died, his mother stepped in. Oma always knew what to do. Without her, we all would have been lost." He ruminated to Helena, who listened while *pijiting* (massaging) his forehead, something she learned living in the Indies.

---

[36] Image of battle in Lombok off of Bali by J. Hoynck van Papendrecht (1858-1933). Retrieved May 23 from:
https://commons.wikimedia.org/wiki/File:Lombok_1894_J._Hoynck_van_Papendrecht_18 58_1933.jpg

"While stern in ways, Oma was very kind and generous and . . . she was funny," he said with a laugh as if remembering something she had said. A tear emerged from his right eye, and he became silent. He had never told Helena why he'd come to the Indies, and he rarely talked of home. With her encouragement and with the idea they may go together, Fransz applied to take a furlough to Germany and to Holland to visit their families. Perhaps they would marry there.

When Fransz's furlough was approved, he and Helena prepared to leave for Europe. Meanwhile, trouble was brewing in Bali. When the Balinese plundered a shipwreck near Buleleng, the Dutch had asked payment for these goods. The Balinese refused, and so the Dutch invaded Buleleng. Consequently, Fransz's leave had been rescinded, and he was transferred to a regiment in Bali. Helena could see that the repeal of his furlough was a great blow, yet Fransz readily rose to duty. There had been talk of Helena joining him and taking both Sarina and Joseph, if not to Bali, to East Java so they would be closer by. However, they needed to be married for Helena to join Fransz. While she was waiting for a divorce, it made sense to see how the circumstances were in Bali. In the end, no one joined Fransz. Sarina and Joseph remained in Padang Panjang and Helena at the plantation.

When Fransz said his good byes, he formally shook his son's hand. It saddened Sarina to see that he could not even show affection to his five-year-old son. In trying to be brave, Yos held back his tears until his father was out of sight.

Bali Campaigns [37]

Led by Major General J. C. Wijck, the Dutch navy invaded north Bali at Buleleng on June 1846 with 1700 soldiers carrying twenty-three canons on nearly twenty large and twice as many smaller ships. A minority of the fighters for the KNIL was European, with the majority being Javanese and Madurese and some African. Three thousand Balinese defended Buleleng carrying lances

---

[37] Particulars of the Bali campaigns were taken from Piet Hagen. (2018). *Koloniale oorlogen in Indonesië: Vijf eeuwen verzet tegen vreemde overheersing*. Amsterdam: De Arbeiderspers, pp. 348-361; 421-424 and "Dutch Intervention in Bali (1849)," *Wikipedia*. Retrieved on March 13, 2019: https://en.wikipedia.org/wiki/Dutch_intervention_in_Bali_(1849)

and fire weapons. They had reinforced the shore with a three-meter high barricade lined with sixty canons with trenches behind it occupied by 600 shooters. In spite of the solid defense, the colonials bombarded the port and marched on to Buleleng, captured its fort, and burned the houses. The Balinese fled to the jungle, and the guns and ammunition left behind fell to the Dutch. The following day, the colonial army moved on to Singajara where the palace had been abandoned. The Governor-General Rochussen requested from the Raja Gusti Ketut Jelanik Dutch sovereignty and reimbursement for the costs of war in the amount of 300,000 guilders.

Bali
November 14, 1846

My Dear Helena,

The circumstances here are forbidding. Our navy has invaded and successfully destroyed the royal palace at Singajara. There continues to be much combat all over the island. We expect with reinforcements to have things under control.

I think of you walking through the gardens or sitting on your favorite chair with a glass of tea and a book. I keep the miniature portrait of you safe inside my pocket wrapped in your handkerchief.

Have you been able to visit Joseph? Has he grown? How is his tutoring coming along? I will write again soon when all is resolved here.

Yours faithfully and affectionately,

Fransz

These letters continued to come faithfully for two and a half years. The fighting in Bali continued, and Fransz never returned to Padang Panjang in Sumatra.

While the Dutch and the Balinese were in supposed negotiation, Prince Dawa Agung from Kloengkoeng secretly had convinced his fellow rajas to ignore the demands made by the Dutch. They continued to plunder Dutch shipwrecks and didn't pay the compensation. This enraged Rochussen needed to show the strength of the Dutch to other European nations that were keeping a close watch. In the meantime, the rajas bought weapons and made plans to expel the colonials from their fort. They cut off the water and blocked delivery of food. At least a hundred KNIL soldiers died of hunger and disease. Others had to be transported back to Java to be hospitalized and were replaced by healthy soldiers. Fransz was integral in many of these expeditions, returning to Java to recuperate, train newcomers, and strategize.

In mid April 1848 there was another expedition against Buleleng, Karangasem, and Kloengkoeng. The Dutch invaded with four steam vessels, five schooners, and eleven transports with seventy-two canons. Fransz was among the troops that destroyed the harbor, villages, and orchards, plundering temples near Bunkulun. With the assurance of artillery backup coming from the sea, the Captain led his men through a small mountain pass to Jagaraga. There 10,000 Balinese with fire weapons and twenty-five canons defended their fort. The Dutch attempted to attack from both sides. As the troops neared the bastion, some Balinese men came around back through a ravine. Hence, Fransz and his men were trapped and had to fight fiercely to get back to the ships.

Puputan (mass suicide) of the Raja of Boeleleng

In March of 1849, General Andreas Victor Michiels led a fleet of eighty-nine war and transport ships with more than 250 canons, many mortars and guns, and with 10,000 men heading from Java to Bali. After Michiels occupied the fort in Singajara, the Raja of Karangasem and Prince Gusti Gede Jelantik were open to negotiate. The atmosphere was tense, and Michiels wanted the Balinese punished for previous deeds. No agreements were made and fighting ensued. The subsequent battles were bloody and the conditions were poor—camps were ridden with illness, especially cholera.

A thousand of the colonial soldiers were hospitalized. More than 2,000 colonial soldiers had already been lost to battle and disease. The warfare continued.

Fransz led a segment marching once again towards Buleleng. Disoriented from exhaustion, he was uncertain as to what he was encountering. *Had another unit arrived before them?* he thought. He continued to march through the carnage with his men, seeing layers of bodies like an emptied box of toothpicks. When he saw a dead man still holding a *kris* connected to his own breast, Fransz understood. The Balinese had committed *puputan* (mass-suicide in preference to facing the humiliation of surrender). The Captain could hear the crying of a child coming from the carnage. Not exactly triumphant over defeating the enemy, the colonials marched back to their camp joining General Michiels.

Bali
May 21, 1849

My Dear Helena,

I find myself back on the ship with many others who are wounded. Before you concern yourself, I am well. However, several of my men are not—with parts of their bodies missing or with gaping wounds in their chests. I hear men call out in French, German, Dutch, and Javanese praying to Jesus, Mary, and Allah. I am sorry to be so brusque.

The Balinese outnumber us, and they are fierce. Yet they have lost tenfold of men, 1,000 to our 100. General Michiels, the iron eater, has been summoned to take over our next expedition.

I hold the lock of hair close to my heart until we are together.

Yours with love and affection,
Fransz

A few nights later, a Balinese leader, Dewa Agung Istri led a surprise attack in Karangasem that resulted in General Michiels being wounded in the leg. The doctor gave the commander the choice of immediate amputation or risking the journey back to the ship to be operated. Michiels chose the latter but collapsed in surgery and died later from infection. Captain Fransz Berg, also wounded, had a deep cut in his right thigh.

This setback along with the strength of 33,000 Balinese fighters forced the Dutch to retreat. A year later, another mass suicide and death of every Balinese prince impeded the Balinese resistance, and a treaty was signed in July 1849 that gave Dutch control of Buleleng and Jembrana.

Meanwhile, Fransz along with his battalion had relocated to Soerabaja on Java. The Captain took a long time to recover, as the wound in his right leg would not heal due to an insidious infection. While he had many times over been able to wash away the ugliness of war, this experience of the mass suicide remained vivid.

Helena Visits Bandung

Letters from Fransz became less frequent, but news of the fighting and conditions in Bali did reach Padang. After months of no word from Fransz, she received a note from a Lieutenant van der Meijden that Fransz had been injured and was recovering in Soerabaja. Needing a change of scenery and hoping to eventually go to him, Helena decided to go to Java to visit her uncle. Oom Carl met her at the Hotel Des Indes in Batavia, where they stayed a few nights before making the overland trek to Bandung. As she saw the familiar face from home, tears formed and her throat thickened.

"*Ach, meisje* (oh, my girl)," he said, and gave her a warm hug. And so they stood for a long while before separating. "You are very courageous."

"I don't know about that," she responded.

"I can't help but feel responsible, as I'm the one who put ideas of travel in your head. Had you never come here…"

"Please, don't," she interjected. "Do not feel in the least bit responsible, Oom. I may have been naïve, but I have no regrets."

So Carl let it be. Just being in the company of her favorite Oom brought Helena to some peace and with more hope.

The trip to Bandung along the *De Groote Postweg* (Great Post Road) took four hours. They were carried in a coach drawn by Java ponies and, when the ascent grew steeper, buffalos were led by dozens of koelies. On route, they passed rice fields scattered with people at work. Her Oom explained how the inlandse harvested the rice. "This is

Groote Postweg

intricate work because the blades are cut one-by-one at the tip," he expounded. "The part that is cut with the hull still on is called a paddy. The remainder of the stalk is then left to enrich the soil. They then till the ground with a large plough using a water buffalo and then let in water to break up the clods. When the plants are four to five inches high, they'll be moved to larger beds. This is why there are so many working in the fields.

"When owners give them sickles, they use it for a day and then go back to their old methods. These methods are part of their religious beliefs. And they are not as bothered by time as we are. I guess I should say that they don't experience it in the same way as we do. They don't see the value of gaining time. They live more in the moment."

As they ascended the hilly slopes, Helena felt the drop in temperature—a cool twenty-one to twenty-three degrees Centigrade (70-75 Fahrenheit.) Between 600 to 1200 meters (2000 and 4000 feet) above sea level, the village of Bandung was beautifully situated in the mountain basin at the foot of the Tangkuban volcano with Citarum Kali (the longest river in Java) running through it. They came to a lane lined with *kenari* (nutmeg) trees that arched thirty meters (a hundred feet) overhead creating a green cathedral. Their trunks were covered with ferns, creeping palms, blooming orchids, and several types of air plants.

Bandung had many tea plantations and vacation homes for those escaping the heat of Batavia. Modest compared to the surrounding properties,

89

her Oom Carl's home had the most beautiful gardens she had ever seen. Carl, now retired from his position at a tea plantation, was a naturalist. As they rode up the driveway to his home, a colorful bird with a beautiful florescent-green neck and a tail nearly a meter and a half long (seven feet) and almost as wide, walked across the greens. Helena almost stood up in the carriage, as her mouth gaped open.

Oom Carl grinned. "I have an aviary of local birds and specimens of the most rare butterflies from all over Java."

A handsome woman with distinct indigenous features and hazel eyes and dressed in an exquisitely patterned sarong greeted them at the steps. Lien, her oom's wife, was Indisch.

"Welcome," she said with a calm ease. "You must be tired from your travels." She then turned to her husband, and they kissed each other on each cheek.

After she was led to her room, Helena freshened up. They had a light meal with both Dutch and Indisch nourishment before returning to their rooms to rest. After the midday siesta, her Oom gave Helena the grand tour of his gardens and then, in an outer building, showed her the large aviary.

He had planted a variety of fruit trees included *pisang* (banana), *pepaya* (papaya), *manga* (mango), rambutan, *kelapa* (coconut), *manggis* (mangosteen), *kedongdong*, (ambarella), and *jereuk* (pomelo). There was an abundance of flowering plants, such as various hibiscus, bougainvillea, low growing begonias, creamy and delicate jasmine, ginger, pink and red roses, cambodja-blossoms of yellow, pink and purple, and tuberose. From trunks or tree branches grew orchids, as well as delicate ferns looking like green feathery tails of chickens. With each turn in the garden, Helena was awestruck. Her Oom grinned with pride. The aviary was like a moving rainbow of colors with scarlet minivets, crimson and black orioles, blue crested Java pigeons, cockatoos, parrots, and pheasants with their long tails. All had their own cooing, chirping, or screeching birdsongs.

It was nearly dark when they returned to the house, where Lien was waiting working on a songket[38] sitting at the table laden with tea, coffee, fruit, and sweets to tide them over until dinner, which would be at eight. Accustomed to the Indisch ways, Helena dressed for dinner, changing from her sarong and *kabaja* (lace blouse for a woman or jacket for a man) to a flowing but tight-waiste European frock.

Oom Carl and Lien intermixed Malay with Dutch, which Lien spoke with an Indisch inflection that sounded soft and musical. Dinner conversation varied from local news and politics, the children and grandchildren, and about their daytime pastimes.

The stay with Oom Carl and Tante Lien was a balm. Helena took many walks through the lush gardens. The three made trips into Bandung. But mostly it was the calm presence of Tante Lien and the jovial company of her oom that cheered Helena. The couple frequently entertained and would play games or read plays or passages from their favorite books out loud. Often their daughters and sons-in-law would come with the seven grandchildren, ages one to nine. The older girls would dress up and perform skits for the adults. It was the little ones, still wanting to sit on Oma's and eventually Helena's lap, who Helena enjoyed most. The extended family sat at the long dining table talking and laughing. While the children knew all too well that, once the coffee was brought out, it was time for bed. They would linger with calculated questions aimed at Opa Carl who loved telling stories.

Helena, with the two-year-old Lettie on her lap, recited while indicating with each finger beginning with the thumb:

'*Naar bed, naar bed', zei Duimelot.*

(To bed, to bed,' said Thumbsalot,)

'*Eerst nog wat eten,' zei Likkepot.*

(Let's eat something first,' said Lick-the-pot.)

---

[38] The word songket comes from the Malay sungkit, which means to hook. Songket cloth is a brocade hand-woven in silk or cotton. The intricate patterns are then picked out in gold or silver threads to create a luxurious fabric that is commonly worn for ceremonial occasions as either a sarong, headscarf, or sash.

'*Waar zal ik het halen?*' *zei Lange Jan.*
(Where do I get it?' said Long John.)

'*Uit grootmoeder's kastje,*' *zei Ringeling.*
(From grandmother's cupboard,' said Ringaling.)

'*Dat zal ik verklappen,*' *zei 't Kleine Ding.*
(I'm going to tell on you!' said Little Thing.)

Of course, this needed to be repeated over and over again before Lettie would go to bed. Soon, she could recite it herself and would try to sit on each of the adult's laps using their fingers and proudly reciting in Dutch.

Chapter Ten

39

Lintang from Soerabaja

Delirium and the Dukun

"No, please, not them too. Stop! Stop!" He pleaded, yelling out loud.

His colleague, George van der Meijden, came to his side. "Wake up, Fransz," he said shaking his friend forcefully. "You are dreaming again."

In his delirium, Fransz repeatedly saw images of the faces of the women and children left slaughtered in their villages and the piles of bodies from the mass suicide. Among them were the faces of his sons.

---

[39] Since I have no images of the fictitious *njais,* I used this one of a Javanese woman from the Tropenmuseum via Wikimedia Commons. Retrieved June 9, 2021 from: https://commons.wikimedia.org/wiki/File:COLLECTIE_TROPENMUSEUM_Studioportr et_van_een_verkoopster_met_een_mand_jambu_bol_vruchten_in_haar_slendang_Nederlan ds-Indi%C3%AB_TMnr_60022730.jpg

The mixed-blood Lieutenant had urged Fransz to try a local healer. Even had Fransz believed in the *guna* (white magic), he did not trust that an *inlandse* would help a military person.

"I know several others who have used the dukun with good reports. I beg you, Fransz, try him." George would not relent.

He finally conceded, and George made arrangements with a *dukun* (healer), Pak Adju. The Javanese term *Pak* is used for an elder or out of respect.[40]

Pak Adju came within a day. Fransz let George, who had fluent Javanese, do the talking. The healer nodded in greeting and then was still for a long while. "You are unsure about this healing," he finally said to Fransz. "This will not work if you do not trust."

Fransz looked at the dukun. All he had known and believed since he had lived in this place felt so uncertain. The dark-eyed man saw turmoil in the other's light eyes. He said in Javanese, while still looking at Fransz, "The illness in your leg can be cured with herbs. Since neither your western nor our methods have worked, I surmise that your trouble is of a spiritual nature." He then paused as he allowed his words to be translated and for signs that Fransz was truly hearing. "Your soul is in battle with itself and this makes you weak, unable to heal. As a result a *setan* (spirit) has entered you, which is causing what you call nightmares. However, the setan is speaking to you.

"I will say a prayer and then insert a gold needle in your scalp and one in your chest. This is to purify. But this alone will not help. Augment with prayers from your own religion."

The dukun spoke soberly, and while his explanation made no sense, something in his tone brought ease to Fransz. And so Pak Adju proceeded with a quiet chant, inserted the needles, and left Fransz with a bag of herbs for the wound in his thigh.

---

[40] In Java, healers and gurus maintain a regular profession as well as that of healer. Their healing work is performed without *pamrih* (self interest) and they take care for their own livelihood. Healers were paid with donations of useful things like chickens or cigarettes. However, the dukun had particular status within their communities.

94

Lintang, 1849 [41]

Many of the main streets in Soerabaja were lined with shading trees, such as the sweet smelling tamarind. Men carried pots held with ropes on a pole—one on each side—to sprinkle the roads with water to keep down the dust. This job would take the entire day, except for a break during the midday hours. There was a *passer* on the greens surrounding a *waringin* (banyan) tree that shaded the shops. Waringin trees have a family of roots that crawl above the ground, and from the large branches smaller ones drop down creating an enormously wide series of trunks. A popular gathering spot, residents came there to shop and to meet. The youth would play games and have rhyming contests. Elders met to exchange news or gossip. Once a week, you would hear the jingling of gamelan, with the singer telling *tjeritas* (stories or historical tales), reciting *pantuns* (poetry), or love songs. In addition, the resonant *alang alang* (reed) would also be heard. This ancient instrument is made of five or eight graduated bamboo tubes cut like organ pipes that hang loosely in a frame. The player would shake or the bamboo would swing in the breeze from a tree branch, producing enchanting melodies.

At this time of day at a kampong in Soerabaja life occurred in relative tranquility. It was morning just after sunrise when Lintang joined the other women and girls to bathe in the *kali* (river) near a tree. As she entered the water, Lintang tied her hair in a knot and then splashed water on her face, arms, and breast. The other women mirrored her movements in the water. Young mothers would slowly lead the little ones into the shallows. Older children splashed and swam, laughing and calling to each other. When done bathing, the women attended to each other's long, black hair in the shade by the riverbank. They finished their toiletry by adorning themselves with flowers. When done, Lintang strolled back to the kampong where she joined others for the

Indonesian man sprinkling road

---

[41] Adapted from Augusta De Wit. (1905). *Facts and fancies*. London: Chapman & Hall, Ltd.

morning meal outside squatting near the cooking pot. With her right hand she scooped rice with vegetables from a banana leaf.

As I describe this sensual and communal morning routine, I wonder what conversations the women shared. What were their hopes and dreams? What was Lintang's family life at home? Was she content with the simplicity in her lifestyle or was she fearful and oppressed by her overlords the colonials? And, if so, how did she cope?

Indonesian women washing and bathing in the kali (river)

Lintang then visited different stands greeting the shopkeepers by name. At the fruit stand, she bought bananas, langsat, kelapa, papaya, and durian, her toewan's favorite. She also purchased fresh spices such as galanga, nutmeg, cloves, and lemon grass, and the stinky *trassi* (made of fermented fish) for various dishes. Most prized was the fish that had been preserved in wet rice fields during the rainy season. Particular, Lintang inspected the goods carefully. She would shake her head and proceed to another vendor either because she was not satisfied with the freshness or to obtain a better price. She then carried her goods to her toewan's house. Like Lintang, many of the inlandse are employed as domestic servants in homes of European residents. Towards the end of the day, many would return to their kampong and again bathe in the kali and meet for conversation, gossip, or to play games.

Arriving at his home, she left her wares in the out-kitchen and then removed her shoes to enter the house and check on Toewan Fransz. Pak Adju, her grandfather, had suggested to George van der Meijden that Lintang nurse Fransz back to health. Lintang approached his room with silent footsteps. She then waited, hunched, until she had permission to enter. Perspiration covered the sleeping blanda's body, which had matted down his wavy hair. Lintang proceeded silently. She set about getting a pan of water to cool him. With her slight hand, she'd reach in the pan to gather water, which she dripped onto the white skin reddened by fever. She repeated this process covering his entire body while singing as if in prayer. She then offered him sips of water from a glass so as to cool his inside as well. As he roused slightly, she spooned the herbal tea into his mouth bit by bit, still singing. She then hand fed him softened rice cooked in coconut milk. He was like a child, as were his tantrums when he did not like the bitter taste of the medicine. Sometimes he would speak to her in his foreign tongue calling her 'mama.' Within the past week, he had become more alert, recognized her, and in Malay mixed with German, he talked of a home in that cold faraway land and a boy and a woman in Sumatra. Being there at a most vulnerable time during his recovery, Fransz became attached to the sound of Lintang's soft voice and her gentle, nurturing demeanor. She was very attentive in that subtle and refined manner that, particularly now, was so vital. In turn, Lintang became quite fond of Fransz. Over time, she did not return home in the evening but remained with Fransz.

Lintang was sixteen. At that time, young women sometimes were wed at twelve. When trying to put myself in her shoes, it is difficult to imagine how she overcame the age gap and crossed the boundaries of her culture to feel comfortable with this military man. Why would she take on the 'job' as his nurse? Was it an opportunity to earn a living? Did she feel fear, at first, sleeping in his home? How did this change her status in the village? She most likely cared for him, but what would induce her to eventually share his bed?

Fransz's Recovery

It had been 20 years since Fransz had to leave his home and had joined the KNIL. A military career had suited his temperament. He had received commendations and enjoyed being an officer. Yet during his several-month recovery, he was no longer able to divert his attention from the past that had been unconsciously driving him. The mass suicide in Bali brought up memories of other battles and of mass killings executed by him and his soldiers. Images of the women and children continued to surface. For the first time he questioned his occupation.

Helena, in hearing of his injury, wanted to come to him. Fransz deterred her. His thigh had healed and the dreams, while had not ended altogether, had lessened. Fransz remained troubled and was not ready to have Helena come. In contrast to the weighty events of the past three years, Helena had become a memory, sometimes quite illusory. He had always been able to manage well, so it was unfamiliar to be so uncertain and full of doubt. Seeing this tone in his letters, Helena knew something was amiss and would not wait any longer. She told her uncle that she wanted to go to Fransz, and so he arranged for Helena to stay with cousins in Soerabaja.

Bandung
22 August 1849
Dearest Fransz,

Reading between the lines of your letters, I know that you are not yourself. It is most difficult to truly understand what has happened to you and to know what to do from afar. I have been patiently waiting and have decided to be bold. By the time you receive this, I will be on route to Soerabaja. I must see you!

I will be staying with the Castricum family, cousins of Rita. They live on the Toenjoengan. Please know that I love you.

Yours affectionately,

Helena

Fransz had mixed emotions about her coming. He was filled with gratitude and a sense of relief. He always felt at home with Helena and he missed her. He would have dismissed Lintang but his second njai was now carrying his child. How would he tell Helena that he once again had fathered a child with another?

Within a week Fransz received another note informing him to meet at the Toko Oen, a restaurant in the quarters near where Helena was staying.

When Helena arrived, she saw Fransz sitting hunched over at a table by the window. His civilian clothes looked disheveled and he was thin. Staring out of the window, he hadn't noticed her arrival. When she called his name, he slowly turned as if in a daze. His formerly bright eyes had become distant, blank. She could not recognize the man she loved. He rose to greet her, but his embrace was tenuous.

In this state, Fransz told her about Lintang. He needed to do that first. Helena was more shocked by his demeanor than his news. She would face the news about the pregnant njai later when on her own. While she wanted to take him into her arms, to console, she knew better. There was still the pride, even now. And so she listened. Slowly he began to tell her of the nightmares, the faces of the women and children, and of the dukun's healing. Her empathy grew as he poured out his story much like a confession, and slowly Fransz became more himself. His posture straightened and he could look into her eyes.

Helena arranged to meet his new njai. The round belly betrayed her youthful face and girlish frame. Helena felt a pang of envy. *Why was it not herself with child?* The young woman's sweetness and innocence assuaged Helena's envy. She knew she had Fransz's love. The two women simply took to each other, not with equality of friends, but more as younger and older sister. When it came time for the birth, most unconventional, Helena was present. On November 18, 1849, Johan Jacob was born, who would be called Jan or Jantje. The attending midwife handed the baby to Lintang. The boy had his mother's round face and his coloring was light, more like coffee with a good amount of cream. While hard to tell so early on, it appeared that his eyes too would be light.

The midwife put some betel nut in her mouth, chewed and sucked, and then walked to the four corners of the house and spit out the red juice. She also closed all the doors and windows. Fransz and Helena began to protest. However, Lintang looked at them fiercely, a first at asserting herself.

"The midwife is making sure no *boerong* enters," Lintang said urgently.

"Boerong?" Both Fransz and Helena echoed.

"A spirit of a woman who has lost her child and out of jealousy steals the children of others. She comes just before sunset." Lintang said this as a matter of fact as one would say if you leave the door open, flies will enter.

So the blandas acquiesced.

Lintang was not at all possessive of her son and happily shared the job of mothering with Helena. And so, Helena became Jan's mother and Lintang became the 'baboe.'

It was auspicious for Fransz that the arrangement worked out so well. He and Helena were still not married, but lived as if they were. Fransz longed to have his elder son join them. He argued that Joseph was now old enough to be away from his mother. "And what of Sarina?" Helena questioned. Fransz refused to bring Sarina to Soerabaja.

Lintang appeared at the edges of my imagination as a young and simple girl, barely woman. She was much different than Sarina, who was what in the west we would call self-assured. Nevertheless Lintang had the facility, with the help of the dukun, to heal Fransz from these physical and traumatic psychic wounds. Lintang was not troubled or anxious. She was a puella. While naïve about some things, she intuitively knew and graciously used her gifts of gentility, nurturing, and joy.

He is walking through the jungle alone. Where are his men? He has no machete to cut through the dense jungle. He feels for a kris, for anything, but has no weapons. There is terror in his gut. He then hears the sound of a child and looks into the clearing. He hurries towards the opening, as the child's cry intensifies. Upon exiting the dense bamboo, the bright sun glares and, at first, it is difficult to see. The crying persists. As his eyes adjust, he sees a wide-open field littered with bodies. Upon a heap in the middle is a baby not old enough to walk. Fransz runs, leaping over arms, legs, and heads, trying not to look into the faces, trying to reach the child, to save the child, but he can't make it. His legs stop working....

Jolted awake, Fransz arose in a sweat. The baby was still crying. Shocked by the images, Fransz jumped out of bed and ran to the adjacent room where Lintang was holding Jantje. He grabbed the child from her, collapsing on the floor and rocking back and forth while holding tightly onto the child he could save. Frightened, the boy shrieked, and Fransz held him yet tighter. Someone was trying to pry the baby from him, and Fransz, now also crying, would not let go. Both father and son wailed in terror. Helena, a heavy sleeper, had now awakened and joined Lintang, both trying to pry the baby from Fransz. Lintang backed up and then pulled Helena away from the scene, gesturing to 'shush' with her fingers to her mouth. She then walked gently towards Fransz, who was still squeezing the frightened child, and carefully stroked the soldier's head, singing softly and intermittently whispering, "Let me help you save the boy." She then parted his arms to reach in and save her son, their son. She handed Jantje to Helena and the baby continued to cry and whimper in his other mother's arms. Lintang positioned herself behind Fransz, and with her small, delicate arms, held the much larger man and rocked, as she continued to sing quietly.

Padang Panjang, 1850

Sarina understood how it was with the men and their njais. In some ways, she should be grateful because Fransz always provided for her and their son. It would be inconceivably difficult to part with Yos. She could not decline. Because Joseph was legally European, he fell under their laws. She would lose her son and never see him again. The grief was insurmountable. With his officer's salary, Fransz was able to make arrangements for a small income, and Sarina could continue to live in their home. That was his way. Good with arranging but not with relations. Sarina, in the end, chose to be with her own people. And, in the end, she also resolved that her son would have a better life in the European, privileged society. She never recovered from the grief of losing Yos.

A few months after Joseph arrived, Fransz received a letter from his sister in Germany that his mother was ill. He applied for and was granted another leave. Fransz embarked to go to Germany by way of Rotterdam in November 1850, a few days after Jantje's first birthday. The couple talked about Helena joining, but her practical nature and sense of responsibility presided. It would be best for the children that she remains with them. It was agonizing to finally be together again and then having to part.

Lintang and Helena, 1850-1852

The two mothers raised the two boys. Helena began to learn Javanese through the stories Lintang told and songs she sang to Jantje. In this manner, she was also more able to understand what she viewed as idiosyncrasies and superstitions of the culture. For instance, Lintang would not allow Jantje to go to the outer gallery after dark. While this made sense due to possible dangers of wildlife, the reason was because a *wewe gombel* (scary supernatural creature) would kidnap the boy. She would also say to Joseph or even Helena, "Don't stand at the doorway, or you may never find a wife (to Yos) or husband (to Helena)."

Indonesian woman with child in a slendang

Astute at intuiting these matters, Helena saw in Lintang's childrearing practices, like carrying a toddler in a slendang, how symbiosis and dependency was encouraged. If left to Lintang's wishes, Jan would not be allowed on the floor. Helena, thinking it had to do with hygiene suggested that Lintang put down a mat where he could crawl and play, but Lintang responded with, "He should not crawl like an animal; it is lowly."

Helena noticed that Lintang also enjoyed keeping the baby near. Only because of Helena's urgings was he allowed out of the slendang to crawl and later walk. However, when the mistress was away, she would not allow the boy to crawl on the floor. Lintang continued to breastfeed Jantje for much longer than Helena was accustomed to witnessing in Holland.

Jan was taught to give in to his brother's wishes, as well as the adults. When he did not, Lintang would not punish but goad him with threats such as, "a tiger will come and eat you." Also threats of bogeyman and supernatural forces where used.[42] Helena would intervene, but realized it was a lost cause, as she couldn't be there all the time. And so each mother raised the young boy from her own backgrounds: Lintang nurtured, indulged, and threatened, while Helena taught and disciplined. In the end, neither interfered with the other.

Helena was the main mother-influence over the now nine-year-old Yos (aka Joseph). Lintang and Yos were much more like brother and sister. She played games with him. Their favorite was a competitive rhyming game. Helena spoke and read Dutch to him and described the places his father was visiting.

---

[42] Niels Mulder. (1980). Mysticism & everyday life in contemporary Java (2nd ed.). Singapore: Singapore University Press, pp. 60-61. Note: In Javanese culture, children learn submissive behavior early in life. After that, the child must learn manners and is pressured to conform, avoid conflict, and repress his or her desires. Western individuality is not valued.

Chapter Eleven

Furlough and Aftermath

Fransz felt chilled throughout the journey between Rotterdam and Dietz. Looking through the fogged-up carriage window, he saw no horizon, only gray, muted, and indistinct scenery. The cold and mist affected his mood, which improved as they headed south, leaving the flatlands of South Holland and Brabant for the rolling hills of the forested green in the duchies of Limburg, Berg, and later Nassau. The old sights brought a grin to his face. He transferred carriages in Maastricht and then in Koblenz, where the coach closely followed the Lahn along the narrow river valley. Upon passing Schloss Weilburg standing high on the hill, Fransz's insides froze. *He would be safe now,* he told himself. His enemy was not the Duke but his vassal henchman, the father of the man he killed.

He arrived at the old house in Dietz now inhabited by his sister and her husband, Werner. Fransz was astonished to see strands of gray in Carolina's hair and the lines around her mouth and eyes. She had the same eyes as his. Of course, he, too, had graying hair and wrinkles. Brother and sister hugged, not letting go of each other. Carolina's daughter, Trudie, was

---

43 Dietz (now Diez) from *Topographia Hassiae* by Merian, Matthäus. Source: scan of the historical book: http://www.digitalis.uni-koeln.de/digitaletexte.html

named after her mother. The near-mature son, Thomas, who looked much like Fransz did twenty years ago, greeted him formally and was most curious about his uncle's adventures in the Indies. There would be time for that later. For now Fransz was happy to sit by the fire enjoying his beer while the good-humored Werner entertained him with local news and stories. Carolina busied herself preparing the meal and on occasion stopped to listen or join in the story-telling and laughter. The effect of the brew and the warmth of the hearth comforted. Fransz had not felt so relaxed in many years. *Would he want to return here for good? Could he bring Helena and the boys?* These thoughts arose, yet he had lived more years in the Indies than he had in his motherland.

Architecture Dietz, Germany, 2016

Early the following morning, Fransz took the cobblestone path up the hill to the churchyard where he found the grave of his beloved grandmother and of his mother, who sadly had died two months earlier. Carolina had sent word to him at the KNIL office in Rotterdam. Fransz followed the somewhat haphazard rows to a stone not distinct from the others. He read, "Our Beloved Mother Gertruida Berg - Korschillsch. 21–12–1791—22–7–1849." The adjacent stones showed the names of his father Pieter Joseph, his grandmother, Augustina, his grandfather, Joseph, and his brother, Leonard. A flood of memories arose. The games he played with his now long-dead brother, teaching his sister to swim, reading with his grandmother, and comforting his mother after his father passed. Grief along with pride emerged when he thought of his father, an honorable and loyal man. No negative words ever slipped from him about his unscrupulous brother who lost the family's money and honor.

Fransz was relieved that no one judged him for his imprudent behavior that could have affected the wellbeing and honor of his family. Being with his sister and visiting familiar places of his youth comforted. As the months passed, the weight he had been carrying lessened. His spirit had a chance to mend. Experiencing the joy with this family brought forth a longing for the same. Now part of his sister's family, Fransz went hunting with Werner and Thomas and helped Werner with chores around the house. Mostly he enjoyed the times sitting around the hearth telling and listening to stories. Some evenings Fransz entertained by reading from the new books he had purchased. He made frequent visits to see his friend, Johan. As what often happens with true friends, they picked up effortlessly from the time they parted. The story of his duel and narrow escape was only addressed once. Fransz was forever grateful to Johan, as he would certainly not be alive without his friend's quick thinking.

Fransz stayed nearly the entire year of 1851 before returning to Soerabaja. He understood that he would never return home again. His life was in the Indies with Helena and his sons. The journey back to the Indies was arduous, but Fransz found himself cheered in anticipation of the future. He would marry Helena, and they would live a good life and have children. He returned to Batavia on the ship *Willem I* on February 6, 1852. The long journey home gave Fransz the time to cogently reflect on life, and he decided to retire from the KNIL.

While they wrote to each frequently, the mail could take months and not all letters arrived. Upon his return, Helena noticed that Fransz was more at ease. Fransz felt comfortable with Helena more than any other women, except perhaps his grandmother.

He told her in more explicit detail of his time with family in Dietz. She shared with enthusiasm the milestones of both his sons and general life in Soerabaja. And they spoke of marriage. While Hans had agreed, there was still no movement towards divorce. Would Helena have to take the trip back to Sumatra? While it would be wonderful to see Rita and her old home, she did not want to be away from Fransz again. Helena decided to ask Rita for help. Why hadn't she thought of it before? Rita must have talked to Hans immediately because Helena received a letter within a couple of weeks.

Padang Panjang
11 July 1852

Dear Helena,

While it saddens me to know that I may never set eyes on you again, I am glad I could be of help. I spoke to my eternal boy-child of a brother that he needs to give you your freedom. He admitted that he held on to the marriage because he could and because it gave him an excuse to never commit to anyone else. You shall have your divorce.

As for the news—Our pet monkey, Guy, died of old age. He was a rascal, but I miss him. Jenny has had another baby girl. And while the couple is happy, our Assistant-Resident has to reconcile himself to having three daughters and no son. Things at the house and plantation are as always. I do miss sitting together in the morning over a hot cup of tea.

I wish you well, dear sister. Congratulations! Finally!

Your loving sister,

Rita

Ambarawa, 1853

And so they could marry. Before he resigned, Fransz had been transferred to the 14th battalion in Ambarawa. The family of four and Lintang moved from Soerabaja to Ambarawa. The city is close to the Lake Rawa Pening that is a volcanic basin in central Java between Semarang and Salatiga and not far from Yogyakarta. Already happy in their new life together, by the end of that year Helena again noticed that her courses had not come. Fransz was elated and pampered her unremittingly.

Both fearing that she may miscarry again, Helena took it easier than it was in her nature to be. Others had to help with the moving and setting up house, the first home Fransz and Helena would intentionally share and reside in together. Fransz retired on May 12, 1853.

108

They returned to Soerabaja for a quiet wedding attended by a handful of friends on the twenty-seventh of May. At eight months, Helena was heavy with child. A month later, on June 24, a daughter was born, Augustina Helena. She could not have fathomed that instantaneous opening of the heart upon first seeing her child, nor the instinct to hold the baby to her breast. Fransz, the boys, and baboes surrounded mother and child, and all in love with little Augustina with her soft, downy, blonde hair. Then exhaustion came upon Helena, and mother and baby slept.

The Berg household had never been so full of cheer. Fransz felt the warmth he had experienced visiting his sister and, understood that Helena played a prominent role in making this possible. Two weeks after the baby was born, Helena had trouble breathing and felt dizzy. Thinking that she had over extended herself, she rested in the coolness of her room, giving Lintang the baby. Lintang, concerned, went to find Fransz. By the time he came to Helena's bedside, her face was terribly swollen. The doctor was called.

Seeing that Helena had eclampsia, he gently said, "It's best that you make your peace. There is little chance that she will survive. I am very sorry."

Fransz shook his head and backed away, wanting to protest. He ran to his wife's bedside, and fell to his knees, first stroking her hair and face, frantically kissing her lips and cheeks, holding her weak hand, and willing her to stay alive. Lintang joined him at the other side of the bed with her hand on Helena's. The other baboes kept the boys away. The two bookended Helena as she lost consciousness. Within moments, Helena died, leaving baby Augustina, Jantje at four, the twelve-year-old Joseph, Lintang, and Fransz cruelly bereft.

Numb inside, Fransz had closed himself from the world and his family. He could not feel; he dare not feel. The events of the past weeks kept repeating in his mind as he interjected the things he could have done, should have done, but to no avail. He could not comprehend that Helena was truly gone. And what of the child? The child? He changed the baby's name to Helena Augustina in honor of her mother.

Local Indisch families came to intervene to help manage the household and take care of the children. Finding no other way to deal with his grief, Fransz took on a job as a warden at the prison in Ambarawa. After an appropriate amount time, the single ladies came to offer their condolences to the handsome widower. Needing companionship that Lintang could not offer, Fransz was appreciative of their company. He particularly was refreshed by the young and also recently widowed Christina Cornelia Cover, known amongst her friends as Tien. She had a baby daughter with her recently deceased husband that was nearly the same age as baby Helena. Tien was from a Chinese Javanese and Dutch family that had an established fabric and rug business and loved to tell the story of how her great-grandfather married into the wealthy great-great-grandmother's family to make his mark in the Indies. Tien's mannerism was typical of the Indisch. He found her social ease, hospitality, and generosity appealing.

She went to the Captain's house to meet the children. Joseph was charming and well-mannered, yet Tien questioned his sincerity. Jantje was nowhere to be found.

"Lintang," Fransz called out. "Where is the boy?"

"Sorry, toewan, he is hiding," she replied, sinking into a squatting position.

Joseph, wisely stepped forward, walked toward the interior of the house, and gestured for Tien to follow. Fransz joined the two as they went into the dining room. There, Joseph, pointing under the clothed and already set table, said to all, "And this is where we shall eat. Pap, are we not to have fruit on the veranda? I think I heard kokkie say she bought durian." He wisely knew what might bring forth his younger brother. However, Jantje still did not appear. Fransz, embarrassed and with a stern expression, walked over to the table ready to lift the tablecloth when Tien caught his hand and gestured at the two males to leave the room. As they reluctantly backed out, Tien got down on her hands and knees. Fransz protested but she continued to wave him away, giving him a wink. When the men left, she crawled under the table, pulling the cloth back down and sat next to Jantje.

"Hello, my name is Christina, but you can call me Auntie Tien," she began. "I hear your name is Johan Jacob. It's a pleasure to meet you." After a moment she continued, "Is this a hiding place or your fort?"

Jantje did not respond. Tien continued to sit under the table with him, talking quietly about herself, about her home and her family, with no expectation for him to respond.

Thirty minutes later, Tien and Jantje holding hands appeared on the veranda.

"Are we too late for the durian?" she asked with a smile.

Striking, with slick, dark hair and blue-green eyes, Tien had a light, easy nature and possessed a great sense of humor. Her slender figure and buoyant personality were appealing. Christina came to adore the Captain and was most willing, with the help of three baboes, to take on raising his sons and the baby Helena. The two were married in Semarang on November thirtieth of that year.

When I first saw the dates conveying the sequence of events, I thought, 'Who is this man, Fransz Joseph?' He marries a Helena Falk years after the birth of two sons with an unknown mother. 'Who were their mothers? Was it Helena?' And then, within only six weeks of marriage and two weeks after giving birth, Helena dies. It's so very tragic. And then another marriage takes place so shortly after. I could have made him out to be a womanizer, but that was not my felt sense. Like many of us, he sought love and was not sure how to find it. I also had to remind myself that early death was more common then than it is today, and a man needed a mother for his children. While I cannot condone his treatment of his inlandse njais, I understand that this was another time. Finally, how often do we seek solace in a new relationship when the old has ended abruptly? I cannot judge Fransz for I have done similar things in my life.

I appreciate the author's journey to get here and her open mind because these last few chapters made me so mad about how all the women were treated.

III – Indisch Community

Not possessing photos of my ancestors living during the nineteenth century,
here is an example of an Indisch family from Wikimedia Commons.

Chapter Twelve

Family Life with Christina

Tien was part of a well-established Indisch culture and community. Aunts, uncles, and cousins surrounded her. She had a zest for life, was very much part of the times she lived in and unequivocally knew how life should be lived. While bright, she didn't have Helena's complexity. She had no time for reflection. To her, poetry was enjoyable as long as it rhymed and left to a few stanzas. She didn't read literature, but enjoyed romance novels and magazines. She had a youthful self-confidence of someone who had a comfortable life with parents that had been affirming. In conflict or when challenged, Tien let it roll off her back. Her husband's inclination to control did not trouble her. While she appeared to acquiesce, she easily went about doing just what she wanted, yet in a manner in which it was difficult to find fault. Her genuine sweetness and generosity was infectious.

---

44 Two women depicting Indisch family relations. Retrieved June 9, 2021 from: https://commons.wikimedia.org/wiki/File:COLLECTIE_TROPENMUSEUM_Portret_van _twee_Europese_vrouwen_waarvan_%C3%A9%C3%A9n_gekleed_in_japon_en_%C3%A9 %C3%A9n_gekleed_in_sarong_en_kabaja_Nederlands-Indi%C3%AB_TMnr_60026865

She loved the children, but left much of the everyday care-taking to the baboes. That was, after all, how she was raised. Those first months after Helena's death, little Jantje withdrew. They would continue to find him hiding in a closet or under a table. From the time he could speak, it had been Helena he called 'mama.' Tien had compassion for Jantje's loss and was attentive and loving to the boy. And, over time, she became his 'mama.' And so Jantje came to believe that Tien was his biological mother. He loved that they possessed the same green eyes. As more sisters joined the family, he became the proud elder brother. At the same time, he keenly looked up to his older brother, Joseph, who was a well-built athlete, had a sociable nature, and was popular.

Things came readily to Joseph. He quickly grew from boy to man, rejecting the need for a mother. He was good with the children and remained close to Lintang. In spite of his capacities, he had little ambition. He saw into the hypocrisies in his social world and felt suspect of the status quo. Fransz, concerned that his son was too much like the uncle who brought disgrace to the family, was hard on Joseph. This just drove the young man further away. As it would have been difficult to rebel, instead he withdrew.

Unlike his brother, Jantje emulated and worshipped his papa and tried very much to behave like a proper European young man. He was short in stature and not as naturally athletic as Joseph, an ability valued in the Berg family. What he lacked in natural aptitude, Jan achieved through hard work and self discipline. He was fascinated with weapons and focused on mastering them, like his father had.

At the age of twelve, in overhearing a conversation between Tien and her sister, Jantje learned that Tien was not his mother. Hurt and confused, he then came to realize that Helena must be his mother. As he deliberated, he unleashed some vague memories of the full-bodied woman. In seeking confirmation as well as more information, he shared his discovery with his brother. Joseph, who knew the family secrets, thought it was time to enlighten his younger brother.

"*Broertje* (younger brother), I shouldn't be the one to tell you, but I will because you should know. Do you know the term *voorkinderen*?"

Not sure, Jan nodded anyway.

"It means a child of an inlandse with a European father."

Stunned, Jan awaited to hear where the conversation was going.

"My real mother is Sarina and lives in Padang on Sumatra," Joseph shared and paused with a piercing look.

"And my…my mother?" Jan began to understand. "Who is she? Where is she?"

"She's been here the whole time. It's Lintang."

"The baboe?" He was shocked into a silence, like receiving the news of a death in the family.

"I knew you would take this hard, but I thought it best you knew the truth," Joseph said. " No one can see it in you, unlike with me, and no one will have to know. Many of the Indos who try to be so European are voorkinderen. Don't take it too hard."

But he did take it hard. He was the son of their baboe, Lintang. *Why hadn't he recognized her as his mother? Wouldn't he know, feel it? Why had she never said anything to him?* Jan never spoke to anyone about it, not even his father and not even his mother, the baboe.

The Family Crest[45]

One day shortly after Joseph's seventeenth birthday, Fransz called him into his office. The young man reluctantly obliged. Fransz was sitting behind a teak desk with a small pile of papers and maps and was looking through a leather bound book. Normally more serious and stoic, Fransz was approachable and animated. He gestured for

Berg family crest

---

45 This fictionalized story is intended to show the rift that can occur between father and eldest son. I do not mean to injure or discredit the actual Joseph or his descendants.

Joseph to sit and grinned eagerly at his eldest.

"Now that you are becoming a man, I want to give you this," said Fransz as he pulled out from a large envelope a detailed sketch that he showed to Joseph.

"This is the Berg coat of arms." He then opened a small velvet-covered box and handed it to his eldest. "And this is the family ring." The gold ring held a blue engraved sardonyx stone. Engraved in the stone, as in the sketch, was a lion inside a shield. On top of the shield was a helmet. And on top of the helmet was another lion. Both lions were in a rampant (upright on two legs) position holding several arrows.

"My father gave it to my elder brother, Leonard Joseph, who you were named after," Fransz continued. "When he died in an accident, it was passed down to me. Now I am giving it to you." He looked up at his son with a kind of warmth Joseph had not ever experienced from his father.

"Our ancestors have a long history of serving kings and other nobles. I can loan you my book that tells in detail the history of the area our family lived, in what is now the Germany Federation. The Bergs ruled this area originally. Then the male line died out, the last marrying a Jülich. Those lands have been in possession of Jülich, Cleves, and Ravensbergs for much of the time since. During the late 1600s,

Photo indicates where the male line of Berg ends, with Mary Berg who weds Gerhard von Jülich. Taken at Schloss Burg, 2004.

one of our forefathers received this coat of arms from Frederick William for courage and valor. Frederick William was the Elector of Brandenburg. See how the lion is holding arrows? That signifies courage in

118

battle. We come from a long line of military men. My own dear father fought against Napoleon." Fransz finished proudly looking at his son.

While Joseph felt honored and appreciative of this attention from his father, it was too little and too late. He would not disrespect his father by sharing his true feelings, that he was not much interested in ancestors in a place he's never set foot and never will, so he kept quiet and accepted the ring. "Thank you, father," he said with deference.

All the while this occurred, Jan was watching from behind the small crack in the door. As much as Joseph did not care for the history of his European ancestors, Jan did care. He would gladly trade places with his brother. When Joseph rose to leave, Jan stealthily disappeared.

A few years later, after Joseph and their father were barely on speaking terms because Joseph had refused to join the KNIL—as was his duty as an eldest son—the ring resurfaced. Joseph, knowing that his brother secretly coveted it, gave it to him.

"You have more use for this than I," he said. "And you deserve it, as you are carrying on the nobility, valor, and courage of the Bergs."

Jan regarded his brother, waiting for a sarcastic look or comment, but he saw nothing of the sort in Joseph's eyes. Jan's return gaze was one of confusion.

"It's not that I don't appreciate and respect our family history. I just don't care enough. I know that you do. You are more like the oldest son our father would have liked me to be. I mean that," he said and put his hands on his younger and much shorter brother's shoulder.

Fransz and Tien had three children together—all girls: Josephina Christina, September 12, 1857; Johanna Christina, December 10, 1859; and Rosina Augustina, August 14, 1866. With Tiens' cheery, extraverted nature, the household was most lively, with frequent visits from friends, family, and the playmates of all the children. Fransz's desire for a warm hearth came to fruition, but not how he imagined it. He could never quite reconcile that the life he sought with Helena he instead had with Tien. He blamed himself for his transgressions and self-centeredness that curtailed a long married life with his first love. As he matured, the bravado and charm of his youthful self had mellowed into a quieter contemplative nature. Some may have said it was melancholia. Fransz retired from his second career in 1877 and died January 25, 1884 at the age of 71 in Ambarawa—11, 494 kilometers (7142 miles), as the crow flies, from his place of birth. He left behind his wife of fifty-one, sons aged forty-three and thirty-five, two daughters of thirty-one, and daughters of twenty-seven, twenty-five, and eighteen.

Chapter Thirteen

Johan Jacob –

Salute the Flag in the Name of Our King

At sixteen, Jan joined the KNIL. He began his career working at the wharf in Batavia. Due to his asthma, he could not go into battle and, instead, performed administrative duties. This made good use of his skills—record keeping, detail, and organizing. His self discipline and eagerness bode him well. And as he learned quickly, Jan was given more responsibility. His work took him all over east central Java, such as Bojolali, Salatiga, Poerbolinggo, Modjokerto, Banjoewangi, Ambarawa, Bangil, and Malang. Some moves were the result of promotions.

Like Fransz, Jan was most dedicated to his military career. He, however, did not possess the natural leadership of his father. His unacknowledged resentment and fear of being recognized as a voorkind often came out in his relations at work. He keenly demonstrated the *beschaafdheid* (manners, culture) of a European. This was apparent from his dress, language, and general behavior. While it was customary for European-born to also speak in Malay, as it was a common language used in an international community, Jan did so only when necessary. He also made the effort to keep from using typical Indisch inflections and cadences in his speech. Having light eyes and hair, he acted as if he possessed little or no Indonesian blood.

In social settings, Jan was often known to say, "Indeed, the entire line of my family in Germany were officers. My grandfather fought under Duke Friederich against Napoleon."

Jan enjoyed his work and was personally satisfied when able to keep track and manage all that was in his charge. At the barracks in Ambarawa, he was responsible for the kitchen and household items. The position for head of shipping and receiving of munitions and weapons became available when the former supervisor retired. Jan coveted the job because he saw it more in line with the image of a military man. However, the job went to a Dutchman who had been educated in Holland. As a consequence of feeling slighted, the then Sergeant Berg affected power wherever and whenever he could. He demanded respect from those in lesser positions and imagined insolence that was not actually there. His manner for handling what he could not control was by dominating. For instance, Jan required that inlander workers perform *dodok*, or drop on their heels and squat and then walk towards him when summoned. This is an attitude of humility and courtesy that the inlander pays to their chiefs, princes, and their elders, but not intended to be used outside their own people.

A typical example of Jan's demeanor occurred with his assistant, a non-military, and government employee called Rhemrev. At that time, some European men who adopted children of their unbaptized inlandse women would not give them complete recognition. The reverse spelling of the father's surname name indicated this. Thus Vermehr became Rhemrev. While Jan Berg and Willy Rhemrev had the same background, Jan was pleased that, at least, he had been fully recognized.

In checking the records of shipment of the last quarter recorded by Rhemrev, Jan caught an error. "Rhemrev," he bellowed into the adjoining room. "Come immediately."

The other appeared instantly, showing his humility by keeping his eyes averted.

122

"What's this? What's this?" he said pointing at the ledger.

"To what are you referring, Mr. Berg?" he said meekly.

"Address me has Sergeant Berg," his superior barked. "You wrote the shipment in the wrong column and your figures don't add up." Jan pointed forcefully at each error.

As Rhemrev came to look more closely, he saw that his work had been done correctly and that his superior was confused. Instead of disagreeing, he said with demure, "My pardon, Sergeant Berg. I was most negligent."

Rhemrev's inlandse mother had raised him to not make waves in order to keep social solidarity and harmony. This Javanese value of "right style of life—quiet and subdued, without startling experiences, predictable, and well-ordered" [46] was essential to Javanese harmony. Not only out of deference to a superior, Rhemrev was wise enough to realize that it was also not practical to argue, because Sergeant Berg was proud, had a chip on his shoulder, and would not admit that he had made the mistake.

Jan was a handsome man and, what was mere bravado, could appear as ease and self-confidence. He easily attracted women and had many lady friends. At twenty-three, he married Johanna Catharina Pichel on September 13, 1873 in Batavia. Johanna, just seventeen, was eager to marry an officer. Jan was only a sergeant, but carried himself as an officer and certainly would become one, as his esteemed father and grandfathers had been. The following May, their first son was born, Franz Joseph Eduard. The child did not live long enough to meet his sister, Eugenie Emelie Rosalie, born October 14, 1875. Then two sons were born, Joseph Carel Leonardo on July 7, 1876 in Soerabaja and August Johan Jacob, December 20, 1876 in Semarang. Joseph, named after Jan's brother, is of an unknown mother but was included into the family. A record of three more children included Johanna Catharina

---

[46] Niels Mulder. (1980). *Mysticism & everyday life in contemporary Java* (2nd ed.). Singapore: Singapore University Press, p. 43.

Wilhelmina, born in Bojolali on March 1, 1878, Theodoor Alex Ferdinand, born in Ambarawa on March 1, 1878, and then much later came Marinus Arnold Hendrik, January 16, 1893, born in Poerbolinggo.

Jan was an attentive father when his children were babies and toddlers, but much less so as they became school age and had lost their innocence. He had trouble with the disorder and rambunctiousness of so many children. Jan needed a regimen. So each morning at six-thirty, the children were to line up in the front gallery from eldest to youngest standing at attention. He would then examine their clothing, hair, and teeth. He also performed surprise inspections of their rooms. At all meals they were to sit up straight, not speak unless spoken to, and display the correct European eating etiquette. The school age children were required to salute the flag hanging on a pole in the front yard and sing "Wilhelmus, " which later became the Dutch national anthem.

Desiring the children to be aware of their heritage, and since he couldn't afford to send them to Holland to be educated, he made certain that they would have like opportunities. All the children learned to play instruments and listened to classical music. The popular krontjong[47] was not allowed to be played. They also learned to dance the Waltz and other ballroom dancing of the time. While he did not enjoy it himself, he made sure the children learn to recite poetry and prose, mainly in Dutch but also French and German.

With his great fascination for weapons, both European and Indonesian, Jan possessed a modest collection. Like his father, he became a Master of Three Weapons. He taught his boys all about weaponries and would sometimes bring out his prize, an old kris that he bought from a dealer. A kris is crafted by first making complicated numerological calculations so that it will fit the hand of its owner as well as his station in life. If these calculations are incorrectly done, the kris may turn against its owner. According to Indonesian folklore, "Magic krises sigh for blood, shrivel and kill plants and animals in their vicinity, and fly invisibly through the air to

---

[47] This music of the Portuguese came to Indonesia in the 16th century and became the music of the colonials. These instruments, especially ukulele pairs, interlock, and apply the Indonesian gamelan orchestral tradition to European instruments.

wreak anonymous destruction on the enemies of their owners." [48] Jan did not believe this nor share this superstition with his boys, yet he kept it in a carved wooden box, just in case.

Johanna, who looked up to Jan, initially went along with her husband's wishes for the children's cultural education. Flexible, she mostly enjoyed her life and relied heavily on the help of her three baboes. Over the years, she almost forgot her youthful fantasy of being the wife of an officer. She was already ill before she became pregnant with Marinus and died at the age of thirty-eight in 1894, leaving Jan with seven children from ages one to nineteen.

I recognize the dominating behavior of my father in Johan Jacob. Although we were never lined up to be inspected, I hear that my Oom Os did do that with my cousins. Jan and my father share the same birthday and have been likened to each other. However, it is my father's brother, Os, who was Opa Jan's favorite. But I'm getting ahead in the story.

---

[48] Anne Richter. (1993). *The arts and crafts of Indonesia.* London: Thames and Hudson, Ltd., p. 26.

Chapter Fourteen

Josephine Susana Paulina Abels – An Enigma

Josephine Susana Paulina Abels (Suus) was born in January 5, 1863 in Madioen, south of Soerabaja. Her mother's last name was Pfefferkorn, but I have not found any other information about her ancestors. She was the eldest daughter in a large family with many half- and step- siblings and aunts and uncles who stayed for long periods, first in the Abels and later the Jansen home. Her mother had married twice, outliving her first husband who was much older than she. The children were divided into sets of the older and the younger generations. Siblings would be most respectful towards the elders and feel camaraderie with their cohort. In addition, the older boys might have demanded extra deference.

From a young age, Suus was keenly sensitive to the moods and needs of those around her. Even before she spoke in sentences, she would console her siblings or cousins with a kiss or a manner she knew would comfort them. She just as readily could be alone, singing to herself or playing with imaginary friends. They were not *just* imaginary friends—both young and old family members who had died would pay her a visit. She had conversations with the adult relatives and would play with the children. While ghosts and spirits and animism was a given in the Indisch culture, Suus' engagement was considered unusual, and her parents discouraged it.

As her mother aged, she deferred to Suus the care of household matters, children, or servants. While Suus didn't have the same starry-eyed dreams of marriage like many of her friends, she at one time had a secret love. His family had someone else in mind, and he would not go against their wishes. Suus barely looked at other men since and never fell in love again.

Jan and Suus Wed

Jan had known Suus when Johanna was still alive—friends of friends in a small, tight community. Suus had taken over running the family pension, where she and three of her sisters lived. Suus had a pleasant demeanor and beautiful, wavy hair that came down to her calves. The courtship was not particularly romantic, and the marriage was one of practicality. Jan needed a mother for the children still at home, and Suus, at 32, wanted children.

So Johan Jacob Berg married Josephine Susanna Paulina Abels in Malang on February 27, 1895. As it was custom after women married to wear their hair in a chignon, Suus cut off her beautiful, long, wavy hair. In losing her best feature, she cried for an entire month. Jan's three youngest children who sill lived at home—Joke (17), Theo (11), and Noetie (1)—created instant family. That same year, on December 21, Suus gave birth to Frederik Willem Karel (Fritz), my grandfather. A little more than two years after Fritz was born, on March 18, 1898, Johanna Catherina Susanna was born. They called her *Pop* (doll in Dutch). Suus had been used to managing a large family. She, like her husband, was good at keeping things in order, albeit she did so with more ease and kindness than did Jan.

Tante Maggie

My Aunt Writes About Her Father's Family

In continuing with the stories of my family and ancestors, I have combined my father's narratives with vignettes from four letters I received from my *Tante* (Aunt) Maggie, my father's sister. Interlaced in the ensuing pages are translated and edited versions (for clarity and structure, yet using her words) of my aunt's impressions of her grandparents and the aunts and uncles on her father's side of the family. Most of my Indisch relatives had one or more middle names as well as a nickname. I indicate the nicknames after first mentioning their full names. In addition, you will see that my father and aunt use words like *Pap* (dad), *Moes* (mom), *Tante* (aunt) and *Oom* (uncle). My aunt, father, and I refer to our respective grandparents as *Opa* (granddad) and *Oma* (grandma) followed by either their first or last names. In this book, I refer to my relatives by their first names when furthering the story. I refer to them using the familial nouns—Pap, Oma, Tante, etc.—when making my own commentaries. When I write about my parents, I use the Dutch words *Papa* for dad and *Mama* for mom.

In her own words, Tante Maggie wrote about her grandparents, whom she referred to as Oma Suus and Opa Berg:

My grandfather had been in the military, but after he retired he was a bookkeeper for a sugar factory. My grandmother was his second wife. Oma Suus was around the same age as his oldest daughter. He was a widower, and the rumor was that he was not an easy man. Like your father, but worse. Oma Suus probably married him to give herself and her unmarried sisters housing. Her name was Susana Abels, but her sisters were called Jansen. I don't know that story.

I never saw her smile. I never saw her angry. Also, I never saw her cry. She didn't want anything to do with dogs or cats. And she wasn't religious. She never went out. When she wore a dress, it was very dull, unimaginative, and in muted colors. Luckily she preferred wearing a sarong and kabaja, which in that time was still worn by Indisch ladies. It is beautiful costume wear. Our Indisch ladies wore different types of sarongs, but always brown.[49] Depending on the motif, the sarongs also had different names, for example, loerik (3 colors of vertical lines), or pagi-sore. The kabajas were always white with broad laced hems. Chinese women wore colored sarongs—pastels with flowers or birds made of batik. They also wore white kabajas.

---

[49] Traditionally, sarongs worn by the Indonesians had symbolic motiefs. For instance, the sidomukti motif, with countless fine lines and a butterfly, symbolizes hope and prayer. Sekar Djagad, the flower of the universe, symbolizes beauty and diversity. Loerik (lurik) is from the Javanese word lorek, which means stripes, but can be stripes or checks or a combinatoon. This motif was traditionally worn by Javanese rural men.

My mother's nickname for Oma Suus was Sarah Bernhard. (In sarcasm, mocking the plainness of her dress.) *But my father admired his mother a great deal. According to him, she was a courageous woman and inwardly strong. I was never close to Oma Suus. Your father would be able to tell you more about her.* (I unfortunately heard no stories about Oma Suus from my father.) *He lived there for more than a year to finish high school when we moved from Malang to Soerabaja. Oma Suus ran and owned a hotel there. I would stay every now and then for a weekend.*

As I said earlier, Oma Suus never left the house. Very early in the morning you would hear her in the kitchen. She was fond of plants and of reading. She took care of her plants as if they were her children. She had various types of chevaliers. Every leaf was cleaned with a feather. Also beautiful orchids and gloxinias of various colors. Because she was always at home, her territory was limited, especially in her old age, where she could be, for instance, in a space of two meters squared (about 10 square feet).

During the time the Japanese occupied Indië and were not popular, I once heard her bring out their good qualities. The few times she spoke to me confidentially she told me some fascinating things. For instance, that when she was young she had beautiful, black, long hair that came down to her calves and that she let hang loose (like Lady Godiva). When she got married and had to wear her hair in a twist, she cut it off just below her shoulders. That broke her heart.

There was a time when many people came to Suus to get readings. She read their palms, or they came with questions that would inspire her to write. Typically women came to query about potential romance, to seek help with willful or wayward children, or to ask advice about pending fortunes. When the questions had to do with relations between two people, Suus found that she could sense the unspoken truth about the other in question. Even when the other was not present, she could serve as mediator. One woman asked her whether to marry the man she loved, who had just proposed, instead of the one her parents wanted her to wed. Suus knew not to influence the outcome by her own thoughts on the matter. She often did not know the answer until it appeared when writing it down. The strange thing is that she wrote in languages she had never learned. She didn't have control over what was written, the language had nothing to do with where the person asking came from, and Suus had not been schooled in European languages except for Dutch. On one occasion, a Mrs. Kok, the wife of a superior of Jan, came to see her. While, quite the lady, she had no airs for she was hard-pressed for help.

130

"You see, *Mevrouw* (Mrs.) Berg," she said. "This situation is most delicate because I don't want to go against my husband's wishes unless it really is the right thing for Humphrey. He wants to go to Holland to study to become a botanist. But my husband wishes that he enter government service."

"What is your question?" Suus asked.

"I'd like to know which career would better suit my son and which would give him more success and happiness."

"I may be able to answer that, but not how to convince your husband."

The woman laughed. "I have my ways."

Suus sat quietly, first blanking her mind and then concentrating on the young man's name. She picked up her pen and paper and began to write. Feeling a sense of calm but also alertness, her hand began to move. Suus was unaware of what she was putting on paper. The answer came in French. She handed it to Mrs. Kok, educated, knew French. The woman read excitedly and then smiled.

"Good," she said. "He will go to Holland to study what he chooses. Thank you so much, Mevrouw Berg."

Mrs. Kok left, and Suus put no more thought to it.

Some months later, Jan came home in a huff and called out from the front veranda, "Suus!" When she did not respond, he bolted to the back veranda where she was attending to her orchids. Before she could turn around, he had grabbed one of her beloved plants and wrenched it from its pot. Suus looked up in shock.

"How dare you get involved with the life of my superior's family!" he yelled.

Suus was stunned.

"*Jij met je verdomde inlandse gedoe!* (You and your damned Indonesian ways!)" he continued. "I've told you to stay away from that guna of yours. You're not only interfering in people's lives, but giving them dangerous advice!"

She now connected that Captain Kok had somehow uncovered what had transpired between she and Mrs. Kok. Suus knew not to argue, nor did she kowtow. Instead, she looked at him with no expression at all and walked away.

Tante Mag tells of her grandmother Suus:

Oma Suus was a medium. She also did automatic writing. She wrote sometimes in languages that she did not know—French, German, English. She had only been to grammar school and had not learned foreign European languages. One day when she had pen in hand, she saw a big, black hand that took her canary, Piet, and wrung its neck. She never attempted the free writing again, not even in cases in which people asked her for advice.

While the *guna* (magic) of the archipelago were commonplace experiences for most of the Indisch and indigenous peoples, stories of how my ancestors connected with the other worlds particularly fascinated me. I believe that Suus' skills in mediumship were uncommon, as her gifts do not sound like the other stories I've heard or read of the local guna. I could see by her manner of telling the story that Tante Mag was frightened and did not approve of her grandmother's dabbling with the occult. It's unfortunate I did not ask my father more about Oma Suus, as I would have liked to have a better understanding of this great-grandmother.

Tante Mag continued with:

Oma Suus had a bunch of step-children. Tante Stans was one of them. My mother and Tante Stans were close friends until the latter died. My father always said, "Stans was a fun-loving girl." Although she was not a beauty, she was popular with the youth. Wim Berg, a first cousin, proposed to her. When they didn't get permission because of the close family relationship, Wim voiced, "If I can't have her as a young woman, then I'll marry her when she's a widow." And that's what happened. Stans first married Nette Kooen. He was extremely jealous. On one bad day he shaved her head bald. She then left him and went home to her parents and he hanged himself. Luckily they didn't have children.

132

So she lived back in the home of her youth. Oma Suus once told me this: "When young men came over to the house for Stans, Nette Kooen appeared for months after his death." I don't know if the others could see him. Oma Suus saw him many times just as he was dressed when he hanged himself—in his pajamas.

Tante Maggie also wrote about a unique friendship that Suus had:

Suus knew Mata Hari (Margaretha Geertruida MacLeod, 17 August 1876 through 15 October 1917, was a Dutch exotic dancer and courtesan who was convicted of being a spy for Germany during WWI). *Oma Suus knew her when she simply was Mrs. MacLeod, the wife of an officer. They lived in the same neighborhood in Rampal, where many people in the military lived in Malang.*

Mata Hari in 1906.

I was most surprised to discover that Suus was friends with Mata Hari, the exotic dancer. Then again, Suus knew her before she became an exotic dancer. Mata Hari formerly was Magreet Zelle and born in Holland. At nineteen, seeking fortune and adventure, she boldly responded to a newspaper ad for a bride. She consequently married Captain Rudolf MacLeod, who was in the KNIL and 20 years older than she was. The then Mrs. MacLeod had heard of Suus' readings and had come to get advice about her marital situation. MacLeod was alcoholic and extremely jealous of the attentions beautiful Magreet received from other officers. He also beat her. Suus and Magreet became friends. Albeit opposites in appearance and behavior, Suus was a good listener, did not judge, and had a calm wisdom that Magreet longed for. The lively woman and her escapades always entertained Suus, happily just an onlooker. Magreet later took on the artistic name when she moved to Paris, divorced her husband, and became an exotic dancer. Mata Hari is the word for 'sun' in Malay. She had learned the dances in Java.

As my aunt said, Suus was mostly a homebody. In addition to her orchid and fern collection, she was an avid reader. She would sit in the back gallery amongst her beloved plants, with a box of ginger candy and a pot of tea, and read. Suus read many of the authors from the Indies, like Maria Dermoût,

Augusta de Wit, Hella Haasse, and Louis Couperus. But she was particularly intrigued by novels that took place in other parts of the world, and those written by female authors like George Eliot, Jane Austen, and the Bronte sisters. Through reading she was able to visit places she would never see and get away from her mundane everyday life.

It was difficult to get a sense of who Suus was. I had trouble reconciling the contradictions—a dreamy medium with a practical capacity to manage well in the material world. In spite of her ability to attend to the needs of others, perhaps it is an emotional distance that I sense in Suus. Was her heart partially impenetrable because she lost her only love? Did Jan's meanness due to his insecurities close her heart more? I wonder if reading novels, befriending an exotic woman, and caring for plants were an escape as well as her solace.

Fritz, My Grandfather

Suus, coming late to motherhood, was overcome by joy with the arrival of her newborn. Fritz was born into the large family and grew up with his half brother Noetie. As they grew older, Suus was keen enough to not make distinctions and favor her own over her step-son. She cared for each in a manner that most suited their temperaments. However, his aunts did not have the same good sense as Suus. Noetie was a *blanke* (light) Indo, with blondish hair and his father's green eyes. Fritz looked more like his mother, with penetrating brown eyes, and the dark hair and skin. As was typical in Indisch households, often the lighter skinned children were (unconsciously or consciously) favored. Hence, Noetie was preferred by his step-aunts and Fritz tended to be censured. For instance, when the two boys were rough-housing and Noetie was hurt, which was more often the case as Fritz was stronger,

Fritz at 17 years with 17-inch arms

134

Noetie would know to come crying to his aunts.

"Boy," they would call Fritz. "Stop picking on your brother. See how he is hurt? Go apologize," the sisters would scold, even though Fritz was the younger. As he obeyed, Fritz would see the gleam of satisfaction in Noetie's eyes.

The sisters often compared the two boys' appearances, manners, and their schoolwork by always favoring Noetie. It was only his mother, who would praise Fritz. Suus, for the sake of harmony, did not interfere much with the adverse habits of the adults in her household, even for the sake of her son. Jan also tended to favor his blanke Indo son. While equally firm and strict with both, Jan, however, tended to notice Noetie's accomplishments more readily.

Fritz and Noetie both did well at school, but for some reason, perhaps his more lively nature, it always appeared that Noetie was the bright one. They were both good at sports and played soccer. Fritz played defense and Noetie offence. Fritz played the clarinet and Noetie the violin. In his teenage years, Fritz became a body builder and skilled at *pencak silat*, an Indonesian version of marshal arts. This is where he could outshine Noetie, mainly because he had the discipline to work out every day.

Fritz was mechanically inclined, always taking apart broken items (and sometimes those not broken for which he'd get scolded or beat if discovered by his father) to see how they worked. As he grew older, his mother or the neighbors often called on him to fix household items. In high school, he was very adept at mathematics and the sciences. He was also a precision draftsman.

Sometimes in the evening, Jan would take out the drawing of the family crest and the book he had acquired from Joseph. Jan then told the boys stories about their grandfather—who had died before Fritz was born and had bravely fought a duel in Germany before he came to Indië. The young boy felt a sense of pride that his first name, like his grandfather, began with a letter 'F.' Once Fritz had taken the drawing and made an exact duplicate sketch. He first showed it to his mother, who admired and praised, but his father could only remark that Fritz had taken the sketch from his office without asking. Quite unusual for a nine year old, Fritz thought about his actions and realized his error. He knew that he was not allowed in his father's room. Fritz saw that he had been caught up in the impulse of the moment. He then swore to himself that he would be better at following the rules. Noetie, on the other hand, had no such scruples.

Noetie, a few years ahead, went on to study pharmacy. Fritz wanted to go to university to become an engineer. "University in Batavia?" Jan said in mocking tone. "What makes you think they'll accept an Indo? Better learn early to be realistic and don't reach for the clouds. It's best you get a job with the civil service." While essentially Jan spoke the truth, his tone was derisive. So Fritz did not attend the university and took a job with the Department of Public Works.

Tante Mag tells about her father's family:

It is said that Pap (her father) *did not have an easy childhood under the regime of three sisters. Moes really disliked Tante Bet* (one of Fritz's aunts). *She was a colorful figure. She often went out for 'Bible lessons.' My father later told me that she was a hardened gambler. She died before the war of cancer in her jaw. Tante Riek died during the Bersiap period. She was buried in a nameless grave in Malang. Oma Suus continued to live for many years even when we lived in The Hague. She kept on going just like the rabbit running on the battery that never dies.*

I only knew one of my father's half brothers, Oom Noetie. He was a bit older than my father. As a kid, Oom Noetie was a slow eater and was not allowed to leave the table until he ate all the food from his plate. My father told me that Noetie would make little balls with his rice. He later became a pharmacist and had a pharmacy in Solo. He was the main supplier for the Susuhunan (the royal family in Solo). He was married to an old, fat widow who owned batik shops (where batik was made). Tante Sjaan and Oom Noetie had two boys and two girls. Oom Noetie was extravagant—every year a new car, and not a Chevrolet like my father, but a Buick. But he died poor in Holland. Pap told me that Noetie was a generous tipper until the bitter end. When he went to the barber in Holland, he would give a 10-guilder tip (about three dollars at the time). *Tante Sjaan died in Indië. Just like with everyone else, the Indonesians stole everything. There would be a sign on your house that said, "In Possession of the Republic Indonesia." You were not allowed to take anything from the homes and the silver guilders were now worth half. Tjeun* (Maggie's second husband) *and I only had 70 guilders, so we lost very little. But the rich felt the loss.*

136

Tante Maggie tells of her relationship with her father's sister, Pop (which means doll in Dutch).

My father had a full-blooded sister, Pop, who was younger. My mother and she could not get along. Their animosity had begun before Moes even met my father. Tante Pop went to the same school as Tante Bon, my mother's sister. My mother liked to tease, most likely more so in her younger years. She would walk behind Pop and, with every step Pop took, she would call out, "Hamba potig." (Google translation from Malay for hamba: slave or servant). *I don't know what it means, but it was clear she was making fun. Pop was a heavy girl and this 'hamba potig' was most likely describing her way of walking, or waddling. So you can imagine that, when they became sisters-in-law, this had not been forgiven and forgotten.*

I often stayed at Tante Pop's house. She thought my mother was over-the-top elegant. My mother liked to dress well and always wore spiked high heels (much like your mother). I should add that, after the war, when Pop and her husband came back from camp and had no home, Moes gave them a room until they repatriated to Holland. Oma Suus also lived with us. She went to Holland together with Tante Pop and Pop's husband. She lived with Pop until she died in The Hague at 90-plus years. I want to honor my mother. She wasn't petty and she often let go of things to help others. Two thumbs up for Moes.

Tante Maggie then finishes the story about Tante Stans:

Tante Stans did marry Wim (Stans' first cousin). *They were well-to-do. He was an administrator at a plantation. Their oldest son was not right in the head. Later he had a job as a chauffeur. The second child was normal but did not want to behave well. I don't know what happened to him. He ended up living in the Indonesian community but not a good environment. Their youngest was a girl, Dorothea, nicknamed Troel. They had a beautiful house across from the monastery when Oom Wim retired. At that time we lived in Malang. Every Saturday, Stans and my mother (along with Troel) went to the SOS (social club for the elite). Troel was at a marriageable age. Tante Stans wanted her to marry an officer, preferably a blanda officer. And sure enough, she married a Dutch Navy officer, Johan Dekker. A nice guy. This all happened when I was still in grammar school. It was a time when there were not many Indisch military men that went to Holland. Troel was very pregnant when they went on furlough to Holland. When she was having her baby there, the nurse did not want to help her because she was afraid that she would get bitten. Troel had dark skin. I could always appreciate this story as very comical, but if it happens to you, it is, of course, not so funny. The marriage did not last. Troel later married a nice Indisch man, and they remained so until he died. She had two good-looking sons with Dekker.*

A Wedding Reception[50]

Wedding party of Troel and Johan Dekker

The large room supported by white columns opened at one end facing the gardens. The marble floors were cool even during the heat of the midday. Rattan and whicker furnishings formed several clusters on the perimeter of the grand room in which guests of various size groups gathered in animated conversation. In the center, people danced to krontjong and popular American music. Formal congratulations, ceremonies and the meal of *rijsttafel* have long been completed. Stans bellowed with laughter at the far end the room where she was sitting with her husband Wim, the doctor, and the Chinese apothecary. Troel, the bride and her captain groom, Johan, sipped cool drinks while holding hands. Oom Noetie had several men trapped with his incessant monologue over the political situation in Europe. Then, Stans called out to the wedding guests. She banged her cane against the intricately decorated brass gong.

"Time for a group photo," she announced and directed the younger men to move chairs to form a line. "The couple should sit in the middle."

---

[50] This story is a partially imagined description based on the photograph shown here of the wedding reception of Stans' daughter, Troel, and Johan Dekker, which took place during the 1920s.

138

Cousin Rudi, who wore a bow from one of the gifts around his head, took the arms of Sok and Stans and walked them to their seats, making sure that he was sitting in between. Family members and other guests gathered in rows, with the tallest in the back and some standing on chairs. It was a noisy, motley crew. These friends and family of the Berg's lived and worked in Malang, a mountain town on east Java. As most were of mixed European and Javanese blood, they are *Indisch*.

Genealogical research indicated two daughters from Johan (Jan) Jacob's marriage to Johanna Catharina Pichel. The daughters were Eugenie Emelie Rosalie, October 14, 1875 and Johanna Catharina Wilhelmina, March 1, 1878. Both these half sister's to Opa were near two decades older than my grandfather. I could not discern which of the two Stans would be. It would appear that she would be a peer of my grandfather to be friends with his wife. But perhaps Stans' youthful personality made her seem young. Two female relatives are mentioned in a letter dated 1982 that I possess from a J. T. Berg, a cousin of my grandfather (daughter of Theodoor Alex Ferdinand). These are Johanna Frederika Constantina (married to a Nettekoven, March 30, 1892) and Josephine Ernestine Louise (married to a Lodewijk Frederik van der Heijde October 8, 1881). I found no record of these two in my search. Stans could be a derivative of Constantina and Nettekoven looks similar to Nette Kooen. Either my aunt or the cousin J. T. could have misspelled the names. If Stans is Johanna Frederika Constantina who married in 1882, she still would be much older than my Oma Sok who was born in 1898, six years after Stans was married. Hence, in age, Oma Sok could be a daughter of Stans. Another possibility is that Stans is a daughter of a step-sister of Opa Berg, hence would be his cousin instead of his aunt.

I'm also not sure if 'Oom Noetie' is the youngest son of Jan and Johanna Pichel. 'Noetie' could be shortened from Marinus Arnold Hendrik, who was born January 16, 1893 in Poerbolinggo. He would have been close in age to my grandfather and a potential peer. Jan married Josephine Susana Paulina Abels (Oma Suus) a year after Johanna Pichel (his first wife) died. Also, according to my records, Suus was born January 5, 1863 in Madioen, thus not a similar age as the daughters of Jan's first marriage as indicated by Tante Mag. They were at least a decade younger than Suus.

Jan and Suus Later Years

Jan's youthful enthusiasm to pursue his father's military career did not unfold as he had imagined, which left him bitter. Over time, the discipline and need for order turned into rigidity. Jan and Suus had settled in the mountain town of Malang where many military officers lived and retired. There, Jan took on a job as a bookkeeper for a sugar plantation. Suus opened another hotel in Malang that was across the street from the Regent's home. She created a warm environment and ran it with efficiency. After he retired, she kept her husband occupied in the back room where he would not bother anyone. It was only during the midday meal that he would come out formally dressed to sit at the head of the table.

Jan died in Malang January 18, 1928. Suus lived on decades after Jan, enduring the invasion of the Japanese and the Bersiap period. She then moved to The Hague, The Netherlands where she lived for another five or six years, living well into her 90s. She died sometime around 1954-1955.

Chapter Fifteen

Adele Ravenswaaij – The Orphan

My great-grandmother, Adele was the mother of my grandmother, Oma Sok. Adele, born in 1878, was the first child of Gerrit Philip Ravenswaaij and Charlotta Frederika Maria van Franquemont who were married in Mutok, Banta in 1876. Charlotta had three boys that were not *erkent* (legitimized) from a previous unknown relationship. Adele's brother, Oscar, joined the family in 1883. Gerrit died when Adele was six and when Oscar was still a baby. Charlotta, unable to manage, sent Adele to Holland with a distant cousin, Frederika Hond, and her husband, Johan Hond. They first resided in Amsterdam and then later in Dinteloord in the southern province of North Brabant where Johan served as a minister. Charlotta died in 1892 when Adele was fourteen and still living in Holland.

Life in Holland

Quite young when she moved away from her high-strung mother, Adele bonded with Frederika. When she called her "mama," Johan corrected her. So the foster parents became Tante and Oom. One of her first memories was of having afternoon tea using the silver teapot, bone china cups, and a blue-and-white-patterned plate with cookies. The tea cups were filled two-thirds from the brim—the proper way to pour tea in society in Holland. The plate of cookies was passed to Adele. She had learned well from her mother—that is, only to take one at a time. When she later reached for another, Oom Johan slapped her hand and said, "Don't be so greedy."

The slap stunned Adele and she blushed with shame. She had never been struck before and never forgot the disgracing experience. From then on, she studied Oom Johan closely for potential corrections in her behavior. As Adele grew older, she attributed his stringency to being born in Holland. Tante Frederika was very much the opposite—easy going and very kind. This saved poor Adele, who had a difficult time in Holland.

She was bright, but a dreamer and sometimes had trouble paying attention at school. Both teachers and classmates, who knew very little about life in the colonies, would question her.

"How is it that your parents are so light but come from the Indies?"

"There are light people in the Indies too," answered Adele, barely seven years old.

"But why are you dark and not your parents?"

"They are not my parents; they are my aunt and uncle."

This somewhat satisfied. Those who knew that Adele's uncle was from The Hague would say in understanding, "Ah, yes, then you must be so dark because you were born in the tropics."

There were other questions. "If you are from the Indies, why do you speak Dutch?" She'd then explain how her parents were not Indonesian but that her father had been Dutch and her mother Indisch and that all the Indisch spoke Dutch. While somewhat troubling, these conversations were relatively benign.[51]

However, less harmless were the names like *zwartje* (blackie), *aap* (monkey), and *bush bush* that some of the kids called out. The pressure to be a good girl and to fit in had its consequences. Adele developed a tick in which she would suddenly grimace or squint. This, of course, exacerbated the teasing.

The family moved from Amsterdam, a far more worldly and liberal place than most of the rest of Holland, to Dinteloord in the southern province North Brabant. Adele was now in secondary school. It was a Christian school. Her history teacher, when covering the subject of European colonies, expounded on the theory of Social Darwinism, which presumed that some human beings were biologically superior to others, that the strongest or fittest should survive and flourish in society, and that the weak and unfit should be allowed to die.

He lectured to the class, "There is a constant struggle between humans and, like with animals, the strongest always win. This is why stronger nations are more fit, the best, and consequently have an inherent right to rule. We Europeans have evolved much further than other races, hence the white, civilized nations have the moral right to conquer and civilize the savages of the world. It is our moral, Christian duty to bring civilization to the backwards peoples, like our colonies of the East and West Indies."

Adele did her best to fit in and to be agreeable. While she did make a few friends, she was mostly a loner. As she became a young woman, an inner rebel emerged. She instinctively knew that this theory of Social Darwinism was wrong, but she would never argue or speak her mind.

Adele's need for solace also set her apart from others. This became stronger in the years that they resided in North Brabant close to the *Volkerak*, which was the delta area of the Rhine-Meuse-Scheldt Rivers that eventually led to the Noordzee and English Channel. She felt more herself while walking along the waterway. The waves, the wind, the trees, the gulls and other water birds were more kin than the humans in her life. At times, she felt so

---

[51] These questions come from stories I have heard my grandparent and parent's generations tell of their encounters upon arriving in the Netherlands.

connected to the nature around her that boundaries disintegrated. On these occasions she was at peace and her difficulties at school or home had no consequence. She had once described this experience to her aunt, "Like losing myself to the wind." Frederika, concerned, told her husband. This was most unfortunate because he saw it as a problem of her character and as a dream fantasy of flight. Adele became more careful about what she would tell her aunt.

Adele returned to Java with Tante Frederika and Oom Johan in early 1897 when she was 19. They lived on the outskirts of the city of Soerabaja. Adele had not realized how constrained her life had been until she returned to the soft air of her original home in Indië. She took walks in nature and through the kampongs. While her elders did not approve, Adele no longer took heed. It was as if the land itself gave her the permission to be herself. Within weeks she lost her tick and let go of her efforts to please. She donned the local dress of sarongs and kabajas, dress that she wore for the remainder of her life.

Return Home to Java, 1897

Adele found herself closely observing the inlandse—those at home that served the family and those in the kampongs. Once she saw Slamat, a sort of butler, remove rust from a kris with pineapple juice. She watched the houseboy blacken her uncle's shoes with old hibiscus flowers. So different from Adele's previous life in the cold north, the inlandse did much of their living out-of-doors. Between six and seven in the morning, while walking along the kali (river), she watched men, women, and children as they bathed. They loved flowers, for adorning themselves and for ceremonies. The women used flowers to scent the water that they used to rinse their long, black hair. Even the men would place flowers behind the ears. She liked to observe how they gathered at the warung for meals. Except for the midday meal, they ate outdoors communally. The warungs were very simple, with two wooden containers, one for the food and one for cooking. They were found everywhere: by the river-side, at the railway stations, at the sadoo-stands, along the canals, at the corners of the streets. [52] At these she would see people of all kinds—*sadoo* (hack carriage) drivers, merchants, government clerks, servants, and even *hadjas* (those who have performed the pilgrimage to Mecca)

---

[52] Adapted from Augusta De Wit. (1905). *Java: Facts and fancies*. London: Chapman & Hall, Ltd., p. 187.

convened at the warung. And not just the men, the women too joined. They would talk and laugh.

She would often go to the passer where she would learn to recognize some of the men and women who sold the wide variety of fruit, vegetables, and meats. She saw men playing board games on makeshift chairs and tables in the *alun alun* (village square) under the wide spread of waringin trees. The children made necklaces of tanjong-flowers and played with their homemade toys. She saw a boy who had tied a string around the leg of a cockroach, taking it for a walk. The adults never shouted, mocked, or quarreled. Even during contests or games, the inlanders remained sedate and quiet. Even for simple kampong dwellers, Javanese etiquette condemned demonstrativeness as vulgar. Emotions were concealed behind outward serenity.[53] From these visits, Adele began to see glimpses of the other life, the non-Western and somewhat forbidden (to her) life of this island. As she observed, Adele felt a sense of longing.

On other occasions, her walks would take her into nature. They had returned just before the monsoon season. Adele was used to rain, as Holland had more than its share. However, on Java it came down in torrents and it took only seconds to get drenched. On one occasion while out walking, Adele was not able to find shelter and came home with her clothes and hair dripping on the tiled floors. The warmth and humidity felt like a balm so unlike the icy cold winds of the North Sea. Walking before or after the rain was an entirely different experience. Before, the earth was dry. Yet, the air was the heaviest and thickest. It's as if she was moving through warm, wet cloth. After the rain, the air became less dense and the grounds emerged fresh and clean.

---

[53] IBID., pp. 154-5; pp. 166-7.

Waterfall

On one occasion, Adele went walking well before the afternoon rains. She enjoyed her jaunt and remained out longer, heading further into new terrain. She ambled higher up the mountainside with its terraced paddies on one side and uncultivated jungle on the other. She came upon a place with a cascading waterfall that fell into a deep, round pool. Next to the falls was a flattened area covered with light moss, where she sat down. Adele looked up towards the fall s, at first holding her eyes in one spot to observe the water passing in full force of white mist. She then followed a segment of water as it cascaded into the dark pool creating foam of white bubbles. She repeated this pattern of following the droplets with her eyes as they fell. The water was dancing before her. Fragments of the falling water became one to form figures like water nymphs. As she experienced the shift, she shook her head so as to see normal again, but the new perception would not shift back. Then water nymphs came out of the falls and flew back and forth down slowly like a feather in the wind. Adele looked to the right where the green covered earth was breathing in and out in rhythm with the dancing water nymphs.

Then her body felt dense and she fell into the moss-covered earth. Adele no longer could feel the boundary between herself and the ground on which she now rested. She was merely a pair of eyes over a nostril that inhaled and exhaled the molecules of air and mist. The eyes focused on the waterfall, as it teemed with life. It was not just plants and insects, but organic matter and molecules and atoms. Adele saw into the space between the solid and into the invisible life. Looking back at the water, she became the water at the very top bend falling over and seeing Adele at the bottom laying there becoming larger as she, the water, came closer. Reclining, Adele watched a single water droplet, and it was as if their gazes met.

Adele had been away for hours. Worried, Frederika called for Slamat to find her. Over the months, Slamat had observed Adele's activities and general destinations. She was an unusual young Indisch lady, which piqued his interest. As he was the chauffer and unofficial butler, they had little conversation. It was not appropriate for them to speak of matters that have nothing to do with the household. Slamat understood this better than Adele.

Slamat knew the path Adele frequented. He began walking slowly yet persistently as the rain continued to fall. It subsided as quickly as it had begun. Slamat took a path up the hillside. The gradual incline became more distinct and eventually so steep even Slamat broke into a sweat. He had been walking for an hour and continued at a faster pace. Slamat knew to head for the waterfall. He understood that Adele would go that way. When he arrived, he found her lying on the moss, eyes closed. It was now close to dusk. As he could not rouse her, Slamat carried Adele down the path back to the house.

By nightfall, which arrives at six and quickly near the equator, Johan and Frederika would normally be bathing and dressing for dinner. Instead, Johan paced back and forth between the columns of the drawing room, while Frederika sat on the rattan chair with extra pillows to hold her upright. She did not lean fully back into the soft cushions. Every few minutes she spoke out her thoughts, not so much for an answer as a way to ease her mind.

"She's probably waited for the rain to stop and then couldn't find her way back in the dark." She paused. "Slamat will find her."

And later, "You don't suppose she would go into the jungle where they've spotted the wild boars?"

And after that, "I should keep a closer eye on her. I shouldn't let her out."

Again, a pause. "Why can't she just find normal interests like other young women?"

After a very long silence, they heard quick footsteps on the drive. Both hurried to the entryway and down the steps. Slamat was carrying the limp Adele in his arms.

"What happened? What is wrong with her?" Frederika asked in Malay.

"I found her like this at *Nimfa Menari* (Dancing Nymphs)," Slamat replied.

Slamat looked at Frederika, knowing she would know what to do, but not wanting to say anything that would cause friction between the married couple.

Frederika caught his glance and pondered how to approach her husband, the minister.

"Take Adele to her room," directed Johan, trying to keep a semblance of control while unsure what to do next.

Frederika followed Slamat and, after he left, undressed her niece of her wet clothing, muttering "*Kasian*," the word for 'Poor thing,' and kept shaking her head in disbelief and fear. She helped Adele's limp body into a fresh nightgown, covered her with a light blanket and then sat holding her niece's hand. Johan then joined her simply looking at his young niece.

"What has become of her? She is too *eigenwijs* (willful, obstinate) for her own good."

Frederika simply nodded, thinking to herself. In spite of her husband's potential protest, she knew what needed to be done and called for Slamat.

He approached quietly on bare feet. "Yes, Mevrouw?"

"You know of a dukun?"

He nodded.

"Get one immediately." She did not explain to her husband, nor did he ask. It was seldom that Frederika would take the position of power in their relationship, and when she did he knew he must acquiesce.

It took nearly two hours before Slamat returned with the dukun. The man was dressed as most local villagers, in a patterned sarong and a *banjo* (jacket) with looped buttonholes in the Javanese style. The dukun was small in stature, but taller than Slamat, with a full head of salt and pepper hair, a wide clean-shaven face and black soulful eyes.

148

Slamat introduced him as Pak Wayan. He bowed towards the couple and then turned to Adele. Johan and Frederika receded from the bed in order to allow the dukun to do his work.

The dukun reached for both her hands and held them in his. He turned them over one at a time to study her palms. He then laid her hands by her side and placed one of his hands on her forehead and the other over the sheets at her belly near the navel. As he did this, he stared straight ahead as if the answers were written in the darkness of the room. Then from an intricately woven bag made of fine cotton, he pulled out several other smaller bags filled with leaves, flower petals, shells, rocks, bones and various other paraphernalia. He took a mixture of these and put them in an empty pouch, which he placed on her chest. Then he pulled out

Dukun (medicine man, healer)

tarnished silver and a glass bottle that looked out of place, as it most certainly was made in Europe. Pak Wayan opened the lid and put the bottle to Adele's nose. As she began to rouse, Pak Wayan turned to Johan and Frederika and said with a smile, "Snuff. It works better than any of my medicines."

They moved in closer towards Adele, but the dukun raised his hand in a motion to wait.

"She will remain disoriented. Give her a moment to adjust. Her soul has been traveling other places. It will take her a few moments to realize where she is and who she is."

Frederika looked firmly at her husband saying with her eyes. *You are now in my country with different rules. I don't want to hear your judgments about inlandse superstitions.*

Adele opened her eyes and her blank stare began to focus on the face of Pak Wayan. She slowly shifted her eyes to behind him were Johan and Frederika stood. Her face and eyes showed composure, but she did not, could not, speak. This did not disturb the dukun.

149

"What is the matter? What has happened?" Now relieved, Frederika could no longer hold back her apprehension.

"I can only surmise that she was called and cajoled by the spirits of the Dancing Nymphs. She is not harmed, but she may not be fully present to this world for many days." Pak Wayan spoke fluent Dutch.

"And," he thought but did not say, "she may never be the same again." He recommended that she eat a non-spicy diet for the next few days, wear this pouch, and drink lukewarm, not hot, peppermint tea. She should not leave the house for a couple of weeks.

"I will return in three days to observe her."

After the experience at the waterfall, Adele's foster parents were concerned about their niece's eccentric ways and fascination of the undesirable aspects of inlandse culture. Tante Frederika knew too well what happened to women who ended up in the kampong. Oom Johan's solution was a husband.

I am intrigued by this dark, *Indisch meisje* (Dutch-Indonesian girl) who lost her parents at an early age and left the Indies to go with strangers to a foreign, cold land. I've heard stories told by my peers born in Indonesia and from relatives of my father's generation about the racism and ignorance they experienced when they arrived as refugees in the Netherlands in the late 1950s and early 1960s. What might it have been like for an Indisch meisje nearly seventy-five years earlier? I could fully empathize when I heard the stories about Adele denying her Dutch heritage and adopting only Indonesian clothing and immersing herself in its culture. Perhaps it takes an experience like hers to 'just say no' to convention and do what your heart tells you. It was a courageous thing to do, especially in the time when women didn't have the freedoms that we do (in the West) today. Yet, she married a full-blooded Dutchman. Reminding myself of the times, I could imagine many reasons for doing so. I see Adele passing on her courage and independence to the eldest daughter, my grandmother Oma Sok, who channeled that into rebellion. I would have liked to have met Adele and learn what she knew about the Javanese and watched how she integrated her Dutch upbringing with her Indonesian proclivities.

Chapter Sixteen

Adele and Adriaan – The Unlikely Couple

The Buttewegs

Carl Butteweg was to study engineering in Delft. When it became clear that he was not suited for academics, his father set him up to start a leather factory in the Indies. He married Adriana Castricum, and the two set off for Java. Carl and Adriana had seven children. Adriaan, the youngest, was born December 27, 1873 in Soerabaja. His mother and father's favorite, the boy had been indulged. Due to a weak heart, Carl turned over the business to his elder sons Carl and Willem. It was a blow to Adriaan to lose his father at such a young age.

Tante Maggie writes about Adriaan's (my grandmother's father) side of the family:

---

54 Postcard of Soerabaja (Surabaya) from my father's possessions

My mother's father, Adriaan Butteweg, was a totok (100% Dutch). His mother's last name was Castricum. The Buttewegs had a leather factory on the corner of Toenjoengan (still one of the main streets in Surabaya today) and a not-through street, Gang Butteweg (named after my mother's family).

Opa Adriaan's father must have died early since the factory was managed by the two oldest sons who both were married to 'Indisch meisjes' (term for Dutch-Indonesian women). *My great uncles were married to sisters (Louise Jeanetta and Henriette Margaretha [Tante Griet] Fournier). The most notorious one was Tante Griet. They were from French ancestry. This Tante Griet was very good looking and had a velvet tongue. But according to my mother's sister, Tante Bon, she was the meanest person on earth, a snake in a flower basket* (sneaky, deceitful person who will stab you in the back).

The Buttewegs lived in a large family home close to their business. Their mother-in-law (my aunt's great-grandmother, Adriana Castricum-Butteweg) *had little power. In this household, the two daughters-in-law were the bosses, and they treated their mother-in-law poorly.*

They were tough and nasty women. You see, their mother-in-law Adriana was a baru, which means 'new' and refers to a person new to Indië. She was not accustomed to local ways. The daughters-in-law made her eat bread with sambal (hot chilly paste). Her son, Adriaan, could no longer witness their cruel behavior and stand living in close proximity to his sisters-in-law. As soon as Opa Adriaan was sixteen, he ran away from home and joined the navy. He couldn't stand it anymore to see his mother suffer at the hands of these two Indo daughters-in-law. There he learned to work on ships and became an engineer (mechanic). He was later known to be very skilled at his work.

Adriaan

Adriaan was very dedicated to his mother. His first stop, after docking port in Soerabaja, was to visit his mother.

"Mam," he would say, kissing each cheek and holding her wrinkled hands.

"My dear boy," she'd say with tears filling her eyes.

"Mama, I have some 4711 for you and some chocolates from Belgium."

152

"Oh, that wasn't necessary." Her enlivened eyes deceived her words. She opened the Eau de Cologne, dabbed some on her handkerchief, and she immediately tasted a bonbon, while offering one to Adriaan.

While he stayed with his mother when at port, Adriaan was more often at sea. Even though his father passed away when Adriaan was an early teen, it did not cross the youth's mind that he could also lose his mother. Adriana died when Adriaan was at sea. He was nineteen. He had always wished he could have been home more to protect her from Griet.

Tante Maggie continued about her grandfather:

Opa Adriaan died young, at 62. I only saw him once. My mother hardly saw her father. Tante Bon told me that once Adriaan said, "If that Griet dares to come to my funeral, God give me the strength to crawl out of the coffin and strangle her!" Sure enough she showed up at the funeral and made a big spectacle. At the coffin she was crying and screaming, "Adriaan, Adriaan, my dear boy!" Tante Bon was shocked by this scene, and thought to herself, 'You never know.'

Tante Griet did not have good fate. She outlived all her peers because she lived until the Bersiap period (this is after WWII when the Indonesian's were fighting for their independence.) (Note: My guess is she lived well into her 80s.) *And, during the fighting between the British and the Indonesian extremists, she died and was buried in mass graves with the killed Gurkhas (British soldiers from India) who were brought in to protect Europeans in Soerabaja.*

It was well known in our family that Adriaan was most prejudiced towards inlanders and the Indisch. This may have been as a result of how his mean Indisch sisters-in-law treated his Dutch mother. At the same time, he was opposed to the snobbish attitudes of some of his Dutch peers. Tante Maggie wrote about the wedding of Adriaan and Adele's youngest daughter, Bon, who married Eddie Matzen:

His family was a bit uppity, what we call in Dutch, kale kak (literal translation, bald shit). *Tante Bon told me that Opa Adriaan was offered coffee at their wedding without a spoon. He let the coffee cool off and demonstratively but his finger in the cup to stir just to shock the 'civilized' in laws.*

I feel little connection to the great-grandfather on my paternal grandmother's side of the family. In my explorations, I felt his absence in the family stories and don't get a sense of who he was. It was common knowledge that he was devoted to his mother and that he wanted sons but had daughters. He was also very good at his profession. In that time, it was often all that men needed to do, and to father sons.

Adriaan Meets Adele

Adriaan was five years older than Adele. He had a good job as a ship engineer (mechanic). Both Frederika and Johan thought that he would be a suitable match for their niece. Adele had lost the ease and sense of freedom she first experienced upon arriving in Indië. She had become somewhat apprehensive and was no longer, as her uncle would say, *eigenwijs* (stubborn, willful).

Adele and Adriaan were introduced at a dinner of friends the two families had in common. Adriaan was home from a voyage to the Dutch West Indies. Sitting next to him at dinner, Adele quietly listened to stories of his travels and description of Suriname. Some of his mannerism reminded her of the Dutch in Holland, a sense of familiarity that could be mistaken for closeness. As Adriaan and Adele spent time together, he came to overlook her dark features and broad nose in appreciation of her European-like conduct and mannerism. At the same time, her demure and humble disposition made it easy for him to condescend her, which in turn made her most attractive. Understanding that inlandse women had strong sexual drives, he assumed that of Adele.

One late evening after they had been at a party, Adriaan kissed Adele good night. She, who had just enjoyed a lovely evening with friends and his attentions, was curious and open to his kiss. Taking this as consent, Adriaan kissed more passionately and grasped at her breasts. Adele tried to back away, but Adriaan, much larger and stronger, held her close. Soon he had her sarong and his pants undone. When all was done, he kissed her softly, as if she was a consenting and affectionate lover. Once at home, Adele tore off her clothes and quietly washed. Shaking fiercely and with tears running down her eyes, she hoped not to stir her aunt and uncle. She would say nothing. Later, alone in bed,

154

she moaned and shook while keeping her face in the pillow so as not to make a sound. No one could know. The following day, she kept up an appearance of normalcy, which in some ways was a relief. At night she would shake as images would arise.

Adele's manner of dealing with the experience was to avoid Adriaan, which was difficult since the relatives were hoping for a match. Feeling alone, she must come to a creative solution, as she knew she would not get support from her Tante or Oom. Her plan was to visit a cousin in Malang, far enough away. When she proposed the plan to her aunt, Frederika agreed noticing that Adele was moody and perhaps in need of a change of scene. She joined Adele on the journey to Malang and stayed on for a couple of weeks. The mountain air was cool. Adele hoped to forget. However, six weeks into her visit she noticed a swelling in her breasts and her courses were late.

When the news hit the families in Soerabaja, the Buttewegs pointed the finger at the loose Adele. Yet Adriaan married Adele on September 18, 1897. The couple had two daughters, Johanna Wilhelmina (Sok or Sokkie), born January 6, 1898 in Magelang and Louise (Bon) on August 18, 1899.

Tante Maggie wrote about her grandfather:

Opa Adriaan was a strange guy. He, I believe, wanted to turn his two daughters into two sons. One time my mother came home crying because a boy had hit her. Opa Adriaan told her to fight the guy until she won. And that is what happened. While fighting, she bit the boy in his thigh, and that was the end of the fight. She came home triumphant to her father's great satisfaction.

The two girls looked quite different from each other. Sok had light-colored, almost blonde hair in tight curls, the green eyes of her father, and broad nose of her mother. Bon—a shortening of Ambon or those with dark skin and tightly curled hair—was more like her mother. The sisters had opposing characteristics, yet got along well. Albeit, dainty and slender like the Javanese in her bones, Sokkie had a rebellious will and was tough. Adriaan and Sokkie, so much the same in temperament, were frequently at odds. If for some reason their father called on the girls to be reprimanded, the younger Bon would

155

already be crying in advance. But to my grandmother he would say, "Lower those cheeky eyes when I talk to you!"

Tante Maggie wrote:

The reason I am well informed about the family is because of Louise or Bon, Moes' only and younger sister. Moes went to the government school, which she called 'skola djonkok' (crouching school). I'm not sure what she meant by that. Tante Bon went to a Catholic school that was rather far from their house. It had become custom that Moes would pick her up, and when Tante Bon got tired, carry her sister home from school.

As contrary as Sok could be with her father, she was most amiable towards and the protector of her younger sister. Tante Maggie wrote:

My mother figuratively carried Bon anytime she had trouble with life. For instance, when Tante Bon's husband lost his job, they lived with us for a year until he got back on his feet. During the war, Tante Bon became a widow and lived with my parents in Java as well as in Holland until she died in The Hague.

Adele with Sok and Bon

Bon (left), Sok (middle right) and two unknown

While holding onto her Indonesian roots, for the sake of her daughters, Adele mostly lived the life of a typical Indisch wife. They spoke mainly Dutch in the home and she fell into the customs of her own childhood experiences.

Adriaan was gone for months at a time. Life at home was more harmonious when it was just the girls—mother, the two sisters, and the baboes. When he was away, certain rules slackened—the sisters felt free to go barefoot, speak Malay, and eat with their hands. Adele allowed these freedoms, for she knew that this time in their lives was short. Perhaps this was conscious, or not, as her own life had changed so abruptly by school age. She didn't want the girls to feel confined, but to play freely and enjoy the innocence of childhood. Sok preferred the outdoors and invented explorative games. Bon played along, but preferred pretend games with her dolls.

Adele would tell the girls Javanese myths and sagas, which are much like European fairy tales filled with animals that speak or supernatural creatures like fairies. The foxes, wolves, and bears we know from western fairy tales are tigers, monkeys, and tropical birds in the Javanese myths. In some satires, the animals would play tricks or challenge the protagonist. Many stories had morals. Adele was a good storyteller, using different voices for the characters and animals.

Akin to the Scottish myth of the silkies or selkies, who can change from seal to woman, or swan to woman, or mermaid to woman, the Javanese version has tropical birds that come from the heavens. They fly to earth, take off their feather costumes, and become young women that swim in a fishing pond. A young farmer steals one of the feather costumes, hides it in his hut, and then returns to take the young woman, who now cannot transform back to her bird nature, as his bride. This was Sok and Bon's favorite story.

The atmosphere at the Butteweg's completely changed when Adriaan was home from a long voyage. Adele withdrew into her own world and became less available to Sok and Bon. Adriaan's presence was like a blaring noise of the radio that Adele needed to shut off to have tranquility. Children often know most goings on that remain under the surface and adapt accordingly. Sok and Bon spent more time in their rooms or in the back of the house with the baboe, or, as they grew older, playing with and visiting friends and relatives with their mother.

Little Bon, terrified of her father's loud reprimands, was a 'good girl' and as quiet as a mouse. Whereas, Sok, almost as if on purpose, would behave in exactly the manner that would aggravate her father. Sok did not like how he talked about the *lui* (lazy) and *stomme* (dumb) *Indische*, or when he called them *zwartjes* (black ones) in front of her mother. He also called them *klipsteen* (don't know meaning) or *blauwe trekhond* (literal translation, blue sled dog). When Adriaan was displeased or Sok disobedient, he would summon her and she approached him with an attitude.

157

Adele paid no heed to Adriaan's prejudices. Yet Sok saw that, when her father was home, her mother's blinking tick worsened and she would suddenly have fits of hooting and grunting and on occasion inappropriate cursing more rancorous than anything her father uttered. Sok later learned that her mother had Tourette Syndrome. But as a child, it was frightening to see her lose control. Adriaan's reaction did not help, because he criticized and became belligerent.

Samina of the Susuhunan Family

Adele was acquainted with the daughter of the prince of Surakarta. It was the type of friendship in which, in spite of their cultural and other differences, they felt as close as sisters. Adele could confide in Samina. In response to Adele's idealization of her Javanese roots, Samina reminded Adele how most Javanese lived. Samina also made clear that, in spite of her privilege, she lived with many restraints and possessed fewer rights than European women had. She must adhere to her father's wishes and marry whom he chose for her. There was also the Javanese etiquette.

Samina shared, "My younger brother or sister must walk on hands and knees to pass me. If a younger sister is on a chair and I approach, she must slip to the ground and bow her head until I have passed. A younger brother or sister must always speak in high Javanese to me and make a *sembah* (put both hands together with their thumbs under the nose). They must do the same if they are talking about me. And they may not touch the food on the table until I have had as much as I would like. Then the same rules apply to me with my older sister and brother, my parents, and other elders." [55]

Once Adele was honored with an invitation to attend a wayang that Samina's cousin, the son of the Regent, was hosting. Sok and Bon sat on the

---

[55] Raden Adjeng Kartini. *(n.d.) Letters of a Javanese princess.* Agnes Louise Symmers (Trans.), p. 20. "In Javanese thinking…men are unequal by definition…. All social relationships are hierarchally associated in fine nuances of relative status. The very use of the Javanese language and its concomitant manners clearly express relative status positions. It is impossible to speak Javanese without reference to the position of the person spoken to in relation to the person of the speaker. In its many complicated and formal gradations, the choice of words reflects position, intimacy or formality, age, social distance and rank, together with all the nuances of relative expectations, obligations, and rights." Niels Mulder. *Mysticism & Everyday life in contemporary Java*, p. 40.

bed as they watched their mother get dressed. Adele wore her finest sarong. The baboe put her thick hair up with two gold pins. She also wore her *akar* bracelet with the gold clasp. These are made of coral called *akar bahar.*[56] Adele received hers from Samina and wore it in honor of their friendship.

Samina arrived with a horse drawn carriage. She joined Adele for tea and cookies, Dutch style. She always brought gifts of handmade dolls or trinkets for Sok and Bon. The girls tried to stay up for their mother's return, but the performance lasted far into the evening. The following day, Adele expertly retold the shadow puppet story and described the gamelan dancers' colorful costumes and fine movements. She also punctiliously depicted the part of the *Kraton* (palace) she visited.

"The grounds had several pavilions that were separated by walkways and the most beautiful gardens. We all sat on chairs in the largest pavilion where the *tulambens* (musicians) were already playing.

After a while, the *dalang* (puppeteer) began his story. He sat behind a very long piece of white cloth with colorful batik surrounding the screen. We couldn't see the fire, but there was one behind the cloth. The dalang used many delicate, beautifully-painted puppets that wore sarongs."

The litho of gamelan performance is made from a drawing by F.C. Wilson.

Bon and Sok's eyes widened. The girls had attended puppet shows before. The shadows were so alive that they frightened little Bon, but not Sokkie.

---

[56] *Akar* means root, whereas *bahar* is Arabic for 'sea.' The two words together refer to coral root. Indonesian coral exists in four different colors: black, gray, white, and red. The Javanese attribute several mystical powers and healing properties to the *akar bahar* and is used by *dukun*s and mystics. Also, the coral is worn around the wrist as a bracelet to treat rheumatism and arthritis.

"The dalang maneuvered the many puppets all by himself. The puppets also had had shields, swords, spears, javelins, krises, and tiny horses and chariots. And there was music, of course. Then the dancers appeared. They had coiled strands of gold around their necks that made their faces look very round and pretty. They wore ear-pendants, tiaras on their heads, and broad silver handclasps on their upper arms, with narrow bracelets on their wrists, and many rings on their fingers."

"Did they have bracelets like yours, mama?"

Gamelan dancers

"No, much finer than mine," she said. "The dancers would make the scarfs float so it looked like they had wings. Then, standing still, their bodies would bend this way and that way so they looked like young trees moving in the breeze."

Then the girls stood up to make the movements their mother described.

"Yes, like that," she said, smiling. "Later, at bedtime, I will tell you the story."

"No, please mama, tell us now," they cried in unison.

Adele told them the story in her own words. This performance was a translation of the Hindu Mahabharata, which is about balance and harmony. Adele explained that it was to remind them not to be too attached to their lives being the way they think they should be and to participate in this world by helping others.[57]

---

[57] The dalang speaks both in Javanese or Malay and Sanskrit. Most Javanese do not understand Sanskrit. Along with the layers of music, Sanskrit is used because it touches the spirit world. The dalang is an intermediary. The puppets represent deities, heroes, and highborn princesses. The dalang is the most skillful of storytellers as he handles the puppet, tells the story, and conducts the gamelan along with the dance. The story consists of a long epic that may be a popular myth or legend. He has the artistic freedom to adapt and improvise dialogues.

160

When Sok and Bon married and left home to start their own families, Adele was very much alone and relied a great deal on her friendship with Samina. At that time she became acquainted with *kebatinan* (Javanese mysticism), which had to do with unity and harmony between a person and God and society.

Samina explained, "The purpose is to achieve unity and *sepi ing pamrih* or to sacrifice your self interest, that individuality so prided in European culture. You come to this through *ria* (non-attachment) and *narima* (to accept life as it comes), and with *sabar* (trustful patience). You become still within to connect with something greater than yourself, and then you are one with *rasa* (your inner truth), which is connected with the truth of the greater cosmos."

Adele learned to become more still inside. Quite soon she recognized and had an explanation for the mystical experiences in her younger years both in Holland and upon returning to Java. This new quietude she was able to find within brought about humility and gratitude, and she became less fearful, which then made it easier to accept life as it came.

Adele was particularly fond of her first grandson, Ton. He was a bright and intense boy, and during the first months of his life cried often. Adele's special bond made it possible to sooth Ton with songs and the same stories she had told her daughters. Ton came to stay with her for a few months as a toddler. That story will come in a later chapter.

Over the years Adriaan and Adele spent little time together, essentially living separate lives. When not away at sea, Adriaan was always tinkering with engines of different sorts, his automobile in the latter years. Adele knew that Adriaan was fond of young inlandse women and perhaps others at ports he frequented. Adele passed away at forty-six on June 24, 1924. Sok, my grandmother, was twenty-six and my father was not yet seven. Three years later on July 29, 1927, a son, Bob, was born to Adriaan by an unknown Indonesian mother.

I was particularly intrigued by the story of Adele returning from Holland not wanting to have anything to do with her Dutch heritage. It also bewildered me that she would then marry a totok instead of an Indo. I have a difficult time reconciling Adele's predicament. I can understand that she might warm up to the company of this Dutch man, who reminded her of things that were familiar. We often gravitate to what is familiar, even when it is painful. While the years in Holland had been difficult, it had been home for most of her life. Yet to be violated and humiliated, how could she agree to marry?

I was particularly interested in how Adele actively identified with her Indonesian roots, which took courage. Through her, I was able to learn about the hidden, unwelcome, and shadow side of myself in a manner that was honoring. Through her and her friend, Samina, I was also able to further portray some of the Javanese culture.

.

Section IV –

My Grandparents'

and Father's Generations

Sok with Maggie, Os, and Ton

Chapter Seventeen

Fritz and Sok – Opposites Attract

She was forbidden to see him. His skin was too dark. Her father's disapproval was as much the enticement as her love for Fritz. He was more worthy than any other man she met at the SOS (a social club or fraternity for the colonials). He was thoughtful, well mannered and, she had to admit, he had a great physique. Who was Pap to tell her whom to date?

Fritz discretely watched Sok who, surrounded by friends, was laughing and telling stories. Her flowing green dress, which matched her eyes, ended just above her slender ankles. On her dainty feet were shoes with crisscross straps and Mary-Jane heels. She noticed him too, dashing, and dressed in a white suit. He shyly approached the slender, petite woman. Her infectious smile, reaching those expressive eyes, gave him confidence and relaxed his

---

58 Left: Johanna Butteweg (Sok) Right: Frederick Berg (Fritz)

formal attitude. His own serious and deep brown eyes enlivened as they spoke. Both were good dancers and circled the room many times throughout the evening. A local band played Hawaiian songs popular at the time—"Oh How She Could Yacki Hacki Wicki Wacki Woo and "Hello, Hawai'i, How Are You?" and "Pretty Baby" originally sung by Bill Murray. The band also played *krontjong* tunes. Sok's favorite was "**Tramboelang**." From that day on, Sok and Fritz were together as much as was possible, often meeting at the club to dance or just listen to the music. Like most young couples of the time, they frequented the theater to see American films, such as "The Cheat" and "The Girl of the Golden West," or they found a quiet place to enjoy each other's company.

Johanna (Sok) and Frederick (Fritz) married on December 16, 1916. While Adriaan did not attend the wedding or reception, he later came to like and respect Frederick Willem Karel Berg. As Tante Maggie wrote:

Opa Adriaan was not particularly fond of Indos. He was against the marriage of his daughter with my father. My father had color. But in practice everything went along fine. Father-in-law and son-in-law had the same hobby. Every hour was spent tinkering on the car; they self-evidently became good friends. My father always spoke appreciatively about his father-in-law. He would say, "I have learned much from the old gentleman." Namely, he was an excellent mechanic.

On November 18, 1917, their first son, Anton (Ton, my father) was born, and on June 14, 1920 the second son, Oscar (Os), arrived. Mildred (Maggie) was born on September 6, 1922. In the late 1920s, Bob Butteweg, the son of Adriaan came to live with Sok and Fritz.

As the story goes, shortly after Opa Jan retired, Sok and her new born, Os, became very ill with influenza. The two went to stay in Malang where it was cooler and Sok with baby could convalesce. Opa Jan was very concerned for the baby boy who had difficulty breathing, which reminded him of when he was a boy with asthma. Opa Jan would hold Os until he slept and insisted on keeping him close so he could check that his grandson was breathing. When mother and child became well and were ready to return to their own home, Opa Jan imagined himself to be ill. The cantankerous and now mostly ignored elder enjoyed the company of this engaging and cheerful grandchild. Sok returned to her family and each time she came for her Os, the old man again believed himself to have an asthma attack. When Opa Jan died on January 18, 1928, Oscar finally returned to his own family. He was eight years old.

Tante Maggie tells:

Moes (referring to her mother) *had a good reason for not liking her in-laws. My brother Os was born during an influenza epidemic. Moes and the baby were sick. My grandparents (on my father's side) lived in Malang (in the mountains), where there was a wonderful climate. Mother and child went there to recuperate. Ton was with Oma Ravenswaaij. He was her favorite anyway.* (Maggie wasn't born yet.) *When mother and child were restored and they were ready to go home, Opa Berg* (their grandfather) *opposed it. He had become so attached to Os that every time the subject of 'going home' was discussed, he had a cat fit. He had asthma and couldn't breathe when he heard the words 'going home.' My mother was told that it would be on her conscience if something would happen to that old gentleman. My Oma Ravenswaaij had a wisdom that made people resilient and peaceful. She gave my mother the advice to leave the child there and let everything take its course. Thus, Os came home after my grandfather died. My mother had a lot of grief around this. With this in mind, it is understandable that she wasn't crazy about her in-laws.*

On the surface, it may not have seemed like a good match. Fritz was meticulous, quiet, interested in all things mechanical, and so well mannered he might seem too proper. In great physical shape, with biceps seventeen inches (forty-two cm) in circumference, Fritz used the Dynamic Tension system for exercise made popular by Charles Atlas. He was very disciplined and also kept a healthy diet. The story goes that—due to his *pencak silat* training—he was so aware that, if Sok threw a pillow on the bed when he was asleep, he'd wake up alert. This story was told by my father in awe and with pride for his father's talent. We were often told stories of Opa's strength. For instance, he once lifted an anvil to kill a poisonous snake and he could rip a deck of cards in half with his bare hands. Fritz was known to fight when he had been taken advantage of or to protect someone who had been taken advantage of. It was a matter of honor, most likely not much different than his grandfather Fransz's behavior leading to the duel.

My opa was a civil engineer for Public Works. In the role of a foreman, he helped build the highway from Banjoewangie to Malang. My brother, Carl, passed on this story Opa had told him:

To pave the road, they used special stone crushers, which were expensive. When his supervisor realized that using inlander manpower would be cheaper (thirty five cents a day), they shifted to manual labor. So when Opa had paid the workers a higher wage than they were accustomed to earning, they did not return the next day. This perplexed his totok boss. Opa explained that they were easily satisfied and, unlike the Dutch, had no interest in earning more than they needed, nor did they feel the need to in save their wages. This may appear to the Dutchmen as indolent or lacking motivation. My grandfather had explained that this was their culture, with different attitudes and values.

Opa was also known for his precision work. One story often told by my father was about the construction of a bridge, which had been built from both sides towards the center. My father said proudly, "When all had been completed, the last bolt would fall in place effortlessly. *Phht* (sound effect typically used in the Indonesian language)."

Sokkie had a great sense of humor, got along with all sorts and, unlike her husband, didn't follow rules too closely. She, too, was fiery, although her approach was more cunning. Early in their marriage they had many arguments, with one or the other leaving in a huff. It's hard to say who was the more proud or stubborn. Both were cajoled by Adele to go home and make up. Because they had great love and respect for each other, the differences between the two softened. And over time, they became accustomed and adapted to each other's ways.

My father told this story illustrating his parents:

168

One day, Moes wanted him to bring home a large barrel left over from work so she could catch rainwater. He obliged and delivered it with a thirty-five cent invoice for her to pay to the Shell Company. That's how he was. Honest, like Abe Lincoln.

Here is another story:

Pap primarily bought his materials from the Chinese. Around the time of Chinese New Year, they would offer free fireworks. "It's bribery," he'd say, refusing the fireworks. But Moes would signal them to come to the back door, where she would happily accept. Later she'd tell Pap that she had bought the fireworks.

Example of inlander selling goods at the home of an Indisch woman

Fritz was loyal, had integrity, and adored his wife. His admiration was a balm for the girl who had to learn how to act tough. Sok helped the serious Fritz lighten up. Once she convinced him to go to the racetracks. He was very much against gambling, and as mentioned, his Tante Bet was addicted. More than once Suus had to bail her sister out of trouble. Sok, on the other hand, was not opposed and sometimes would play the horses. They were invited by friends to go to the races. Opa, encouraged by Sok, made a daily double bet. The race was close, the crowds were screaming, and as their horse came forward during the last bend, even Fritz was jumping and screaming, "Go, go, go!" Even though they won, Fritz never gambled again.

Sok – The Rebel

My grandmother was not a traditional housewife. She was averse to the frivolous life that many housewives loved, with hobbies like embroidery and growing orchids. Conversely, she performed many of the household chores that were typically left to servants. She had always wanted to study dentistry, but did not have the opportunity. She was a midwife, assisting a doctor, when they lived in Malang.

By dealing with the wives of Indonesian notables during her stay in small towns in the interior (as part of being the wife of a civil servant), Sok

169

learned to speak Malay, Javanese, and Madurees quite well. Like her mother, she was interested in Indonesian culture. Mrs. Soebroto, the wife of the mayor of Soerabaja and granddaughter of the prince of Surakarta, was her friend. Mrs. Soebroto's sister lived with the Berg family and was treated by Sok as her own daughter. Unfortunately, I don't have any stories about that relationship.

Sok would often lend a hand to people in the community, particularly the underprivileged members of the colonial society—Indos and inlanders, as well as Dutch. She not only had a sense of social justice, she was skillful in dealing with many types of people.

Tante Maggie writes of her mother:

Moes had a great love for the underdog. At the beginning of every month she had a set group of people who received support from her. Strangely enough, this was not affected by her antipathy against the Dutch, as she also supported low-life Dutch military men. A regular customer was Beertje (diminutive of Bear), *a drunkard married to an inlandse woman named Fien. The money Beertje received from my mother was always accompanied by a warning: "If I hear from Fien that you have kept the money for yourself, I will teach you a lesson!" Moes went regularly into the kampong where Beertje and his wife lived to see what happened to the money.*

At the outbreak of the war, Beertje was called to arms. He was in the same internment camp with Pap. He was then part of a trafficking gang that went out of the camp to smuggle food. He gave Pap some food, but thought it necessary to remind my father, "Do not think that I do this for you, because you are an asshole but you have an angel of a wife."

Here is my father's version:

Moes knew how to handle people according to their culture and class—how they needed to be addressed. You couldn't treat an inlandse baboe like you would a Dutch servant. The inlanders have their own customs and pride. For instance, they would take off their jewelry and shoes when coming to work for us. That was their custom and not imposed by us.

Retired Dutch soldiers had a meager pension and would often disappear in the kampong and marry an inlandse. One of them would come by the house to sell postcards and pencils. Moes would pay and say, "Don't you drink that money away. Give it to Fien." And she would go to the kampong to check that Fien got the money. She had empathy but was strict. She loved to bargain with the Chinese vendors, down to a quarter of a penny. She might be blunt or familiar, but they all liked her. No one took advantage because she could see right through their deceptions. And they were too afraid of getting on my father's bad side, because then they'd get beat up.

Tante Maggie goes on with:

The 'kleine boeng' (literal translation little brother) had a special place for my mother's heart. She had the gift of being kind without being condescending. Behind the main building of our house we had a long, covered, wide hallway that led to three guest rooms, the kitchen, the bathroom, the W.C., and the servant W.C. I still see my mother standing in admiration while our dendeng (beef jerky) seller gave a demonstration of how well he could dance. It was a Viennese Waltz. "I can turn left and right, Mrs. Berg." There he danced around, black as the night, with his expensive English name, Worthington. Later in the Bersiap time, he was murdered by Indonesians—getientjanged (cut into pieces).

Moes would converse readily with the poor inlander men. I have had the privilege of listening to the following conversation with an inlander man: "Mevrouw, do you want to buy W.C. smoking?" My mother said, "Dahna, njo, apa itoe W.C. smoking?" (What is W.C. smoking?) After some going back and forth, it turned out he was selling deodorant. Then after the sale was closed, Moes asked him if he might like to work for my father. After some worried consideration, he said, "Nah, never mind, ma'am, I prefer just being a birdbrain."

The Berg household was often busy with folks coming and going. There were always dinner guests, as Fritz had many colleagues and friends and Sok tended to attract people of all creed and colors. In addition, various family members and others in need would come to live with Sok and Fritz.

Tante Maggie wrote:

Tante Bon and her husband, Oom Eddie, lived with us for several years. Eddie Matzen was a large man—tall and fat. His father came from Sweden, if I am not mistaken. During the sugar crash in Indië, Oom Eddie lost his job. He was an accountant on one of the sugar plantations. Even though my father couldn't stand him, they came to live with us when he lost his job. But in those days people had respect for each other. Every night we had dinner together at our big table. My dad sat at the head of the table and Oom Eddie at the other end opposite my father. I never heard a harsh word or argument.

I didn't get to ask why my grandfather couldn't stand Eddie Matzen. My guess is that he didn't pull his weight. That would have been dishonorable.

My aunt went on about Eddie and Bon:

When Tante Bon and Oom Eddie lived with us, he'd get an odd job once in a while and he'd be gone for a few weeks. When he wasn't there, I would sleep with my Tante Bon. She lived in our large, converted two-car garage. Luckily there was also a carport for my father's car and our bicycles because my dad loved his car. Tante Bon had a real big bed, bigger than a king-size. Our beds in Indië are high off the ground and had klamboes (canopies). We called the bed our desert island. On this island, I heard lots of stories about the family. Tante Bon and I were much closer than my mother and I. She was a sweetheart. Oom Eddie died during the war. He was on a transportation ship on its way to another camp when the Allies torpedoed the ship. As far as I know, none of the prisoners of war on that ship survived. Bon then stayed with my parents until she died in The Hague in 1954.[59]

Tante Maggie offered this perspective of her mother:

We called my mother Moes. She had green eyes. She would look at us with those fierce eyes when, for instance, we were at someone's house and candy or cookies were offered. That look meant for us to say, "No thank you," because children should not be greedy. We weren't allowed 'tamba' (seconds). At meals we were allowed to help ourselves to as much as we liked, but we could not take tamba. At the same time, if we had really a lot of food on our plates, she would say, "Do you have to eat like a koelie?"[60] *But when it came to it, my mother could mix with everyone. She was open-minded. The opposite of my father. I was more like him, and she had a hard time with that.*

I remember that she didn't like going shopping with me because I would remind her that she had at least forty pairs of shoes and I don't know how many scarves and that she

---

[59] My grandparents and their peers would have been in their late forties to early fifties after WWII. They went to the Netherlands about five years after WWII ended.
[60] In Javanese culture, children are taught to be content with *cukup* (enough). This applies to many things like ambition, which should not be exaggerated.

really didn't need anything new. Strangely enough, my second daughter has the same mania for shoes. Moes often wore a silk kimono in Indië. She remained petite and delicate until she died.

My mother must not have ever forgiven her father. It would come out in expressions and her overall attitude. She called him a 'blanda met flink vizier,' meaning a 'Dutch one who thought much of himself' (like a high official). *My grandmother Adele died very young, and I never met her. She lived in Holland from the time she was quite young (but returned to Indië). I believe she was always an inspiration to my mother.*

Moes was Orange-minded (pro Dutch royalty). She had a firm trust in the integrity of our Queen. Later, in Holland, she was interviewed twice to talk about the pension of the surviving widows of the Ambonnezen (Moluccans) *who had participated with her in the resistance. Yes, that resistance caused my mother a lot of trouble. After the war, she received two honors personally from Queen Juliana. Both honors related to her courage and how she had faithfully shown up as resistance fighter. Your father has them. I have no need of them. I have seen the misery from up close.*

Even though I often didn't agree with her, I admired her. She was morally courageous. She dared to do things without being concerned about public opinion. She had an inner standard of right and wrong, and she adhered to it. She was well aware of the fact that we have to take account for our actions.

With this I want to conclude: At the gymnasium (college prep high school) *I was a good student, eights and nines, even a ten for Mathematics. I am very well informed, and I do not mean that I have read all the novels of Courts Mahler. Thanks to my classical education, I prefer literature of a better genre. I have a realistic self-image. I always considered myself above average. But if I compare myself with my mother, who only had 'skola gjonkok,' I'm just a little girl. My hat goes off to you, Moes. You were a good person. You did your duty for the family, your fellow man, and your country.*

I am sorry that Oma Sok's dislike for blandas remained when she lived in the Netherlands. It was evident that she did not accept my mother (who is Dutch). I didn't have a close relationship with Oma Sok. It is known amongst my cousins that she preferred the boys. I don't remember any intimate or personal conversations with her. I have no stories that I heard her tell about

Indië. I could have benefited from her wisdom, experience, and perspective. I was much like her in my early twenties—that is, wanting to help the underdog.

She is the only relative I remember speaking Malay in full sentences. She often sang songs in Malay. She had a good sense of humor. Much like Tante Maggie described, she was tough and had a sardonic manner. By the time I was of an age that I would have been less intimidated, she was no longer able to communicate with words. In her later years she had Alzheimer's.

There is the story that goes around the family about her Chinaman. I remember the large (eighteen inch; forty-six cm), wooden statue of a Chinese man that stood on the mantel. She was quite attached to the statue and would gesture and talk to it (even before she had Alzheimer's). The story is that she wanted the Chinaman to be buried with her. For unknown reasons, no one obliged or perhaps it was not legally permitted. It ended up with a cousin who is a bit of a collector. Over the ensuing years, he became concerned about not following our grandmother's wishes and also about the bad luck it could bring to family members for not adhering to her wishes. Since it was too late to place it in her grave, the Chinaman has been clandestinely laid to rest at an Indisch monument in the Netherlands.

Due to effects of Alzheimer's, Oma Sok was in a nursing home for more than ten years. My grandfather visited her every day. As the story goes, he would faithfully go through rain, cold, and snow by bus. On some days, Os would take him by car. Oma died in the nursing home on May 16, 1987 at eighty-nine. From her, I have a small whicker box with several elegant gloves; some I've mended and I still wear on occasion.

Opa Berg – As Honest As Abe

I formed a deeper relationship with Opa Berg when I became an adult. I found him to be gentle, kind, and with much integrity. It is difficult to reconcile the youthful, body builder and the stories of his fighting nature with the man I came to know. Perhaps life experiences softened, humbled, and hopefully brought him to peace. Perhaps he learned new ways to be an honorable man. In my late twenties when vacationing in the Netherlands, Opa took me to a shop in his neighborhood where he bought me a wall clock.

Meticulous as he was about time as well as other things, it was fitting. I had that clock for twenty years. It was the only item of his I possessed except for a silver key chain I received after he passed away.

Here is Tante Maggie's summary about her father:

Pap was a great guy, completely honest. But he was strict for himself and whomever he was dealing with. I loved him. I did a lot of things behind his back, but I never resented his authority over us, his children, and I never doubted his integrity.

Opa Berg

Our car was my father's prize possession. He maintained it himself. The chauffer was allowed to polish it, but every Sunday my father was under the car to keep the engine in perfect condition. If we closed the door too hard (for his thinking) when we would get in, he always responded with, "Don't think you're in a taxi!"

Pap was a Chevy-man. According to him, there was nothing better than a Chevrolet. He repeatedly told me this story about the Bromo-stairs, which he had built. These stairs reach the highest point of Bromo, a volcano in East-Java. The stairs lead to the crater. Once in awhile his highest boss would come to see if the work was proceeding well. His boss had a Mercedes Benz, but to reach the highest point, the Mercedes had to drive backwards.[61] Then, Pap would drive our Chevy with a smile on his face and without any trouble getting to the top (where the stairs were).

During my trip to Indonesia, I went to the Crater Bromo. It was quite an adventure. I rose before sunrise to leave the hotel in Malang. Having been told to dress warmly, I wore the one long-sleeved blouse I had with me. I hadn't brought warm clothing a since the average temperature on Java is around eighty degrees with seventy-five percent humidity. It, however, was

---

[61] This may be because, at that time, there was no front wheel drive. The road to the Bromo volcano was up hill. Perhaps the Mercedes had more power driving backwards.

cool at 2329 meters (7641 feet). We left before dawn. We had spectacular views of the sun rising, with fog hanging below the volcano peaks like a foaming bubble bath. The Jeep took us down to a low sandy plateau where we then entered another vehicle with very large wheels that could manage in the sand. When it stopped at a ridge of sand dunes, dozens of turbaned riders on small horses[62] squeezed against the Jeep like fans against the stage at a rock concert. We could hardly get out. They were offering rides up the sand dune to the rim of the crater. Taken aback and not realizing how arduous the walk would be, I opted to not accept a ride. Walking on loose sand up hill made the 45-minute walk feel longer. Once there, it was quite surreal to look up the stairs my grandfather had built seventy-five years before. I then ascended the 240 steps to the rim of the Crater Bromo.

Bromo Crater, 1996

As if he knew the end was soon, Opa had asked Tante Maggie to come to Holland and stay for a while. At that time, her eldest daughter just learned that she had Multiple Sclerosis and so Tante Maggie didn't go. Opa Berg also had asked my parents if they could come live in Holland for half a year. My mother still regrets not going. Opa tragically died at home alone. Not able to reach the telephone attached to the wall, he crawled to the front door, where he waited in hope that someone would come. Later that day, Oom Os arrived for his daily visit. By then Fritz, Pap, Opa was gone. He passed away before his beloved Sok at eighty-nine on March 28, 1985. **Sok and Fritz had then been married for sixty-nine years.**

---

[62] The Sumbawa Pony was originally bred on Sumbawa Island in Indonesia. Some say that they came from native ponies of Arabian breeding or from Mongolian horses and ancient Chinese stock. Most ponies average 12 hands (48 inches). Retrieved November 11, 2019 from https://en.wikipedia.org/wiki/Sumbawa_Pony.

Chapter Eighteen

Anton – From Loner to Leader

Anton (Ton) was a difficult baby who cried a great deal, as if he was uncomfortable in his skin. As was custom, the baboe carried Ton in a slendang much of the time; it was the only way he would remain calm and quiet. Already early on, Ton had a thirst for knowledge and he played in a most focused manner. As already told, his mother went to Malang to recover from influenza when Ton was not quite two. Ton stayed with his grandmother Adele. Os was an easy, cheerful child who readily engaged those around him. When Moes returned without Os, she was miserable, missing her second child. This acutely affected the elder boy Ton.

Luckily he had a bond with his maternal grandmother whom he would visit often in his early years. Adele saw deeply into the boy and could appreciate who he was. When they played together, he would say, "No, Oma, like this," show her how it was to be done, and then go back to whatever he was doing. Sometimes she would tease and do just the opposite. He'd then

Os, Ton, and Jack the dog

stand up, barely past her knees and say, with his hand on his hip, "Oma you're not doing it right."

They created books in which Ton would make drawings and dictate a story for his Oma to write. Sleeping in her bed was a special treat. Like she had done with her daughters, she told him stories she made up or would recite Javanese myths and sagas. She spoke to him with honest answers to his constant questioning. If he was puzzled, he was allowed to question. Sometimes she did not have an answer, and she would ask him what he thought.

He always had questions after she had told a story. One of his favorites was *Koopman dan anak harimau* (The Vendor and the Tiger Cub):

The vendor, Jan, walked his cattle to market. The route took him through the jungle where he came across a young tiger. He tied the tiger to a clump of bamboo with a batik scarf from his wares hoping that its mother (who must not be far) would be detained by unraveling the scarf. He hoped that no tiger followed him as he worked his way through the jungle. He successfully sold his wares at the market and hoped to get home through the jungle before dark. On his way back, the vendor ran into a woman wearing a slendang holding a baby. The slendang looked much like the scarf he had used to tie the baby tiger. The woman asked if he had left the scarf with her baby, which he affirmed. She then invited him to come to her family's home for dinner. Jan, having heard of these tiger-people, was wary and said "No." She was insulted and became angry, so he acquiesced. The village, deeper in the jungle and far from any path, was just like any village. Jan enjoyed a meal with the tiger-people. The elder of the village also thanked him for the scarf and for gracing them with his company. The elder then asked if the vendor had a request. Jan said that he wished to be able to pass through the jungle without being stalked by tigers. His wish was granted, and he never ran into another tiger.

178

After Oma Adele was done telling, Ton would sit still, his brows together in thought. "Oma," he would say, "Why did the tiger lady get mad at the vendor?"

"I don't know. Why do you think?"

He paused and then said, "They didn't ever have company for dinner and she really wanted company."

Oma Adele laughed and said, "That might just be so."

Only with his Oma could he ask for just one more story or one more turn at having his back tickled. He adored her. Sadly, Adele died when Ton was not yet seven.

Ton was also very fond of their dog, Jack, a German Shepherd with whom he played endlessly and who also consoled him when he was sad.[63] My father described himself as a *zonderling* (eccentric loner). He most likely kept to his own because the family moved often—every year because his father worked on the highway from Banjoewangie to Malang, which is 500-600 kilometers (311-373 miles).[64] When he was just starting to make friends, they again would move. But Jack was always there; the Shepherd was his best friend.

Papa liked to reminisce about his childhood. On one of the days I was visiting them in Las Vegas, I was able to record some of his stories. They were told in a mixture of Dutch, Malay, and English. I translated the transcripts to English. He shared the following:

---

[63] My father remained fond of and most compassionate with animals all of his life. I have seen him stop the car and get out to check on a bird he had accidently hit while driving. He collapsed to the ground and wailed when a car in front of our house hit one of our dogs. He held another of our dogs in his arms for hours as she was dying. He was also against killing the mice/rats that came into the house in California.

[64] Between 1800 and 1950, Dutch engineers built 67,000 kilometers (42,000 miles) of roads, 7,500 kilometers (4,700 miles) of railways, bridges, irrigation systems, covering 1.4 million hectares (5,400 square miles) of rice fields, several harbors, and 140 public drinking water systems."Dutch Empire," *Wikipedia.* Retrieved March 13, 2019 from https://en.wikipedia.org/wiki/Dutch_Empire

When Pap worked on the highway we lived in seven places and I went to seven schools: Pasoeluwar, Probolinggo, Lumajang, Gember (Gambar), Worektetok and Bangel (?). That last place was the best, with marble floors, a front gallery (living room) so large we could play tennis. We had twenty klapperbomen (coconut trees) and a long drive-up lane edged with flowers. It was about two acres. We lived quite comfortably with nine servants: cook, clothes washer, driver, gardener, nanny, houseboy, and house maids. Even so, your grandmother helped with the household chores.

After living a year in Malang, we moved again to Lumajang, but I lived with my Oma Suus (who ran a hotel in Malang) so I could attend high school. Later my parents moved back to Malang.

Growing up with a household filled with people with different backgrounds and ideas helped form Ton into being a free thinker. They lived amongst Moluccan and other Protestants, Indonesian Muslims, both subscribing to the inlandse animism including their *guna* (white magic), *guna guna* (black magic). There were also atheists, Jews, Chinese (unsure of their religion), and Catholics.

My father often told the story of how he changed from a quiet and studious boy into an extroverted leader.

I was a shy kid and a loner up until then. In one of my classes was a good-looking girl named Vera van Belsum. She had an older boyfriend who was the best looking guy in the school. Broer Sibrandi. An Indonesian girl with long pigtails sat in front of me. She was the smartest girl in the class. Her father was a teacher. She'd always raised her hand when the teacher asked a question.

One day Vera stopped at my house on her bicycle with the pretense of asking a question about the homework assignment. When I saw her coming to the door, I hid in my room.

Moes came and called, "You, get out here!" So I went out and sat at the table not knowing what to say or do.

Vera, about a year older, said, "Why are you always so quiet? Why don't you ever come to any of the dances?"

I just raised my shoulders in an 'I dunno.'

She then said, "If I didn't already have a boyfriend, I'd want to dance with you."
She was, of course, trying to pull me out of myself. Smart girl. That changed my life. I
wasn't shy anymore. I became popular and even became the chairman of the TAVENU
(Tot Algemene Verpozing en Nuttige Uitspanning. In English: Towards A
General Peace and Useful Relaxation*). I had more votes than there were members.*
That's because they voted for me more than once. Most of the kids chosen in these positions
came from families with fathers in high positions, like Iffe Bijhoud, the daughter of the
Governor, or Koos, the son of the Commander of the Army. All the guys had girlfriends,
too. Not me. Yet, I was still voted in.

He sat up straight with a proud look as if it happened just yesterday.
Papa then explained that within the year he would dance with all the best
looking girls at school, the SOOS, and TAVENU dances and, within another
year, had a girlfriend. By his last year of high school, he was voted the student
body president.

Track team with Ton in the middle

High School

My father explained that *de Hogere Burgerschool* or HBS (Higher Civic
School) is for those going on to college. It's secondary education that
included languages—French, German, English and Dutch; math and
sciences—physics, chemistry, biology; analytical geometry, algebra; and

181

trigonometry; and history and geography. At the university level, they had the same schools on Java as in the Netherlands for medicine, technology (like engineering), or law. The Dutch brought these institutions to Indonesia so that those living there would not have to go to Holland to study. The universities were all in Batavia (now called Jakarta).

Papa continued to live in Malang when his parents were taken to another town as Opa continued to work on the highway. This was during my father's last year of the HBS. By the time he graduated, he was fluent in the four languages. His sister, the bookworm in the family, learned Greek and Latin as well. Many, like my father, also spoke Malay and/or Javanese, most likely learned at an early age from their baboes. As told previously, these languages had three to five different forms depending on what class of person you were referring to or addressing.

My father and aunt also told how they learned children's songs and stories that referred to scenes in Holland, such as snowy winters, ice skating on the canals, and the flora and fauna that was non existent in the tropics. The Netherlands is at a latitude further north than anywhere in the continental US except for Maine. Indonesia lies on the equator. Although the Indonesians had their own schools, the HBS attracted students from diverse ethnicities living on the islands. Papa often told about this ethnic mixture at his HBS:

In my class of twenty students, there were four Chinese, five or six Javanese, and a couple of foreigners that weren't Dutch, Chinese, or Indonesian. For instance, there was a German whose name was Keizer. The rest were Dutch. More were Indisch. The Chinese and Indonesians were often wealthy and the more serious students. The Chinese owned factories and were millionaires. There were also less wealthy kids. It was a hodgepodge of people. Everyone had to go to a secondary school. We had the HBS and the MULO. Where you attended was based on an entry exam you took in the sixth grade of grammar school. The HBS was a higher level, but you could transfer to a HBS from the MULO if your grades were good. You'd just have one more year of secondary school, seven instead of six.

The parents of students in Soerabaja were businessmen, a different sort. Malang was high in the mountains and where many retired and well-to-do people lived. They were more bescheiden (literally it means humble, but is also used to mean civilized).

In antithesis to the formidable academic load, he fondly tells humorous stories of the fun he had:

I graduated in 1938. I remember all my teachers. The chemistry teacher had nicknames for us: giant with glasses was Max. Guy with cowlick was me. Teacher Dresser taught Dutch and wasn't liked by the students. Once he left class to go to the bathroom and forgot to zip his pants. One of the girls, Elaine, gestured with her fingers closing her nostrils. (My father demonstrated.) *So he sent her out of the class and then we all followed her.* (He laughed.) *Pitiful. Another time someone cut the seat out of the whicker chair, so when he went to sit down he fell through. Of course, the class burst out laughing. He didn't know how to handle us. They fired him.*

Our German teacher was telling us about words in Dutch that were German words expressed in Dutch. He called it a 'Germanisme.' And he'd say, "Afbranden in German is abbrennen." (Afbranden is a Dutch word for burning down.) *Then the German kid, Keizer, said, "No, in German it is niederbrennen." The teacher then said, "No."*

Papa continued while imitating the gesture he described his classmate making:

Keizer then made the form of a pistol with his hand and held it up and said, "Is it niederbrennen or abbrennen?" Of course, we all burst out laughing. Those were good times.

Papa recited this story with the glee, pride, and bravado of his teenage self at the time.

Every Saturday we had a dance party. Every three months there was a big party at the SOS, with mostly the wealthy crowd. We always held it in a big dance hall. There was a girl named van der Zoubrouwer who came from a good family and was one of the best dancers. She invited me to pick her up and take her to the SOS. So I did all excited. Then this really handsome guy, Jimmy Lot, came to sit with her. They used me because her father didn't approve of Jimmy because he was of a lower class. She later married an officer.

I'm amazed that he remembers so many first and last names. In part this may be because it identified ethnicity, which, in spite of the melting pot he described, must have had significance.

We had a trivia contest between different High Schools—Batavia, Bandoeng, Semarang, Malang, and Soerabaja. At the meet, we needed to have een tafelmeisje (a girl at our table). *At that time, Emmy Tibot was the prettiest girl. So I said to Koetsveld, a Dutch guy who was part of the meet, "Why don't you invite her?"*

He said, "Why? Do you like her?"

"No," I answered, not wanting to admit it. "You know her and I don't. But if you won't, I will."

So, later, when we were heading home, I pulled up to her with my bike and asked her if she'd come.

"Of course," she replied and smiled.

So she came to the contest and after that we continued to date. She was the stepdaughter of a retired governor. He was Indisch. Her biological father was from Friesland (province in Holland) *and her mother was Dutch. When her father died, her mother remarried. Anyway, I completely changed. I was a great dancer. We did ballroom dancing. We had good bands at school. I also became the champion in track for 400 meters.*

Emmy Tibot and Ton must have broken up. During his last year at the HBS he met another great dancer, Louise Adelaide De Haas, or Wies for short. Vivi told me that it took some convincing for Wies to go on a date with our father. But when she saw him dance, she gave him a second chance. Wies and Ton married October 24, 1941.

Melting Pot

Classification by race, ethnicity, and class was set deep in the societal structure. My father told:

Pap's best friend was Chinese, Liem Wei Chu. His son became a Dutch citizen, but he stayed in Indonesia after the Dutch left. The Indonesians had their own legal system that fell under the Sultan of Susuhunan. The Indonesians also had their own Dutch grammar school where they could learn about Islam. Or they could go to Islamic schools. Some of the Dutch did not hang out with Dutch-Indonesians, and some Dutch-Indonesians did not have anything to do with Indonesians. It just depended. My parents were open to everyone, and so that's how we were.

184

As teens and into adulthood, my father, aunt, and uncle listened to classical or the pop music of the times on the radio or record players and attended dances and balls. However, they also had their own music—krontjong (now *keroncong*). Papa reminisced about the local music and his mother singing:

Tramboelang, de maan aan de kant van de rivier.

[The moon is on the side of the river.]

Je moet niet altijd geloven wat je man vertelt want hij verzint wel eens dingen.

[Don't always believe what your man says because he makes things up.]

Then he told of the local Indonesian kids that did something similar to contemporary rap:

Eh dai jo net te kol

Eh per no ko sol

Eh klos ol ne per daal

Eh taba nopola

Eh taba nebotol

It's a children's game. Everyone took turns and had to add a phrase. I memorized them. I was always good at remembering songs and poetry. (He then recited a German and a French poem.) *These I learned in grammar school. I'll never forget.*

The lifestyle of the Dutch-Indonesian colonials was more free and worldly in certain ways than that of most of their Dutch contemporaries living in the Netherlands. A continuous influx of people from many parts of the world, east and west, and the already dynamic mixture of cultures, albeit within a structured class system, allowed for the inflow of diverse ideas, culture, arts, music, and fashion. Music and dance was significant in the Berg family. Jan played classical flute, Fritz played classical clarinet, and Ton played guitar. The family owned both a radio and a gramophone player, so there was often music and impromptu dancing with school friends or between generations at home. In addition to krontjong, the latest music from the US and Europe came to the Dutch-East Indies. My father joined a krontjong band with some of the local young men.

Classic Stories

The house was active with many visitors, dinner and/or long-term guests. As told, Sokkie had a way with people and was savvy. Some of the guests were not always on the straight and narrow. My brother, Carl, tells:

There was a guy who lived with Oma and Opa before and during the war, who was Indisch with a German father. His name was Helmut Schirmer and he was a lichte (light-skinned) *Indo. Because he was German—a supposed ally to the Japanese—he was allowed to roam freely during the time Java was occupied by the Japanese. He was a bit of a conartist. During the occupation he collected old broken watches and would tinker with them so that they looked functional. Then, just before approaching a Japanese military person, he shook the watch so it would tick, and then put it against the ear of a Japanese soldier in order to sell it.*

I often heard a story told about Sok purchasing materials from a vendor. As it was told, there was something suspicious about the materials. After inspection, my grandfather refused to pay and told the vendor to take it back ASAP. When the vendor refused, Fritz punched him in the face. (Here is an example of my grandfather's hot temper and violence that was told by my father with pride. Was that how it was in those times? Was this a way to show power when feeling powerless?)

A few days later, Sok went to bathe the baby Maggie. Thinking that it was taking her a long time, Fritz went to check and discovered Sok in a trance moving her hand back and forth as if washing, but Maggie had slipped out of her other hand and was under water. He was lucky to arrive just when he did.

The explanation was that Sok had been put under a spell. Many inlandse and Indos resorted to guna to acquire, to influence, and guna guna for revenge. My grandmother was not well for a week. My grandfather

186

contacted their doctor who, as soon as he saw my grandmother, knew that her condition was as a result of guna guna. He advised Fritz to consult an Ambonees and gave him the address in Soerabaja. Fritz had to drive ninety kilometers (about fifty-five miles) and back to pick the man up. Upon arriving and inspecting Sok, the dukun told Fritz to look under the mattress at the left top of the bed. There he found a fabric doll with bits of Sok's hair. The dukun knew just how to bring Sok back to this world. As the story goes, she had to stand naked by the entrance of the house where Fritz had hit the man, and there the dukun covered her with seven species of flowers. It took about week for her to get back to normal, and so she remained except that once a week, always at the same time, she'd have an itch under her arm.

When Tante Mag told me the story, she warned that one who uses magic, whether for good or evil, would have to pay in turn. The way I understand it is that one can manipulate life events to go the way the ego desires. Whether this is done using shady means or not, in forcing an event that is not ripe or true, there is a consequence. In Javanese mysticism,

> (t)he exercise of *tapa* (ascetics) and meditation are possible means to achieve purely worldly and magical purposes that may even be destructive to others, and that are clearly guided by *pamrih* (ego motives). This type of mysticism is generally rated as sinful, as an attempt to interfere with the prevailing cosmos order or the divine will in order to achieve a temporary result. It is 'black magic', and its practice will certainly meet with *karmatic* retribution....[65]

Indos often took on many of the beliefs and superstitions of the inlanders. And many witnessed the guna of the inlandse. Tante Mag told me to never plant a bougainvillea in the front of the house because it was bad luck. It is known that a kris takes on the power of the owner. Opa Berg explained to my brother that one could test which kris was more powerful. Make a fist with each hand, putting the thumb on top and extended over the closed fingers. One places each kris on top of the extended thumbs and then slowly moves the two fists together bringing the knives closer to each other. The kris (not the fist) that is more powerful will, without any human attempt, place itself on top of the weaker one. This reminds me in the Harry Potter

---

[65] Niels Mulder. (1980). *Mysticism & everyday life in contemporary Java* (2nd ed.). Singapore: Singapore University Press, p. 17.

novels when the wand maker explains the relationship between wand and wizard—that is, that the wand choses the wizard. In Java, oneness of existence carries over to objects, which "are possessed by the spirituality of their owner or maker and may contain a power of their own." [66]

Military

About his military career, my father began with:

Ton playing his guitar.

I wanted to be an entertainer. I played on stage in a small band. I sang well. I played guitar. But Moes didn't want me to take it seriously. She said, "I'll break that guitar on your legs." (He laughed.) *She, of course, didn't want me to become a krontjong player. "You'll become a poeaja." Which meant someone of lower class. It was the tradition for the oldest son to become a military officer. I didn't learn this till later. It was a Berg tradition. I was told that my grandfather and grandfathers back until 1200 were all military officers. My father wasn't an oldest son, so he wasn't a career military officer. But his father was and retired as a captain.* (Records show that my father's grandfather retired as a Sergeant Major. My father may have been mistaken, thinking of his great-grandfather. As we know, his Opa Jan also was not an oldest son.) *Then he became a bookkeeper for a sugar factory. Danny, of course, couldn't because of his hip. So it ends with me. My grandfather and great-grandfather had many sons. I know that, of the family in Indonesia, there are ten to fifteen Bergs in the KNIL, from captains to generals.*

Oom Chris told me that Fransz Joseph's father fought in the war against Napoleon. At Schloss Burg (a castle near Solingen Germany that housed Bergs since the 1200s), *they said that our family crest is the only one with a lion. All the other*

[66] IBID., p. 24.

German heraldries have eagles. Adolf Berg, the first Berg, came from Limburg, which used to be Germany but now is part of the Netherlands.

This information and the family crest were given to my grandfather (Fritz) by an uncle Chris who, my father indicated, was the oldest brother of my grandfather.[67]

After HBS I went for officer's training, which took three years. That was in 1938. In 1940, WWII began in Europe. I had just completed officer training and then I was trained to be a pilot. There was an exam. We had to sing the Dutch national anthem. I remember the doctor looking at my skinny legs saying, "Can you use those legs?" I said, "Lets go to the stadium and we can both run the 400, and then let's see who can use their legs!"

---

[67] In my genealogical research there is no Chris or variation of Chris. With common use of nicknames, it could have been a son or even a grandson of Joseph Carl Leonard. He then could have been a great uncle or uncle of my grandfather, Fritz.

Chapter Nineteen

World War II – Prisoners and Spies

Summary of Events Leading to War

Although the Netherlands had proclaimed neutrality when World War II broke out in September 1939, Nazi Germany invaded the Netherlands on May 10, 1940. The Dutch government (Dutch Queen and prime minister) went into exile in Great Britain and the Dutch East Indies remained under control of the Dutch government. Had the Dutch collaborated upon surrender to Germany, the **Dutch East Indies** would have been surrendered to Japan (Germany's ally). The Dutch didn't collaborate because they wanted to hold on to the financial interests of the colony. It was rich in resources, such as oil, rubber, and tin. "By December 1941, the Dutch force in Indonesia numbered around 85,000 personnel: regular troops consisted of 1,000 officers and 34,000 enlisted soldiers of whom 28,000 were

---

[68] Ton and mates preparing for paratroop training.

indigenous."[69] After the Japanese bombed Pearl Harbor, the Dutch realized that the Japanese would try to occupy the archipelago. On December 8, 1941, the Dutch declared war on Japan. According to my father, the Allies wanted the Dutch to declare war so that the Japanese would try to take Indonesia, which then would give the Allies in Australia time to prepare for an invasion on Japan. In other words, from my father's perspective, The Dutch East Indies was sacrificed. At that time, the KNIL had 389 planes, which were mostly outclassed by the Japanese.

The Japanese Imperial Army invaded the Dutch East Indies on January 1, 1942. Since they were occupied by Germany, it was difficult for the Dutch to defend colonial interests in Indonesia. In spite of help from American and British forces, Japan took the archipelago in the Battle of the Java Sea at the end of February 1942 and drove the Allied naval forces out of Southeast Asia.

As a consequence, the Dutch colonial government vacated Batavia, and Japanese soldiers marched in carrying both Indonesian and Japanese flags. Captured Dutch military were taken to Singapore and later to camps in Japan and all over Southeast Asia. Roughly 65,000 Dutch and Indonesian soldiers (fighting for the Dutch) were sent to labor camps, working on the Burma Railroad and in mines in Japan where many suffered or died as a result of ill treatment and starvation. According to the Library of Congress (1992), between four and ten million Indonesians became *romusha* (forced laborers).[70] In addition, 80,000 Dutch, British, Australian, and US Allied troops went to prisoner-of-war camps where death rates were between thirteen and thirty percent. Twenty-five percent of the Dutch-Indonesian POWs did not survive.[71]

Dutch administrators were sent to concentration camps and Japanese or Indonesian replacements were installed in senior and technical positions. Japanese troops took control of government infrastructure and services such as ports and postal services. Opa Berg, Oom Os, and Oom Tjeun (Maggie's

[69] *Royal Netherlands East Indies Army (KNIL)1814-1950*. Retrieved August 18, 2019 from https://www.youtube.com/watch?v=KENqdtUqKNI
[70] "The Japanese Occupation," *Indonesia: World War II and the struggle for independence, 1942–50*, Retrieved July 15, 2019 from http://www.country-data.com/cgi-bin/query/r-6196.html
[71] Jean Gelman Taylor. (2003). *Indonesia: Peoples and histories*.

husband) were interned in Burma and worked on the railroad leading to the bridge over the River Quai.

According to figures from the Netherlands Institute of War Documentation in The Hague, the Japanese interned more than 110,000 men, women, and children of Dutch ancestry. Those who could prove that they had Indonesian ancestry could live outside of the camps. While many may have had Indonesian ancestry, they could not prove it because often this ancestry was hidden, or some simply did not want to own their Indonesian heritage. Women and children were put behind barbed wire in old prisons or in barracks. Boys over the age of ten were separated from their mothers and put in camps for boys and men. All possessions, except things like clothes, a few pots and pans, etc., were to be handed over to the Japanese.

With slogans in of support ("Japan is our older brother" and "Banzai Dai Nippon") of the Japanese invasion, revolutionary Indonesians killed groups of Europeans (particularly the Dutch) and were informants for the Japanese. Many of the Indonesian ruling class, who had been local officials and politicians working for the Dutch colonial government, also joined Japanese military authorities. During the occupation, Indonesians received support and encouragement from the Japanese for nationalistic sentiments. These events, along with the Japanese destruction of much of the Dutch colonial state, were fundamental to the Indonesian National Revolution that followed World War II.

Sok's Story – The Housewife and The Captain

Before the Japanese occupation in 1942, my grandparents lived on Tegalsari 78, a home with open verandas and a large garden in a wealthy neighborhood of Soerabaja. My grandfather had been promoted to the head superintendent of Public Works and earned "a very good salary." By 1941, after Pearl Harbor, the Dutch were anticipating attacks on Indonesia. Oom Os and Opa Berg were called up for military service with the KNIL, and my father had been flying missions. Oma Sok volunteered as a telephone operator at the headquarters at the Air Defense Service (ADS) opposite their house. During those first months of relative quiet in Soerabaja, no one anticipated or expected that in only two months the Dutch would capitulate to the Japanese. Once the Japanese were in Soerabaja, the ADS became the *Poesat Keibodan* (PK) (Vigilance Corps), an auxiliary police force run by the

Medal Oma Sok received from Queen Juliana for her work resisting the Japanese.

Japanese intended to help maintain order and security and watch out for spies and saboteurs. Staff of the original ADS was now working for the Japanese. Closely watched, the head commander of the ADS was arrested and accused of listening to news broadcasts from Allied radio stations. Other European and Dutch-Indonesian staff was arrested as well. Oma Sok was not arrested, most likely because of her friendly ties with the royal house of Soerakarta. This may also be the reason she was able to remain in their home during Japanese occupation. However, she became involved in communications with prisoners of war and was soon asked to join the resistance. She didn't want to take the risk because her daughter, Maggie, and much younger brother, Bob, lived with her. After witnessing arrests, humiliations, and general bad treatment of internees, and more so seeing what the *Kenpeitai* (Japanese military police) had done to her husband, convinced Sok to do something. Hence, Sok became a messenger for those working in the resistance. She worked closely with a Captain Meelhuysen, who had gone undercover after his plane crashed on a mission. Meelhuysen used the pseudonym Tahir and was a master of disguises. After meeting Sok Berg, he became her 'gardener.' The two clicked, a close friendship arose, and it appears that she was his most important confidant and advisor.

194

On 21 December 1942, Wil Meelhuysen, captain-pilot of the Military Aviation of the KNIL and one of the leaders of the underground movement in East Java, cycled for the last time through Surabaya. He was on his way to the police headquarters at Paradeplein, to report to the PID.[72] With this deed, he hoped to get Mrs. Berg, a close associate who had been arrested the day before. Mrs. Berg was obviously not released. Meelhuysen would commit suicide the following night. After an attempt to deprive himself of life by taking cyanankali, he managed to hang himself at the bars of his cell in the Werfstraat prison at night.[73]

The Dutch, Indisch, Moluccans, Minahassers, Madurees and Chinese, within the internment camps or elsewhere, wanted to continue the fight. Some collected weapons and distributed news reports, and others provided civilians and ex-military personnel with weapons inside and outside the camps. The organization led by Meelhuysen under the code name Corsica was preparing for the Allied invasion that he expected would be soon. The organization obstructed strategic positions such as bridges, railroads, barracks, police stations, and logistics centers.

Meelhuysen also worked on building an espionage network because military and general information about the occupying forces were of great importance for the success of the Allied campaign. Members of Corsica improved the overall condition of those occupied by smuggling food, money, and clothes to internment camps, helping hidden soldiers around Malang, financially and materially supporting families of prisoners of war, and providing the groups of soldiers in the mountains around Malang with weapons and other goods in the hope of keeping the guerrilla struggle going. They gathered weapons that were left by soldiers and others who had ignored the Japanese command to surrender all weapons. These had been buried, hidden, or thrown into the *kali* (river).

The organization grew quickly, some say to 750. The organization's 'foot soldiers' consisted mostly of Moluccans and Minahassian KNIL soldiers

---

[72] *Politieke Inlichting Dienst* (Political Intelligence Service)
[73] B. R. Immerzeel and F. van Esch. (1993). *Verzet in Nederlands-Indië tijdens de Japanse bezetting 1942-1945*, Den Haag: SDU uitgeverij Koninginnegracht ISBN 90 12 06847 9. Ensuing story is my translation from this publication.

loyal to the queen and flag. Many women joined and were used mainly for courier services. Sok had the function of contact person and was involved in the recruitment of new members for the organization, and her house became a center of clandestine activities. Various resistance fighters also found a safe shelter in her home. Reluctantly, Bob and Maggie participated in subterfuge at the house, mainly by not telling anyone. The movement was comprehensive.

Despite disguises and due caution, their activities were known to many. Too many, as there were those who did not sympathize with the Dutch colonists that secretly worked against the Japanese. The Kenpeitai waited to go after the group when they were certain they had identified key players in the resistance and the repository of firearms. Meelhuysen, along with many others, were arrested, and eventually through torture, my grandmother's name came up. She tried to save herself by declaring that she did not know the captain, instead admitting that she knew Tahir (one of his disguises) with whom she had an amorous relationship. Months of painful interrogations followed. The story I heard growing up was that she was questioned about her involvement in the resistance and despite the water boarding torture, she denied all accusations and did not give up anything that her interrogators did not already know.

When the message that Sok had been arrested reached Meelhuysen, who was not yet identified, he realized that the game was up. He gave himself up in hope of freeing Sok and the others. From the Keibodan, he and my grandmother were transported together by car to prison and were able to exchange a few words. Meelhuysen told her he had taken cyanide tablets. The poison, however, had lost its effect because of water boarding done to him. On that same day the guards had found him dead; he had hanged himself from the bars of his cell.

My Aunt Maggie, who at the time lived in her parent's house, wrote about her version of her mother's experience:

At the outbreak of the war, Moes had offered her services as a telephone operator. Coincidentally the Luchtbeschermingsdienst (LBD) (Air Protection Service) station was down the street from us. Hence, Moes became a telephone operator at the main LBD station. After the capitulation she was retained, probably because she knew Indonesian languages very well—high and low Javanese, Malay, and also Madurees. Van Hutten brought her into contact with the underground work. He was called Paatje (Pops) *van Hutten.*

From the beginning I told her, "Stop that craziness, it will not go well." And, unfortunately, I was right. I myself never participated. I have a sacred respect for authority. If something is not allowed, I will not do it. In addition, I am no hero. I had seen enough of the Japs to know that there was no playing around with them.

When the people from the underground came to gather, I locked myself up in my bedroom; hence, I did not know anything about what was going on in the underground. Unfortunately, I was right about my fears. All the men who were involved in this conspiracy were beheaded, except Captain Meelhuysen, who committed suicide. The interrogations took place in the third section at Boeboetan where Moes was temporarily locked up. I could bring her clean clothes once a week. The Sumatran commissioner, who was the head of the third section, let slip, "Miss Berg, that mother of yours is 'bani mati' (she dares to face death)."

On the birthday of Tenno Heika, the Japanese Emperor, my mother's death sentence was converted into life because she was a woman. But before this verdict was pronounced, both the Ken Pei Tai (her spelling) *and the Politieke Inlichting Dienst (PID)* (Political Intelligence Service) *tortured my mother severely. When she came out of prison after two and a half years, she was completely gray, all her beautiful teeth were loose, and she had two strange black-and-blue spots on her back that remained until her death. (They had hung her by the arms.) When she later mentally deteriorated, she had an explanation for that: "Those Japs have played soccer with my head."*

She confided to us how she prepared herself for these interrogations: "You have to look at them right in the eyes (which she learned as a child when summoned by her father), *and then you say ferociously: 'Kon asu, akoe matjan.'* (You are a dog and I am a tiger.)"

Corsica continued for another three months under another leader, and, by early March 1943, about two hundred people were arrested. Six leaders were then sentenced to death and beheaded by the Japanese court in Batavia. The other men and women got off with long prison sentences.

Fritz's Story – The Death Railway

All men that were able were called to join the KNIL to fight the Japanese, and most wound up in camps, primarily in Indonesia, Burma, and Japan. My Opa Berg, Oom Os, and Oom Tjeun worked on the 'the Death Railway' in Burma, which ran from Ban Pong, Thailand to Thanbyuzayat, Burma, passing through the Three Pagodas Pass that runs for 415 kilometers (258 miles). Of the 60,000 allied POWs who worked on this railway, nearly 13,000 died during the construction.[74]

Between 180,000 and 250,000 South East Asian civilian laborers and about 60,000 Allied prisoners of war, including Dutch, Indies British, British Indian, Australian, and Americans, were subjected to forced labor.

From postcard in my father's possessions of internment camp prisoners working on railroad in Burma

Construction camps, that housed at least 1,000 workers, were established every eight to sixteen kilometers (five to ten miles). The camps consisted of open-sided barracks made of bamboo poles and thatched roofs. Two hundred men were housed in each barrack with a two-foot (sixty-one cm) wide space to live and sleep. About 90,000 civilian laborers and more than 12,000 Allied prisoners died. The Indisch were better off than their western counterparts because they tended to be more resistant to tropical diseases and more acclimatized.[75]

[74] East Indies Camp Archives. Retrieved April 14, 2019 from:
https://www.indischekamparchieven.nl/en/general-information/about-de-camps/daily-life-in-the-camps
[75] BridgeRiverKwai.com. Retrieved April 14, 2019 from http://www.bridgeriverkwai.com/

After the railway was completed, the POWs had to wait almost two years before returning home. During this time, most of the POWs were moved to hospitals, and those who were fit went to relocation camps where they could be available for maintenance crews or sent to Japan to alleviate the manpower shortage there.

An American engineer later commented after viewing the project:

What makes this an engineering feat is the totality of it, the accumulation of factors. The total length of miles, the total number of bridges —over 600, including six to eight long-span bridges —the total number of people who were involved (one-quarter of a million), the very short time in which they managed to accomplish it, and the extreme conditions they accomplished it under. They had very little transportation to get stuff to and from the workers, they had almost no medication, they couldn't get food let alone materials, they had no tools to work with except for basic things like spades and hammers, and they worked in extremely difficult conditions—in the jungle with its heat and humidity. All of that makes this railway an extraordinary accomplishment.[76]

In Java, at the start of the war, my grandfather was assigned to a vandalism corps. He was captured by the Japanese and resisted by fighting back. The soldiers struck him hard on the back. As a consequence, he suffered from back pain throughout his time in the POW camp and the Bersiap period following the war (eight years). One may surmise that his broken back led to a broken spirit. The helplessness and incapacity to demonstrate his strength by fighting was unfamiliar to my grandfather. Over time, Fritz perhaps wisely accepted his situation by becoming thoughtful and observant. He watched his fellow prisoners, the guards, and the dynamics at camp. Fritz was not the type to complain. Anticipating how their situation would deteriorate, he taught himself to think of one thing each day for which to be grateful. This became his new discipline and it saved him.

Unlike Oma Sok who called the Japanese *gladakkers* (scoundrels), Opa Berg did not have bad feelings towards the Japanese. Perhaps one explanation is that the commanding officer in his camp demonstrated integrity and impartiality, characteristics very important to Opa. Carl repeats Opa's story of a young English prisoner who frequently got into scuffles with the Japanese guards.

The Japs had a designated cell for unruly prisoners that was less than a cubic meter, meaning that one could not lie down or stand up but had to squat or sit for the length of the imprisonment. It had no windows and was unbearably hot. The defiant English prisoner had often been sentenced to the 'bad hut.' Upon being released after two solid weeks, one of the more hostile guards pushed and handled the very weakened prisoner with undue force. The commander, having seen this, called everyone in the camp to gather. He called out the guard to come forward and ordered him to get on his knees. Then the commander pulled out his Samurai sword, held the sword up, and swiftly bought it down on the guard's neck. Everyone thought he was going to behead him, but the blade hit the guard sideways. Nearly as punitive, the guard had been humiliated.

Another of Opa's stories took place at the end of the war:

The Allies wanted to bomb the railroad as well as the enemy. So as not to bomb their own who were imprisoned, the Allies sent scouts to see where the Japanese military camps were in relation to the Allied POW camps. However, the Japs knew what the Allies were up to and switched camps with the prisoners, so when the Allies came to bomb, the prisoners instead of the Japanese would be killed. When the Ally bomber planes flew over dropping bombs, one of them went astray, hitting an oil tanker. So then, the Allies dropped the remaining bombs in that same area. This is how the bridge was destroyed and the Allied prisoners were saved.

Fritz was in camp for another year after the war ended. Under the command of Mountbatten, the British, Americans, and Australians were liberated before the prisoners from the Dutch East Indies. My grandparents, who had not been in contact with each other for four years, corresponded for the ensuing year while Fritz waited to go home. Carl says that heir letters have been saved, but no one knows where they are or who has them. I'm most curious to see what the two would have shared.

Anton's Story – POW Camp in Japan

Lieutenant Anton Berg flew ninety operational missions as a flight commander. His flight group came out of Yogyakarta, Java. After the Japanese had infiltrated the Dutch East Indies, he was trained as a commando and dropped behind Japanese lines in New Guinea for sabotage work. My father narrates what happened when the war broke out:

We, Jaapje, Rambelje and I, were the first three to fly when the war broke out. I was the paratrooper leader. Jaapje was my right flyer and Rambelje, my left. Jaapje was shot down. From my position, I saw him and the Japanese who shot him. The Japanese pilot did like this. (My father salutes.) *When people badmouth the Japanese, I tell them this story: A Japanese pilot was shot down in Singapore. He wasn't dead, so an English soldier simply shot him dead. It says in the Geneva Convention that you may not kill someone who is shot down.*

My father was able to evade the Japanese for three months, but was eventually taken prisoner when he was unable to make connection with his rescue boat. He was captured March 8, 1942 and taken on one of the 'hell' ships to Nagasaki. For the first nine months the Japanese moved prisoners around so the POWs wouldn't figure out how to escape. After nine months, people tended to give up. Papa spent three and a half years as a prisoner of war, with most of this time in Fukuoka, Japan[77]. He was hospitalized for acute colitis at the Itozu-Branch of the Kokura Military Hospital on April 26, 1943 and remained there for three weeks. At Fukuoka, the POWs worked at On'ga Mining Station, Nippon Mining Co. Ltd. There were 1,062 POWs (764 Dutch, 138 Americans, 117 British, 41 Australian and two of other nationality) that were still interned by the end of the war. Seventy-four died while imprisoned, and one Australian was shot to death due to his escape attempt.[78]

In Japan, there were seven main camps, eighty-one branch camps, and three detached camps at the end of the war. In total, 32,418 POWs were detained in these encampments. Most camps were set up in mines and in the industrial areas such as Keihin (Tokyo and Yokohama) and Hanshin (Osaka and Kobe). As with my father's camp, at the end of the war, some were moved to areas closer to the Sea of Japan in anticipation of an invasion of

---

[77] Fukuoka is 153 kilometers (95 miles) from Nagasaki. The US detonated two atomic bombs over the cities Nagasaki and Hiroshima on August 6, 1945. My father did not mention anything to me about the bombings. A friend of his and fellow pilot also captured, Paul Jolly, was in a POW camp in Nagasaki and had saved many lives. See: J. Stellingwerff (1980). *Fat man in Nagasaki: Nederlandse krijgsgevangenen overleefden de atoombom.* Amsterdam: T. Wever B.V. Franeker

[78] Stichting Oorlogsgetroffenen in de Oost: Met Japanse archieven en contacten (SOO). Retrieved August 4, 2019 from http://pow.s-o-o.nl/Camp/

Japan due to air raids by the US Air Force. The camps usually consisted of two-story wooden buildings with a compound surrounded by barbed wire. The POW quarters had rows of bunk beds with woven straw mats or mattresses. The lights were bare bulbs, and fires in shipping drums were used for heat.[79]

Many of my father's stories have to do with his time as a POW in Japan. Documentation, the literature, as well as dramatizations such as *The Railway Man* and *Unbroken* depict the behavior of Japanese towards prisoners as extremely brutal. My father, like my grandfather, had respect for the commanding officer of his camp and considered him more *beschaafd* (civilized) than some of his fellow imprisoned officers. Pap was particularly disdainful of

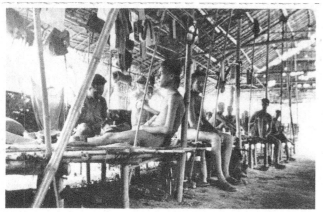

the British, who, he said, thought they were better than others—certainly the mixed-blood Indisch. He also respected the Japanese commander's sense of honor and pride. Papa explained that, while punishment was at times severe, he believed that the commander was just.

From postcard in my father's possessions of a camp barracks, most likely in Burma

Perhaps the connection with the Japanese officer was also because they both ran track (the commander had been in the Olympics, running the 500 meter), played tennis, and loved music—the commander played violin.

While his stories were always a scattered stream of consciousness, I now weave them in relative sequential order. Below is one tale about his time in camp that depicts his attitude. In the officer's section were Dutch (which included the Indisch), British, Australian, and Americans. My father was one of the first Dutch-Indonesian officers to arrive.

---

[79] "Prisoners of War of the Japanese," *Forces of war*. Retrieved April 14, 2019 from: https://www.forces-war-records.co.uk/prisoners-of-war-of-the-japanese-1939-1945

Those British officers complained about sharing with darkies. That was me! They didn't know that some of my colleagues, who were lighter and had blue eyes, were Indos too. Only we *can recognize another blonde Indo. What did those stuck-up English know? But the Japanese had no time for these Englishmen and their airs. One was particularly unreasonable and got a 'binta' (hard slap) from a guard. Of course that wasn't very smart. It created bad feelings.*

When telling the story, Papa stopped to take a sip of his *koffie tubruk* (Indonesian style in which one puts ground coffee in a mug, then the boiling water, and then waits for the grounds to float down). *But the commander was a wise man. The soldier who slapped the Englishman was punished. Some of the guards were brutes.* He took another sip and his eyes glazed over. *There was one Indo who knew guna guna. So when the guard was unreasonably brutal, he made the gun look like a snake, or made the guard think it was a snake. So the guard always stayed away from him.* He chuckled to enjoy his reminiscing.

There were close to 200 US soldiers that came out of prisons, like San Quentin. They volunteered, and, if they lived, they'd get their freedom. These were real criminals, Mafioso types. Two tough US sergeants from the military police kept them in line. A lot of gambling was going on, and one of the guys, he was from Polish heritage, would win everybody's rations and cigarettes, etc. He'd clean them out.

I got along well with the Americans. But not those stuck up British. They were the worst. That Japanese commander had it over the British. He was a fair and honorable man. He used to play violin in the evening. I would do my work quietly, or, when I was off duty, I would lie in my bunk and listen. It always reminded me of Pap (his father). *He played clarinet, you know?*

I was responsible for the housekeeping and kitchen supplies. We were to give each prisoner a certain amount of grams of rice a day. We would get a bowl of rice, a cup of miso-soup, and pickled vegetables. Once a month or so we'd have fish. As time passed, we had less and less food. It was difficult to measure the right amount so there was a huge margin of error. If prisoners didn't get the allotted amount, they'd go nuts. So I would undo the hinge of the locked cupboard and steal rice, but not so much so it would be noticeable. Of course, eventually they would figure it out.

Well, people knew, including the Japs. But those dammed Englishmen. While they were so above everything, they'd quibble over small things and would use a matchstick to ease out crumbs of food from the cracks of the table. And these were officers! He said this in disgust. *One of them ratted on me. I know because he wanted my job.* His eyes turned fierce and he sat up straight. *The commander already knew, anyway. He understood everything. When I was brought to him, of course, I admitted what I'd done. You know what he said?*

Even though I'd heard the story often, I shook my head.

He asked me how I did it. I could see in his eyes that he had respect for me. But, of course, he had to punish me. I lost the coveted position and was sent to fetch water, which turned out to be a super easy job. We collected water in the ocean and spent half the time swimming. He sat back again, laughing. *We were getting it for the salt. This was at the end of the war. They knew the allies were coming, so they kept us busy.*

Papa closed his story, remembering the Japanese commander: *He was much more of a gentleman than those British officers. He had real class.*

When the war ended and before they were sent home, the commander gave my father his father's ring, which had a black stone. Papa ended the story with, *Like I said, we had an understanding.*

My father was released on September 18, 1945 and was handed over to Colonel Griffin at Nagasaki Harbor. At the postwar B and C class Criminal Trial in Yokohama, the Fukuoka POW camp commander, Colonel Iju Sugasawa, and the Mizumaki Branch Camp Commander, Captain Suematsu, and a guard were sentenced to death by hanging. [80]

I was quite taken aback when I read that the camp commander was tried and hanged for war crimes. All those times I heard my father tell stories of his time in Japan and of the commander, I had an image of a fair and honorable man and thought that, in spite of what I heard about war crimes, there are good people everywhere. I don't think that my father knew the commander had been tried and hanged. If he did know, then perhaps he

---

[80] Stichting Oorlogsgetroffenen in de Oost: met Japanse archieven en contacten (SOO). Retrieved August 4, 2019 from http://pow.s-o-o.nl/Camp/

purposely only remembered or exaggerated the good he saw. If he didn't know, I wonder how he would feel to have heard the news.

Literature in the Netherlands regarding World War II explains the effects of Japanese prison camp and internment camps. Most former POWs and those in the internment camps hated the Japanese and were silent with their families about their experiences after the war. Also, many experienced periodic outbursts of rage as a result of PTSD.[81] My father had rage, but, as I stated earlier, he did not hate the Japanese.

Bersiap Period

Two days after Japan capitulated (August 15, 1945), Sukarno and Hatta proclaimed the Republic of Indonesia independent. In spite of this, the Dutch continued to consider itself sovereign over Indonesia and sent tens of thousands of troops for a tour of duty in Indonesia.

Indonesians in resistance. Photo taken at Bronbeek Museum, 2018

Upon returning to Indonesia after POW camp, my father and many of his peers continued serving in the KNIL as pilots. From 1948-1950, my father worked in intelligence and counter intelligence.

On September 29, the first British troops landed on Java with commander Mountbatten in charge. Not prepared to fight a colonial war for the Dutch, he limited the British presence to large cities on Java and Sumatra, such as Batavia (Jakarta), Soerabaja, (Surabaya), and Palembang to assist

---

[81] Tanja Harper and Wilmar Dolman. (2002). *Achter mijn glimlach: Vanuit het donker naar het licht.* Diemen, The Netherlands: KKJJB '40-'49.

Dutch citizens who were interned in the camps. Mountbatten sent Recovery of Allied Prisoners of War and Internees (RAPWI), an allied military organization, to track down, help, and support prisoners of war and internment camp victims. Meanwhile, thousands of Dutch prisoners of war were waiting in Japan, Thailand, Burma, and Singapore. The POWs in Japan were transferred to the Philippines, others were sent to Bangkok and Singapore. Opa Berg told Carl that it took several months to a year for Dutch prisoners of war to return to Indonesia. The Netherlands did not have sufficient means of transport for their men who had been in Japanese camps. Dutch transport vessels that were still in operation were at the service of the Allied forces. At the same time, the re-occupation of British territories in Southeast Asia and the removal of British prisoners of war had a priority.[82]

My father remembers:

We came back to Java on August 15 or 16, 1946. (This is an entire year after the war ended.) *We had been picked up in Nagasaki with a Japanese ship and went to Formosa (Taiwan). We had to be disinfected, deloused, etc. Then we were put in an American camp to wait for planes to take us to Manila. There was an American singer there. Not Doris Day, but the one who sang, "Money is the Root of All Evil."* (Andrew Sisters?) *We left for Manila in a B26 and were there with POW's from all over. In three to four months, we left on an English aircraft carrier on to Balikpapan, which is on the east coast of Borneo at a big oil port. It was part of the Dutch colony not rebelling. There we got instructions for flying B25s. I had to get newly trained because I hadn't flown in four years. After that, we went to Tjililitan close to Batavia. We landed on August 17 with seven B25s.*

In the overall post war confusion, with so many displaced military and civilians and months of waiting to be taken home, they received conflicting stories (rumors) about what was happening in Indonesia. Due to the experiences of the past four to five years, along with the anticipation of finally

---

[82] Indische Kamparchieven. Retrieved May 6, 2019 from:
https://www.indischekamparchieven.nl/nl/bezetting-en-bersiap/bevrijding-en-evacuatie;
"Redelijk inzetbaar: Overlevenden van de Jappenkampen moesten meteen weer vechten," *ncr.nl.* Retrieved May 6, from:
https://www.nrc.nl/nieuws/1998/10/03/redelijk-inzetbaar-overlevenden-van-de-jappenkampen-7417255-a174354

coming home, they were not prepared for the situation at home. When traveling for the first time as a free officer in Indonesia, Pap came across some rebels. Pap shared, "I was in a Jeep and was stopped by an inlander who was pointing a rifle at me. I reacted out of instinct by grabbing the gun and slapping the man for his insolence." It was how it had been before the war. This must have occurred once he was back in Java on route to his base in Tjililitan.

My father and his then wife, Louise (Wies), were able to reunite. They lived in Australia for the first year. On January 14, 1947, Danny was born in Batavia, and a year later, on January 9, Virginia (Ginny for short) was born also in Batavia. The only stories he told me about that period had to do with his military experiences, not about family life. He continued his story with:

After Tjililitan I went to Bundaberg, Australia. We had to fly from Australia to do our missions. I flew people back to Indonesia or to bring engines to the Philippines. I'd be in Indonesia one week and then two or three weeks in Australia. We did that for about a year. Then I was sent to Sumatra. I was the commander of the reconnaissance squadron.

We were at war with Indonesia and had to determine where and when they would attack. At one point, I flew the General Cox on a Piper Cub, a small plane, to the harbor where the

Lieutenant Berg in a B52 with General Cox

ship was. I didn't know, nor did he, that I had to land on a quay, and to get to the quay I had to fly over huge barrels. I did it and got him to his destination. (He says this with pride). *I still have the photo of us. Eventually we were back in Tjililitan until we were thrown out of Indonesia.*

After a four-year struggle, the Netherlands was, as my father told, "forced by the British and American allies to let go of the colony." At an exhibit I viewed in the Fall of 2019 having to do with Dutch colonialism in Indonesia at the Wereld Museum (World Museum), it stated that, "During the Battle of

Surabaya, the allies remark on the strength of the Indonesian nationalism. For that reason, Commander-in-Chief Mountbatten urges the Dutch to negotiate, and especially not to intervene militarily." [83] In addition, the US reminded the Netherlands of the Atlantic Charter (1941), which dictated Freedom for all Nations.

According to my father, he remained in Indonesia for two years, to help with the training of Indonesians for the transfer of the KNIL to the Indonesian National Military Air Force. The KNIL was disbanded by July 26, 1950, and those of Indonesian heritage were given the choice to terminate their service or join the Indonesian military. Of the 65,000 members, 26,000 were incorporated into the new Indonesian army. Not my father. He joined the *Koninklijk Landmacht* (KNL) Royal Dutch Army and went to Holland.

Danny, Wies, and Ginny (Vivi) on a ship to the Netherlands

Wies with the toddlers Ginny and Danny took a ship to Holland without my father. We are not exactly sure as to when that was. According to Vivi, they went to Holland and returned to Indonesia because my father had not come as soon as he was expected. There is a photograph of Wies and the children (roughly ages six months and a year and a half) on a ship that would confirm this story. According to the stories Pap tells, they left for Holland in 1951. When he was two years old, Danny fell and injured his leg, which did not mend correctly. It may be that Danny was in a cast too long and, consequently, his injured right leg was not able to grow correctly. In Holland, Danny was sent to a sanatorium in Scheveningen near to where his parents lived. He was there for five years. The story is that he also caught tuberculosis; however, Vivi says

---

[83] "Dossier Indië," Wereld Museum, Rotterdam (November 2019). https://www.wereldmuseum.nl/nl/zien-en-doen-in-het-wereldmuseum/tentoonstellingen

that was not the case. We have heard many versions of this story, and it remains a mystery. My father didn't speak much about that time period. Tragically, Wies died from complications of a surgery on December 11, 1951. Danny would turn five and Ginny four within a month of her passing.

While my father often told and retold these stories about the war, I did not hear any from my grandparents. For years after World War II when living in the Netherlands, Oma Sok was in communication with government agencies seeking unpaid revenue for the years of service by those involved in the underground. As my aunt said, she supported the Dutch Royal house and was a nationalist. Oma Sok also was an advocate for social justice.

The story about Oma Sok's involvement in the underground, her torture, and imprisonment was commonly known and a source of pride in the family. Perhaps it was not so for Tante Mag, but certainly for my father. This attitude did not include or allow for the terror. To be honest, until the writing of this book, I had not stopped to think or to feel for what my grandmother experienced. She never spoke of it. She was tough and angry, which came out in sarcasm. My experience of Opa Berg was of a calm and gentle man. Although stories exist about his strictness around timeliness, honor, and honesty that continued to occur while living in the Netherlands, Opa had become a tender man.

While my father was not silent about the war and Bersiap period, all his anecdotes were told with a humorous or positive spin. Pap relished in telling stories about his time in POW camp. There was no pause, no sign of sadness or anger when telling about his friend and right flyer, Jaapje, who was shot down. Instead, he only showed admiration for the Japanese flyer because the soldier had saluted him. The negative feelings were directed at the stuck-up British officers and in sudden fits of rage when we, as kids, somehow slipped and set my father off. After researching the history and revisiting the horror and terror in these stories, I can understand wanting to forget and to bury or perhaps change the past.

Research in the Netherlands shows that internment and prisoner of war camp survivors lived out their lives with an undercurrent of rage and depression. Most were silent about their experiences, but the repressed trauma came out in other ways and often with their children. I understand that my father and grandmother and, most likely, most of my relatives that had experienced the war and Bersiap period had PTSD.

Harpe and Dolman estimate that 64,000 children of Dutch colonial prison camp veterans in the Netherlands have serious psychological complaints. The children lived with their parents' silence and learned to hide their pain "achter hun glimlach" (behind their smile). Harpe and Dolman write, "Wie het verleden verzwijgt, blokkeert de toekomst," which loosely translates as "whomever doesn't speak about the past blocks the future." [84]

Many of the children felt isolated and had to make up for their parents losses experienced during the war and aftermath. The message was: "be brave," "don't feel what you feel," "do it yourself," "you don't need anyone," "don't trust anyone," keep at it until you drop," "adjust," "fit in," and "don't be noticed." The psychotrauma of the children of the concentration camp and POW camp survivors has been compared to that of the children of holocaust survivors.[85]

---

[84] Tanje Harpe & Wilmar Dolman. (2002). *Achter mijn glimlach: Vanuit het donker naar de licht.* Diemen; KJJB '40-'49, p. 10.
[85] http://www.stichtinginog.nl/

Chapter Twenty

Ton and Anne – Restless and Adventurous

My mother, Anne, grew up in a village not far from Rotterdam. Her father, Hugo, owned several bakeries in the surrounding area. She proudly would share, "Aside from the doctor, we were the only family in our village with a car." Hugo's father, Theodore, had 'done well' and had retired early. Hugo's sickly mother, Geertje, came from a wealthy local farming family. He had one sister, Yasprina, or Sprien for short. My mother's mother, Anna, was the twelfth of fourteen children and lived in the neighboring village. Anna was complying, nurturing, steady, and faithful. Her soulful brown eyes and nice legs attracted Hugo, who was fun-loving, musical, and charming. Having a mother who was ill, dampened the atmosphere at home. Hence the liveliness of Anna's large family buoyed the young man. Hugo and Anna were twenty-two when they married in 1926. They had six children and two died. The four living were Gery, Anne, Theo, and Ineke.[87]

---

[86] Anton Berg and Anne Speet marry October 29, 1952 in The Hague.
[87] I'm only describing enough of my mother's family to present a sense of her background and character. Perhaps a book about her family and ancestors will follow.

Anne, Anna (my grandmother), Theo, and Gery

While most unusual for the times in the Netherlands, Hugo and Anna separated. This transpired just before the Germans occupied Holland and when my mother was eleven. Hugo was what today would be called a sex addict, and his indiscriminate digressions were known all over the village and beyond. Anna was aware of and endured Hugo's transgressions—that is, until Anne told her mother that she had seen her father in an embrace with an employee of the bakery. Cajoled by her family, Anna and the four children moved from their village to the big city of The Hague where several of Anna's brothers and sisters lived. She would never have left of her own accord. My grandmother never stopped loving Hugo.

Gery, the eldest, was a favorite of her paternal grandparents and spent a lot of time with them before and after the separation of her parents. At the early age of eleven, my mother took on the role of caretaking her mother, who was bi-polar and suicidal. Until this day, my mother fiercely defends her mother. Anna and the four children lived in The Hague during the German occupation. Anna remained there until she passed away at ninety-two. All four children immigrated to North America in the mid 1950s, leaving Anna behind alone.

Anne was nearly seventeen when World War II ended in the Netherlands on May 5, 1945. My mother has shared stories about the five-year German occupation and of the exhilaration felt when American and Canadian soldiers, in their well-cared-for uniforms and straight, white teeth came to The Hague. People were dancing and celebrating in the streets. American and Canadian soldiers handed out chocolate, cigarettes, and silk stockings (like in the movies), and much-needed food came down with parachutes. My mother

212

described how, during that last very-cold winter, many were hungry and nearly starved to death. Rations were running out, and some people consumed things like flower bulbs for nourishment. The children were sent to the country to board with famers so they could gain their strength eating wholesome, fresh food.

When I visit the Netherlands and am there on a May 4th, my mother and I will watch World War II documentaries and commemoration ceremonies that take place all over the country. In Amsterdam, the King and Queen, as well as veterans or ancestors of veterans from WWII, lay wreaths in honor of those who died. At eight p.m., two minutes of silence is observed that occurs throughout the country. All public transportation stops and those working, at home, or out-and-about pause to honor and remember.

After the isolation of the German occupation and war, an inflow of new ideas and the exuberance of new freedoms emerged. In spite of her Calvinistic upbringing, or perhaps because of it, Anne had many adventures during those post-war years. At seventeen, she and her childhood friend, Marijke, trained to become nurses. Within a year she was encouraged by one of her teachers to receive on-the-job training at the elegant Sanatorium Les Rives de Prangins near Geneva. My mother found a replacement for her current job and off she went to Switzerland arriving in the dead of winter to nearly two meters (six feet) of snow that ruined her newly purchased high-heeled shoes. Here Anne received training as a psychiatric nurse. With her earnings she was able to save for and purchase a fur coat. In the ensuing years, Anne had a series of jobs: teaching Dutch to the young, white-Russian wife of the Dutch ambassador in Greece; nurse at a hospital and in a doctor's office in The Hague; and governess, first in Belgium and then in England. In between jobs, she would always return home because she was very attached to and concerned about her mother.

During one of these interims at home, she became a nurse at a Rudolf Steiner hospital in Scheveningen. There she met a doctor who, seeing her aptitude, gave Anne on-the-job training way beyond her current nursing skills. For instance, she assisted him in surgery. Working closely together, they fell in love. As stories go, the doctor was in a loveless marriage and divorce was still illegal in Holland. More than the young Anne could bear, she left the relationship and the job.

Anne and Ton

My mother was quite open to new ideas and was influenced by her friend, Janna, who delved into artistic, bohemian viewpoints. My father was interested in esoteric philosophy, religion, and metaphysics. Both Anne and Ton, having recently experienced loss of loved ones, attended a metaphysical talk in search for answers. Ton was immediately taken by the pretty and witty Anne. In turn, Anne was drawn to his uniform, excellent manners, and self-assuredness. *"Hij was een heer,"* or *"He was a gentleman,"* she would tell me. Yet, uncertain and on the rebound, Anne left Holland for a position as a governess in England.

My mother in her nursing uniform

Attractive, my mother was often approached by men. Due to the behavior of her father, she was particularly distrustful of their intentions. Yet, in ways she was still quite naïve. At a dinner party in London, Anne was introduced to an aristocratic gentleman. Attracted to her expressive eyes, fine nose, and figure, he asked if she would be willing to pose for photographs. They made an appointment and, on his calling card, he wrote down the address of his studio in a part of London with which she was unfamiliar. Upon entering the neighborhood, Anne felt that something was suspicious. That uncertain feeling told her not to knock on the door. So Anne made an about face. Ton had someone follow the supposed aristocrat and found out that the man had connections to those working in the sex trade.[88] Ton came to London to inform Anne who then realized she made a lucky escape. While she had realized something was amiss by her own deduction (or intuition), she felt rescued by the well-dressed, gallant gentleman. Anne returned to The Hague and the two continued to court. When Ton learned that he was to leave for a NATO

---

[88] I almost didn't include this story because it sounds too much like a mystery story or romance movie. However, it does reveal more about my mother, who was able to take care of her mother, work, and travel at a relatively young age post WWII, yet in ways was still a naïve, young lady.

214

position in Fontainebleau, he persuaded Anne to marry and join him. They had a simple, civil ceremony on October 29, 1952.

Shortly after, they moved to Fontainebleau, France. My father shared: *Cox, my commander during the war, was in Paris. He was the administrative head. I said to him when he wanted me to work in the NATO, "Lex, I can't come because of my 'smoel'"* (crude word for face, meaning his mixed-blood features). *Cox was also an Indische jongen* (Dutch-Indonesian boy), *except with blue eyes. And he had the English last name, Cox. He responded with, "And then which country bumpkin will they send instead? You're coming!" So I went to Fontainebleau. There the commander said, "You are only a captain and I need a colonel." So I was given special permission to perform the duties of a colonel.*

Ton enjoyed his work in intelligence and the international sphere of his workplace, and both Anne and Ton took to the international social life. Ton's daughter, four-year-old Ginny, joined them in Fontainebleau. They changed the shortened version of her h name, Ginny to Vivianne, probably giving it a French variation. Danny, his son, remained in the sanatorium in Scheveningen and later lived with our paternal grandparents in The Hague. Two and a half years later, on April 26, 1955, I was born. By then the family lived near a military base close to Eindhoven in the Netherlands.

While in many ways my father enjoyed a stimulating and suitable career, he was not satisfied and could not overlook the discriminations that occurred. Upon returning to the Netherlands when his assignment at NATO ended, Ton was given work that did not utilize his capacities and skills. While he had more flying hours than any of his Dutch colleagues, he was required to take courses and examinations he had already completed and passed. Similarly he was not promoted according to his capacities and experience, because *ik had een donker smoel* (I had a dark face). A General Norstad, an American, encouraged him to immigrate to the US where he could perhaps continue with intelligence work. Norstad appreciated Ton's keen intellect, and, with his facility with languages, believed my father would be an asset in the US military intelligence.

Upon leaving a disappointing meeting with his chief officer about the unfairness he was experiencing, Ton ran into a friend from the Indies. After making brief exchanges, his friend Paul said, "I'm moving to the United States. I just left the emigration office. There are special circumstances for Indos under the refugee clause. America here I come!" After consulting with General

Norstad in Fontainebleau, my father followed the procedures to immigrate to the US and was referred to a sponsor. He then visited the emigration office in The Hague and within a month formalized his decision to leave Holland. A pattern I've witnessed many times growing up, he did not consult Anne. She did not want to leave her home.

All these years later, it's unclear to me why General Norstad would recommend emigrating from the Netherlands if my father was too old to join the US military. Certainly the general would have known that. My father was thirty-nine when we immigrated to the US and the cut off age for joining the US military was thirty-five.

Once in the US, my father's sponsor suggested that he could, instead, find executive work in a company. However, when Tony (Americanized version of Ton or Anton) went for interviews, they told him that he was over-qualified. He also applied to be an airline pilot, but was just a year too old for their maximum age limit. So, instead, he went door to door with pots and pans, the *Great Books of the Western World*, and eventually to sell life insurance and real estate.

My resourceful mother had applied and been selected to be contestant on *Queen for A Day*. On television, the contestants were interviewed and they told their stories—often about recent financial, medical, and emotional hard times. They were then asked what they needed the most. My mother asked for the age limit to be waived for my father so he could join the US military and continue to work in intelligence. According to Wikipedia, "the winning contestant was selected by the audience using an applause meter; the harsher the contestant's situation, the likelier the studio audience was to ring the applause meter's highest level." [89] My mother did not become Queen for A Day.

---

[89] *Queen for a Day* originated on the radio in 1945 and ran until 1957. The show then ran on NBC Television from 1956 to 1960 and on ABC Television from 1960 to 1964. Retrieved 2/8/2020 from: https://en.wikipedia.org/wiki/Queen_for_a_Day

Land of Opportunity

While adventurous, both Ton and Anne also held onto convention for dear life. My mother enjoyed the security and social standing of being an officer's wife. My father had lost his home twice while living in the Indies and then again, albeit by choice, by leaving the Netherlands. He hoped and believed that there was less to lose by leaving the country that was not really home and that there would be more potential in 'the land of opportunity.'

Photo from newspaper clipping of Danny, Pap, Mam, Astrid, and Vivi when we first arrived in Michigan, November 1956

Once they moved to the US, my mother had to work full time while caring for three children and had lost the comforts to which she had become accustomed. With her wit, charm, and nursing background, Anne readily found a job. She most often would work a night shift as a nurse. Tony had a harder time finding employment that matched his qualifications. This brought about more insecurity and resulted in frequent job changes and moves that triggered contention between my parents. My mother felt powerless and a victim. Both of their unexpressed frustrations were difficult to bear as a child. In witnessing my father's dominating attitude and raised voice with my mother, I became aligned with her. I now understand that my father's repressed pride emerged in shame and guilt that was camouflaged by bravado and a need to control. With his frustrations and dissatisfactions, his decision-making and choices became impulsive.

The Unexpressed

While they hid their anxieties, fears, and frustrations with us children, the conflict between them was palpable. My parents fought, but not about the true issues at hand. There was no couples therapy or methods for recognizing and working with the PTSD of my parents' respective war experiences ad home life. My parents did not grow up with the psychological sophistication we have today, nor did they find many opportunities for help. They played the charade of 'we are doing fine.' We were well groomed, had great manners, lived in homes tastefully kept, and they both had an elegance and style that presented well in the world.

I situate my childhood memories based on the houses in which we lived. During the eighteen years I lived with my parents, we resided in as many homes. I remember living at the end of a driveway in a house in back of a main house. I was three. I had a playmate, Tommy, who was my age or slightly older. One of us decided that the neighborhood cat needed a bath. I can see us trying to lift the captured pussy up into the washing machine. Luckily we were too young to actually turn on the washer. I can't remember how we were discovered or how my mother reprimanded me.

That evening, when my father came home from work, my mother and I were on the sofa in a sunroom with the heavy drapes closed and the standing lamp switched on. I don't remember how the incident about the cat came up. I didn't get in trouble, but my Mama did. I can still see the fear in her eyes, the way she played with the loose skin on her parched lips as Papa's voice increased in volume. I wanted to reassure her. I was so sorry I had caused all this trouble, but I dared not speak. Now more than sixty years ago, I don't remember the content of my father's lecture to my mother except for one phrase. "And stop playing with your lips!"

They didn't realize what a child of three takes in. I may not have understood all he had declared, but I could feel his rage and her fear and isolation. This was the underpinning of my need to protect my mother. In the ensuing decade, I had strong feelings about how he dominated her and urged my mom to assert herself.

I can now look at my parents' lives with the wisdom of my own life experiences. Having come to the US with high hopes, his disillusionment was impossible to admit, not only because of his pride, but because he was too busy figuring out a way to support his family. My mother, frustrated and most displeased, was furious that she was cajoled into leaving the comforts of her more privileged lifestyle and the support of her large family in Holland.

218

Immigrants

It was in November when we immigrated to cold Michigan where we had a sponsor. Within six months, my parents drove the family across the US to California where my mother's younger sister, Ineke, had immigrated with her husband, Ronnie, and son, Francis. My mother's other sister, Gery, and her husband, Peter, had also moved to the area. My Uncle Theo and his partner, Dio, moved to Vancouver in British Columbia, Canada. We moved often around the northeast end of Los Angeles—Alhambra, a couple of places in Pasadena, and in Highland Park. My father's sister, Maggie, and husband, Tjeun, along with their four kids—Inge, Maarten, Johanna, and Esther came five years later. Oom Bob (the half brother of Oma Sok who was raised by her as a son) also immigrated with his wife, Iet. Only one aunt and uncle, Os and Nanda, remained in the Netherlands. Other relatives and friends of the Indo side of the family also immigrated to the LA basin.

Tante Maggie, Oom Tjeun, and my cousins lived next door to us in Highland Park from January 1961 through June 1964. My cousin, Johanna, and I, near in age, walked to school together and were best buddies. With eight kids in the two families, there was much activity within the two homes. My mother worked, but Tante Mag was home and watched us after school. She was strict, tough, and I was a bit afraid of her. Yet, she allowed us to make a mess while playing in the house, which my mother would never allow. For instance, we made forts from blankets and furniture turned every which way. Other Indo family members or friends would come by on weekends. From this, I experienced the Indo culture and lifestyle and the differences between the Indisch and my Dutch mother.

As a child, I didn't question why so many relatives had emigrated from the Netherlands. Many Indisch came because of the less hospitable circumstances of their (compulsory) move to the Netherlands from the Indies. The Netherlands at that time was recuperating from WWII and German occupation. There was a major housing shortage and the cold weather was difficult for the Indos. Many Caucasian Dutch people also emigrated to Canada and the US in the decade after WWII.

Danny, Vivi, and I spoke Dutch at home. We had a connection to our European and Indisch relatives and roots. In subtle ways my mother distinguished us from Americans, and we were raised with a slightly different

Carl (age 3) wearing his cowboy outfit

set of values. At the same time, my father proclaimed how lucky we were to live in the US of A. Three and a half years after we arrived, my younger brother, Carl, was born on April 4, 1960. My father declared, "Carl could become a president. In this melting pot, all creed and colors can be successful." While I wholeheartedly believed what my father and teachers proclaimed, as I grew older, my experiences were somewhat contradictory. From the looks and comments adults made thinking children do not hear or see, I gleaned that there were differences between whites and those of color, and understood that I was lucky that my ethnicity didn't show. At the same time, like any immigrant, I was teased for our exotic customs and mannerisms.

My parents both came from cultures that had more convention around behavior than I experienced from the 'American' culture in California. My mother was taken aback by what she thought was a lack in 'proper' behavior of Americans and which she attributed to class. I now realize that immigrants can misunderstand the norms and behavior of their new country. We lived in California with fewer restrictions, more freedom to behave as one chooses, and less formality than was possible in Holland at that time.

Like my forefathers in Indonesia, I grew up with the stories about our noble family in Germany. We had the ring with our coat of arms. My father told the story about my great-great-grandfather who fought the duel and killed a nobleman. In later years, he took each of us kids to the Berg Castle near Solingen, Germany. My mother supported my father's notions with her own values around class and nobility.

Beschaafdheid (culture, being civilized) was important to my parents and was used to describe people they admired and valued. The lack of *beschaafdheid* in people was deemed as undesirable. In spite of her sometimes pejorative ideas of some Indisch habits and characteristics, my mother agreed with my father that the Indisch were more *beschaafd* than the average Dutch person. As

220

a child growing up in America, I questioned these outdated ideas around class as being from the old country. Yet I did want to be *beschaafd*.

Return to Holland

After nearly ten years living in the US, we moved back to the Netherlands—but as American citizens. While we spoke Dutch, stayed with and visited family, and for that first year we attended a Dutch school, my brother and I weren't quite Dutch. It appeared to me that both parents were noticeably happier. My mother was back home where she rekindled friendships, lived in the same city as her mother, and preferred the Dutch lifestyle, convention, and culture. While my father glorified the American dream, he also sought the *beschaafdheid* familiar to his upbringing and appeared to find it more readily in Europe.

During the ensuing seven years, we moved back and forth between California, the Netherlands, and Spain. As I wrote earlier, that first visit to Holland was an extended vacation that went into my fifth-grade-school year and a scouting trip for my father to see if he could set up a business to sell Hawaiian real estate to the Indisch community in the Netherlands. Six months later we moved to The Hague and lived there for a little over a year. It was the five of us: my parents, Vivi, Carl, and myself. Danny had graduated from high school and remained in California. Soon after that he married. Vivi had also graduated and worked for Bechtel, an international engineering company. After the first year in The Hague, she returned to California and later moved to Hawai'i to be a tour guide, and within a year married a Hawaiian.

After the selling-of-Hawaiian- property venture in the Netherlands, my father gained employment with a real estate development company in Madrid. We lived there for a little over year and, after that, roughly another two years in the Netherlands. During that time, we made several trips back and forth between Madrid and The Hague. I have very fond memories of these European road trips.

During this more prosperous time, my father purchased a new vehicle each year. The first was the yellow Volvo station wagon in which we traveled from the Netherlands to Spain via Paris. My father and Oom Os sat in the front, and my mother, Carl, and I were piled in the back with the seats folded down to create a cozy area with lots of extra cushions to lay against. Perhaps due to the lighter side of my uncle's nature, I remember laughing and joking a lot during that trip.

Then came a Mercedes sedan, a Toronado, a souped up Mercury Cougar, and finally an Audi. My favorite was the dark blue Mercedes. I remember Papa proudly driving the front-wheel-drive, silver Oldsmobile Toronado through the narrow cobblestone streets in Holland and testing its speed on the autobahn in Germany. When passing Heidelberg, we got the thumbs up from American troops we'd pass. There was an American NATO base in Heidelberg. Sometimes we drove straight south from The Hague through Belgium and the length of France entering Spain either from the east or west. I think my father had an affinity for Spain—their hospitality, the flamboyance. I could feel the shift in him when we crossed that boarder from France into Spain.

There was such an atmosphere of adventure during those trips. At the end of the day, we would stop at a restaurant, which, even in a village, had a 'classy' French menu. My father could read and order in French (and in German), would enjoy a glass or two of wine, and sip coffee after dinner. Note that my mother read French as well, but my father would be the one to order. I had never seen this side of him. We had never been out to dinner as a family in the US. These meals would last a couple of hours over pleasant dinner conversation. Both parents were in good spirits. I imagine it reminded my father of the pre-war years in the Indies, the infamous *tempo doeloe* (time of old, good old days) period when there was ease and affluence. My mother may have revisited the post war years and her travel adventures that continued early in their marriage. I discovered different sides of my parents and I experienced a taste of the discovery and adventure that goes with travel. I remember first using a bidet in French and Spanish hotels or the less pleasing holes in the floors that were toilets at pit stops along the drive.

Carl and I discovered castles along rivers and on top of hills, and could see the towering of church steeples as we approached villages. We drove past lavender fields, bailed hay, and on mountain roads with hairpin turns. Once at a gas station in the Pyrenees in Spain, we saw a family of twelve get out of a Seat. The Seat was a Spanish model automobile much like a small Fiat of that time. We didn't visit tourist or cultural sites, for example the Eiffel Tower or Louvre in Paris. I'm not sure why. I don't think my parents thought about a cultural education or of making these trips more like

222

a vacation, as we never had been on vacation in the US. We drove straight through, only stopping to overnight at hotels.

Later, in my early adult years when I traveled to Paris, my father advised me to visit, not the Louvre nor the Notre Dame but the Sacré-Cœur, which was special to him. More than once when traveling on his own (which he did often in years to come), he visited Lourdes to see Saint Bernadette. He brought me back the booklet and shared the story of her well-preserved body in the glass casket. For those who don't know, Lourdes is a place where many visit to be healed. I've never been.

These family trips occurred during the Vietnam Era when many Europeans were opposed to the US being involved. Our various automobiles had recognizable US tourist license plates. Once at a service station in France, the attendant refused to pump our gas because we were Americans. This was before the self-service, pay-by-credit card era. We had to drive on to the next village to get petrol.

Going through Paris was always very confusing, the roads in Germany were better than in France, and my father liked the no-speed limit autobahns. Therefore, he preferred going east through Germany and then south through Switzerland and southern France, entering Spain from the northeast. On one of those trips, we stayed in a lovely lakeside town called Meersburg, which means, "Castle on the Sea." Meersburg is a medieval town in the southwest of Germany at Lake Constance. On the other side of the lake is Switzerland. The *Unterstadt* (lower town) and *Oberstadt* (upper town) were reserved for pedestrians only and connected by two stairways and a steep street (Steigstrasse).

Old Castle of Meersburg (by Mike Chapman, 2006)

This place had special meaning because it was where I was conceived.

223

My frugal parents generally stayed and dined at three-star hotels and restaurants. But on this occasion, our accommodations were more luxurious. We dined in the hotel restaurant where a band was playing. After dinner, my father asked me to dance. As a little girl, I stood on his feet and followed his steps. On this occasion (I was twelve), he skillfully guided me and we glided through the room. To me, this was my father at his best.

De Posada de Castilla (The Castle Inn)

Pap was in his element when we lived in Spain. He was the sales manager of Terrenos de España, a real estate company developing a vacation haven, Posada de Castilla, for northern Europeans seeking sun. That first year of its inception the company had built an Olympic swimming pool, tennis courts, and a restaurant. Land, villas, or bungalows could be purchased for investment purposes or as summer homes. At that time, many Dutch, Germans, and English came to Spain on vacation to score some sun.

One of the owners and founders was from Los Angeles and loosely connected with the movie industry. Actors like Bill Cosby and Robert Culp from the 1965 TV series *I Spy* (some episodes took place in Madrid) were visitors. Burt Reynolds and Clint Eastwood also frequented the Posada. David Niven had bought one of the first villas, and Elke Sommer was a regular. In addition, parts of *The Return of the Magnificent Seven* were filmed at the castle ruins in the village next to the development.

The sales crew of Terrenos de España were eccentric outcasts looking for a way to earn a living: Carmen, a former hairdresser, would solicit taxi drivers to bring potential buyers to the property; Emelina, a divorcee, had been married to a bull fighter; Suren, was a flamenco dancer; Ute came from the family of the Mercedes racing team; Jaime, the Argentinian, was a soccer player who had been injured; and Boris, was a count with no castle or money. Perhaps the misfits of decades before who sought help from Oma Sok along with the cross-cultural experiences in his early years shaped my father towards a natural affinity for this motley crew. He led with charisma, was visibly liked and admired, and became a confidante to the sales men and women.

Each weekend we would go to 'the property,' which was an hour outside of Madrid. Much like the Hawaiian luaus before, my father organized events, this time with Spanish food and entertainment. The company

224

chartered planes from Holland and Germany to bring potential buyers for arts and entertainment, which would include a Lipizzaner horse show and a bullfight, as well as golf, sailing, and horseback riding. Having Suren connected to the flamenco music and dance scene was a plus.[90]

On those weekends I rode horses. My favorite was Morro, the black Arabian stallion. I rode English and not the Spanish or western saddles. I learned to jump, which I enjoyed tremendously and which offered me a sense of competence. More than anything I enjoyed having that silent communication between Morro and myself. I also watched the horse trainer work with two beautiful Lipizzaner—stallions with long, flowing, silver-white manes and tails. These beauties were a young, adolescent girl's dream. Originally warhorses bred and trained by Habsburg nobility in the sixteenth century, Lipizzaner horses are trained to make stylized jumps and other movements known as the "airs above the ground." I would watch the two white stallions practice in the ring. They might begin with the *passage*, a hesitated or slow motion walk. From there they would go

Astrid riding Morro, the black Arabian stallion

into the *in two tempeeze,* in which the stallions change lead every two strides looking as though they are skipping. In the *piaffe*, the Lipizzaner trots in place and then into the *trot half pass,* which is a flowing side step in which they move diagonally. I would have liked to continue with horseback riding once we had moved back to the Netherlands.

The scene at 'the property' was full of flair, splendor, and flamboyance. When decades later my parents moved to Las Vegas, I could

---

[90] The theatrical flamenco dance and music is based on the various folkloric music traditions of Southern Spain, and includes singing, guitar, dance, vocalizations, handclapping and finger snapping.

never understand the attraction. Then again, the showy, glitziness is perhaps an American version of those times at the Posada de Castilla.

We returned to the Netherlands a little more than a year later, where my brother and I attended the American-International School of The Hague. While in Spain, we were expats, but in Holland we were not. We spoke Dutch, had family and friends in the Netherlands, and mostly lived as the Dutch did, whereas my classmates lived in international communities and had little to do with every-day Dutch life. Most of my friends were other Americans (I regret now not getting to know more classmates of other nationalities). We weren't quite Dutch and we also did not fit in with the American ex-pat community. I shadowed my father's desire to be American. My mother, on the other hand, preferred the Dutch conventions. These conflicting influences became part of a teenage identity crisis. As an adult, I grew to appreciate more these different perspectives and experiences within.

The last year in the Netherlands was also my last year of high school. I don't know what work/business adventure took my father there on this occasion. We had been living in California for a year and a half. I had fallen in love. Upon hearing about another move, I was quite angry with my folks. We were to live in The Hague for just a year. Since we'd left in the middle of my junior year, it meant that I would be in two different high schools during my senior year. I begged my mother to find a way that I could graduate mid-term. She did, and I doubled-up on coursework those two semesters, graduating early, leaving nine months (what would now be called a gap period) before I was to begin university. When we returned to California, I found a part-time job and took adult education courses in oil painting, fabric design, and auto mechanics, the latter so I could tune up my own car.

My parents would return once more to the Netherlands seven years later. I had completed college by then, had birthed a son, and was onto my own adult ventures. Carl interrupted his college education to join them. When my father passed away, I moved my mother to The Hague and lived there for two years. I visit her every year, and the impressions, sensibilities, and happiness of those early years are with me each and every visit.

My relationship with my father during those teenage and early adult years became distant. I always had great respect and an (unconscious) sense of responsibility for his happiness. His outbursts of rage continued when I'd visit

226

my parents as an adult. He wasn't actually angry with me or other family members. He steered dinner conversation to politics and then proceeded to argue, even if you agreed with him. Beware if you questioned or did not agree. Whoever was the chosen victim would be cornered receiving the same kind of enraged lectures I had experienced as a child. He directed his fury, one time too many, at my (former) husband during a Christmas dinner. As we headed home, my son was crying and my husband said that he would never come to their house again. It was then I saw how much the family had normalized my father's behavior. Over the years, I sought ways to connect. The only means I was able to relate was by listening to his stories.

Section V – Integration Towards Healing

Balinese Mask

Chapter Twenty-One

Unleashing the Dark Side

I was forty-one when I stepped onto the island where my father was born. As I deplaned, I entered a long, red-tiled hallway with windows on each side that exposed the rich, green fauna of this tropical place. The air was thick, heavy, and more humid than Hawai'i. Or was it something else I was sensing? My father had told me that when the anthropologist Niels Mulder arrived in Java, he could feel the heaviness of its magic. According to Anne Richter, in the indigenous Javanese tradition,

---

[91] I made this mask in Bali during a cultural tour with Daniel Deslaurier and Fariba Bogzaran in 1996. Daniel, from Quebec, had an affinity with the Balinese, learned their dance, and had connections to Balinese artists and performers. Each participant performed with our masks. For me, it was poignant to be exploring my inner self in the land of my forbidden ancestors. During the unrehearsed performance, I began by peaking out at the audience from behind the curtain. I then slowly expressed delicate nuances of the Indo-self I was discovering.

...birds inhabit the upper world of intellect and spirit; the realm of the gods and ancestors. Reptiles symbolize the lower world of fertility, instinctual energy and supernatural forces, which may not only be creative, but demonic. Human beings occupy the space between the upper and lower worlds, and in order to prosper, much draw strength from both. [92]

My Indo relatives did not frame their experiences with magic in terms of animistic upper and lower world cosmologies that I later came to understand in a graduate program in East-West Psychology at the California Institute of Integral Studies (CIIS). However, they had personal stories of the island's magic. While most Indisch are Christian, some practiced and many hired those who practiced the local magic. Since I was raised in the West, they did not expect I would understand. My elders almost disbelieve their own first-hand experiences, since memories of these encounters no longer conformed to their current Western lifestyles in the Netherlands or the US. Was it that they could never go home that affected distrust in what they had once experienced?

The circumstances of my mixed blood, half-breed, Eurasian, Indo, Indisch, Dutch-Indonesian relatives can never be revisited except through story and imagination. The Java they knew at the end of the three hundred and fifty years of Dutch colonization is gone. Most Indos moved to the Netherlands in the end of the 1940s and into the 1950s after Indonesia gained its independence. Most of those with mixed blood were neither completely at home in the indigenous culture of the Indonesian islands, nor with their European ancestry. While they were educated alongside their European classmates learning western history, science, and four European languages, they were not meant to be intimate with Europeans. However, exceptions were made and boundaries were crossed. And this is where interesting stories emerged.

Integrating the Shadow

I had very little connection to my Indonesian self during childhood. I rarely heard Malay (Maleis) or Javanese (Javaans) spoken. I had only a slight relationship to Indonesian or Indo/Indisch customs and culture. Community

---

[92] A. Richter. (1994). *Arts and crafts of Indonesia.* San Francisco: Chronicle Books, p. 9.

my father had with Indo friends and relatives faded over time, as our nuclear family moved away from the neighborhoods where fellow immigrants lived. Both my parents appeared culturally European, and the Indonesian influences were subtle and silent in my Indo father. We became US citizens as soon as it was possible. I was educated in western schools.

The longing for connection to my Indonesian origins was unconscious. Not until I was forty did I become curious about this other: the colonized side, the magical side, the dark side, the slow side, the delicate side, the graceful side, the non-Western side, the forbidden side, the non-privileged side, the shadow side. Who is she? Could the answer be found in the culture of the Javanese? Not knowing what the exploration of Eastern philosophies and religions in my graduate studies would bring, it led me to a fatherland I didn't know I missed. While writing my dissertation, I made the intuitive connection between a loss of the imaginal (imagination, intuition, mystical) with that of my Javanese roots. Concurrently, I visited two of the islands in this exotic place.

Having been raised in the West and encouraged to value its customs, I had yet to learn more about the thick, invisible air that permeates the island of Java. Centuries denying the value of the delicate nuances of my Javanese ancestors were pleading to be unleashed and honored. The hubris and practicality in my Dutch-self lacked the appreciation of that which is unseen, unproven, subtle, and changeable. The densely philosophical musing of my German ancestors needed to make way for that which is not from thought—where another wisdom exists and can be experienced, those in the dense air and in the secret, shadowy places of the jungle. The fact that my ethnicity is imperceptible may have offered an ease my father did not experience in his striving to attain recognition as an equal. Does my privilege provide just enough solace to allow the Indonesian-self to slowly and unobtrusively come forth, express itself, and potentially cultivate a new self?

Visit to Java

In Jakarta (formerly Batavia) I stayed with an American friend and his Balinese wife. I then took a train to Yogyakarta in the center of the island. Even at dawn the air felt like a sauna. I entered the exclusive-class, air-conditioned car and got situated. As we left this city of thirteen million, with both modern hustle and bustle and its darker side of rats, roaches, and poverty, I was refreshed by the contrast of the countryside. We passed through flatlands of rice paddies. Surrounding the wet rectangular plots were raised pathways that farmers could use to get from one paddy to the next. They were hunched over inserting the grass-like plant into the shallow pools of water. Just as in the picture books of my relatives, they wore wide brimmed hats. I occasionally saw a man guiding an ox pulling a plough akin to the paintings I'd seen on walls of Indisch families. Small grass huts occupied the intersection of paths. Later in the day, when the sun was at its peak, workers found shelter in these resting places.

My attention turned to the inside of the train. Most of the co-passengers looked familiar, yet foreign. Somewhere in the setting of their cheekbones and the deep, dark almond eyes, I saw my grandparents, aunts, uncles, cousins, and the face of my own father, and now my grandchildren. Yearning to connect, I wondered if they could see the same when they looked at me. Or am I just a blanda tourist? I spent several days in Yogyakarta and Malang walking and absorbing the land and the faces of its people as I looked closely, but not intrusively, in hope of recognizing something familial. We don't know the names of our Indonesian relatives. Yet, based on DNA results, my father is about fifty percent Indonesian. When I have asked my elders, they only could recite those of European ancestry: Berg, Butteweg, Abels, Mons, Pfefferkorn, Ravenswaaij, Castricum, van Franquemont, and Falck. We have no known relatives left in Indonesia, as most of the four- to six-hundred thousand Indisch colonists went to Holland when Indonesia became independent. I almost wrote, 'returned to Holland,' but most had never set foot on the Dutch, sandy soil. However, their education, religion, and culture were Dutch and they were Dutch citizens. Identification and familiarity with the Javanese or other Indonesian cultures varied. As I've written, many of indigenous people were of a 'lower class' fulfilling servant roles—maids, chauffeurs, nursemaids, gardeners,

Group of curious Indonesian children, 1996

234

cooks—or plantation workers and other laborers. While trapped within societal demands, the lives of my Indisch forefathers included wealth and material ease: comfortable homes with servants on large pieces of land. Their material lifestyle was more luxurious than their contemporaries in Holland.

By the afternoon, the terrain changed to terraced paddies cut into the hills. Seeing this spectacular landscape, I imagined centuries of farming of this island and began to grasp the history and depth of the Javanese culture before the Europeans arrived. Images of stories told by elders reminiscing about their homeland

Terraced rice paddies (flooded fields), 1996

came forth as I stared out the train window. Children appeared from behind the trees and brush, seemingly out of nowhere, to wave at the passengers. Older children carried the younger ones—with their big round eyes—on their hips. As I became more accustomed to the dense foliage, I could see the kampongs on the other side of the trees. Richter describes Java as follows:

> …the heartlands of inner Indonesia, the intricately terraced green rice fields have supplied substantial surplus and wealth and supported glittering courts and vital traditions of orchestral music, dance and drama. Borobudur, the Buddhist mountain-mandala, and the Hindu temples of Prambanan in Java, are thought to be among the greatest works of religious architecture.[93]

---

[93] IBID., p. 7.

Buddha statue in front of stupas, Borobudur, Java,1996

Around and in Yogyakarta, I visited the tourist sites of the Kraton, the 1200-year-old Buddhist temple of Borobudur, the 1100-year-old Hindu temple of the Prambanan. Near Malang, I visited the crater of an active volcano at Mount Bromo. All the while I continued to seek the familial in faces or gestures of women who sell the wide variety of fruit in the markets, of men playing chess on improvised chairs and tables in the plazas under the umbrella of waring trees, of young, modern, veiled Islamic women riding motor scooters, or of vendors cooking food in large wadjans on the side walks. My contact was limited to those who served tourists. I satisfied myself with this small bit of connection. I brought pictures of Indo family members and showed a hotel reception clerk, a waitress, a *becap* (rickshaw) driver, or whomever. But mostly, I was the tourist that needed a guide, a ride, a place to eat and sleep, or to purchase locally produced wares.

Photos of Malang taken in 1996

Warung (street vendor) on the alun alun (town square)

Vendors at the pasar (market)

My father's HBS (high school)

Toko Oen Restaurant

238

Exploring Malang with Pap's Map

Before I left for Java, my father had drawn a map of Surabaya, where he was born, and Malang, where he attended secondary school. Surabaya—on

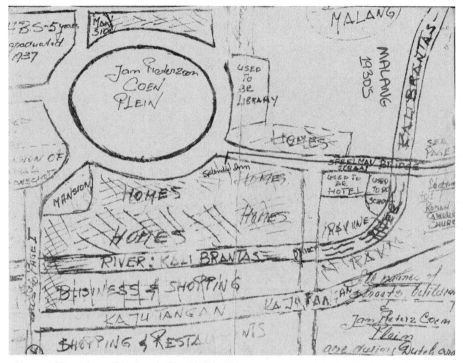

Map my father drew of Malang before I left for Java.

the eastern side of Java and Indonesia's second largest city with a population of 3.1 million—was unrecognizable in relation to my father's hand-drawn map. But Malang, in the mountains, had not changed much from his drawings, except for some newer buildings, and the Dutch streets were renamed in Bahasa Indonesian. I could easily follow my dad's map to the *alun alun* (village square), his secondary school, the streets where he had lived, the track field where he had run the 400 meter, and various other landmarks like the churches and Toko Oen—a restaurant, still with its colonial ambiance and where I enjoyed *Gado Gado* (parched vegetable salad with peanut sauce). Since more than sixty years had passed, there were many new buildings and houses. My hotel, the Splendid Inn, had décor (most likely original) of the time my father lived there. I found out later that my grandfather had something to do with building this hotel.

239

With map in hand, I mostly explored the small city on foot, feeling, imagining, and remembering my father's stories. He was full of stories, which he told often, especially during his latter years. I've conveyed how he liked to make light of his secondary school years with tales about dances, playing pranks on teachers, or of his popularity. Race and culture played significant roles. The stories my father shared about his childhood portrayed cultural acceptance, understanding, and experiences, but they also posed discrepancies.

Gamelan musicians carrying instruments, 1996

In Malang, I was able to imagine into the lives of my father and ancestors. When I ran into a small group of girls walking home from school, I could see my Tante Maggie or Oma Sok and her sister Bon returning from their schools. At Pap's old HBS, now an Indonesian school, I envisioned my father and his friends coming and going on their bikes or in class playing pranks on the teachers. On the alun alun with the banyan trees, I could glimpse traces of Lintang, Helena, Suus, and Adele at the pasar. Viewing the homes from the now gated driveways, I caught sight of the large verandas where so much of my ancestors' daily lives were lived.

Uncovering What Had Been Lost

I felt a strong connection to these roots by way of the arts. One evening in Bali, I heard the sound of fast-beat gamelan. The instruments used, predominately percussive, were metallophones (tuned metal bars similar to the xylophone), *kendhang* or hand played drums as well as xylophones, bamboo flutes, and *rebabs* (a bowed instrument). The music flooded the silence of the balmy evening. I left my hotel room and ventured down the street following its sounds. Local tulambens were rehearsing under a pavilion. As I was

240

now in Bali, they were not playing the more melodic gamelan of the Javanese. This is a fast-paced sound called *Kebayar*. This strange and foreign music was somehow familiar. I found myself moving closer until I was on the platform with them. The music reverberated in my body, and I longed to be one of the players. They abruptly stopped. Sadly, I thought it was over, but then they began playing drum-like instruments. The *balanganjar* was louder and more intense and moved in and through me. Tears ran down my cheeks.

In Malang, I came upon a group of young girls with slight bodies and round faces moving gracefully. Their delicate fingers, eyes, and heads made subtle movements. Wearing striking sarongs, they were dancing to gamelan. I have not learned this traditional dance, and yet it was so familiar. I saw in their gestures, the behaviors and attitudes of my relatives. Later I learned the Javanese words for what is expressed in the dance. *Alus* is the refined, subtle, and ethereal, not only in gestures, but embedded within Javanese beingness. In their way of thinking, the development of alus *makes* one Javanese. In addition, "...the ability to create objects of beauty and significance

Indonesian girls performing gamelan (dance), 1996

was...thought to demonstrate fine character..." [94] For the Javanese, "[i]t is through the making of art that a complete and adult understanding of social and religious thought can be expressed." [95] The delicate expressions and gestures of alus in the Javanese dance are like those I have seen in Indisch family members. The inner refinement I experienced mostly through the arts in Java and Bali activated a deeper understand of what I intuitively knew.

---

[94] IBID., p. 13.
[95] IBID.

Many Javanese intellectuals and mystics are quite emphatic in pointing out that Western (scientific) knowledge only deals with reality by use of the ratio (capacity for rational understanding); contrarily Javanese understanding grasps the essence of reality directly through the *rasa*. In their view, the rational scientific way of understanding demonstrates its impotence by the fact that yesterday's theories are rejected today and that today's knowledge will be invalidated tomorrow; *rasa* understanding, however, penetrates directly into the heart of the matter of the truth. [Bonnef, 1976b; 223-24]. [96]

Rasa is an inner intuition that captures the essence of living in the moment and by enjoying life's beauty. For my father and other Indisch ancestors, living in a country dominated by Westerners and yet influenced by Javanese tradition induced opposing values and characteristics. The integration of alus and rasa with the more straightforward and rational western behavior must have been a challenge. Reconnecting with my roots—the dark, unavailable Indisch side—unleashed what had been partially lost in my father, his Indisch ancestors, and within me. The palpable felt-sense of being there became an opportunity for joining East and West, indigenous and modern, shadow and persona. The experience of the subtly familiar alus in Indonesian music, dance, and behavior as well as walking the land had a healing affect on me. Will this felt-sense have value to those of the next generation—to my American son, grandson, and granddaughters? Will *alus* show in their gestures as well? Will *rasa* be a significant value in their lives?

Nobility

Part of the reason for writing this story was to surround and familiarize myself with my ancestors—those who lived in the Dutch East Indies. It has also been an exploration of culture and how cultures blend and do not blend. On a more personal note, this process has revealed how the 'sins of the father' were transmitted from generation to generation. For the Bergs, the impetus leading to sin (dis-ease of the soul) was honor, pride, and a reverence—but also idealization—for what is noble. Fransz Joseph was preoccupied with restoring his family's honor. Johan Jacob fiercely identified with the honor and nobility of his European ancestors, and Frederik Willem

---

[96] Mulder, N. (1980). *Mysticism & everyday life in Java* (2nd ed.). Singapore: Singapore University Press, p. 16. Marcel Bonnef. (1971). "Gama: Portrait d'une Universite," Archipel, v. 2., 223-224.

Karel upheld the family's honor by keeping his word and principles. All three took pride in these honorable actions. In the telling of his stories and his ancestors' stories, my father also reflected these values, as did Tante Maggie with hers.

What particularly caught my attention when visiting Java and Bali and that I witnessed in the arts comes out of the *prijaji* [97] worldview with its "high art and intuitive mysticism," which, in my father's time and beyond, "remained the model not only for the elite but in many ways for the entire (Javanese) society." [98] Proper behavior in Indonesia is not like the Western preference for individuality and personal accomplishment. Prijaji implicates individual deference, loyalty, and subordination for the sake of social harmony. The mystical aspect of prijaji relates to an inner refinement that develops from spiritual practice, as in meditation and meditative prayer. Prijaji that arises from spiritual practices is not a prescribed behavior (like good manners) one learns from family and culture but an innate refinement—these are to be humble grateful, compassionate, and present. Behaviors distinguished in the metaphysical language in Javanese mysticism were the social "measuring rods" of *alus* and *kasar*.

Alus means pure, refined, polished, polite, exquisite, ethereal, subtle, smooth. A man who speaks flawless high-Javanese is *alus*, as is the high-Javanese itself. A piece of cloth with intricate, subtle designs painted onto it is *alus*. An exquisitely played piece of music or beautifully controlled dance step is *alus*. So is a smooth stone, a dog with his hair petted down, a far-fetched joke, or a clever poetic conceit. God is, of course, *alus* (as well as visible spirits), and so is the mystical experience of Him. [99]

Whereas *kasar* is the opposite, like being "impolite, rough, uncivilized... a badly played piece of music, a stupid joke." [100] According to Mulder, the term *prijaji* used for "refined people," refers to art and mystical practice as well as etiquette.[101] While the term relates to class, in Javanese

[97] Here I am not referring to the prajaji noble class in Java.
[98] Mulder, N. (1980). *Mysticism & everyday life in Java* (2nd ed.), p. 16. Parenthesis added.
[99] Marcel Bonnef. (1971). "Gama: Portrait d'une Universite," Archipel, v. 2., 223-224.
[100] Clifford Geertz, (1976). *The religion of Java*. Chicago: University of Chicago Press, p. 232.
[101] IBID., pp. 30-33.

mystical practices and as a cultural tradition it is intricately woven into centuries of Javanese behavior (for all classes). It not only distinguishes the refined, privileged class but the behavior and values prescribed for all Javanese. This inner refinement I witnessed in the people I encountered on Java and in my Indisch family and the Indisch community.

In Dutch, the word prijaji loosely translates as *beschaafdheid*, or civilized in English. Because my early forefathers were taught to value the superior world of the Westerner, the European blood they so identified with, they discounted and overlooked the inner refinement of their inlander nature. This then, I believe, surfaced as a preoccupation with honor or the 'beschaafd' behavior of a noble person of class, position, and status.

Integrating the Forbidden

My exploration into the family has unleashed the forbidden, the ugly, the shadow—dramas and traumas. Perhaps telling my father's story with all its losses as well as the cultural and racial inequities of colonialism brings that which was hidden and denied to light. The particulars may be different, but most Indo histories contain the ugliness of war, imprisonment, brutality, loss of family and home, prejudices, classism, and racism. These unprocessed life experiences, unprocessed fragments, or 'the sins of the fathers' were passed on to the ensuing generations to bear and integrate.

I have focused on the male line of Berg because that is where my energy was drawn. However, while writing, I noticed that the female 'supporting' characters were often powerful, wise, and courageous women with a sense of adventure. In many ways, they carried 'his' stories.

We live the aftermath of our parents and ancestor's unconscious choices and experiences, which are reflected in how we have been raised and how we then raise our children, make decisions, and behave in relationships. When not aware of trauma, it becomes karma—the unconscious energy that governs our lives. My telling the story of the past is a step towards healing family trauma and, in a minute way, humanity. Reclaiming my Javanese ancestry is helping to integrate the colonized, the magical, the dark, the slow, the non-Western, the forbidden, the non-privileged, the shadow, the indigenous, the hidden, the unwanted, and the shadow side.

Spiritual Path

Now 24 years since that journey to my roots in Java, I revisit and reflect: have I embodied the Indisch side of myself? Have I been able to integrate, internally accept the shadow that perhaps my father and his forefathers (and mothers) were not able to? While psychological literature discusses the effects of war, imprisonment, and repatriation for the Indisch, I have not found much on the inner colonization. I've lived with the internal dialogues between the cultures for much of my life. I am beginning to value what each has to say. Continued exploration of rasa has served to unleash more of the forbidden Indisch in me. The development of prijaji, as it is meant in its mystical sense, has become a life path. Over the decades, I have come to trust the *batin*, or my inner realm of experience that comes from quietude. I concur with Clifford Geertz who, in describing kebatinan mystical practice as a method of knowing or understanding, says:

> The final appeal is always to (emotional) experience which carries its own meaning. God, forms of worship, and views of the nature of man, are always validated on these grounds—never grounds of logic or essential rationality...never on pure belief...never in terms of social consequences...but always on the quality of experience which is self-validating and empirical.[102]

In trusting this inner knowing, I have often gone against my better rational judgment and the conventions of society.

The subtle process of inner development included witnessing and then letting go of ego attachments of status, position, identity, and roles. I have slowed down my modern, Western pace, work ethic, and ambitions. Yet I noticed impatience when part of me would rather remain with the status quo. I have experienced a source of tension, struggle, and shame in the lack of that drive to accomplish that I had come to expect and value in myself. Over many years, these outer forms have lessened their hold on me, and prijaji, or a more true noble behavior that is innate, authentic, and natural, has slowly been emerging. For myself, the development of prijaji, in its mystical sense, has been a lifelong quest aligned with meditation practices in which 'honorable' or 'good'

---

[102] Clifford Geertz. (1960). *The religion of Java*. The Free Press of Glencoe, as quoted by Niels Mulder. (1980). *Mysticism & everyday life in contemporary Java* (2nd ed), p. 19.

behavior arises from within and for which humility, gratitude, compassion, and presence are the process and the goal.

Addendum

103

Indonesian History, Geography and Culture

The Republic of Indonesia has five main islands: Sumatra, Java, Kalimantan (Borneo), Sulawesi (Celebes), and Irian Jaya (New Guinea).[104] It currently has the fourth largest population in the world with 269 million human inhabitants, and it is the largest Muslim nation. Indonesia is about a fourth of the size of the continental US and fifty-five times the size of the Netherlands.[105]

The majority of Indonesian languages are Austronesian (from Latin *auster*, or south wind, and Greek *nęsos*, or island), which spread throughout the

---

[103] Merapi Volcano, Litho from "De Indische Archipel," The Hague, 1865-1876. Retrieved June 9 2021 from:
https://commons.wikimedia.org/wiki/File:COLLECTIE_TROPENMUSEUM_De_vulkaan_Merapi_TMnr_3728-470.jpg

[104] Bali, a popular tourist destination, is a small island off the eastern coast of Java.

[105] Worldometers. Retrieved April 2, 2019 from: http://www.worldometers.info/world-population/indonesia-population/

islands of Southeast Asia, Madagascar, and the Pacific. The Proto-Malays landed in several waves followed by the Hindu-Buddhist Kambujas, or Indo-Persian royalties, and traders from southern China—all intermarrying with the aboriginal people to form a group known as the Malays. On the larger islands, separate kingdoms had distinct languages: for instance, on Java there was Malay, Javanese, and Madurees. These languages have up to five forms of expression—one for each class of people. The archipelago was situated on the trade routes between China, India, and the Middle East, where merchants

came to trade the island's wealth of resources, such as wood, gold, gems, and spices.

The people of Java, Bali, and Sumatra (the western islands) are typically short, have black hair, a medium brown complexion with the high cheekbones and almond-shaped eyes. They are a mixture of Mongols, Malay, and Polynesian, with some Arab, Indian and/or Chinese. Most Indonesians are genetically close to Asians. Those of the more eastern islands are similar to Melanesians. The ethnic

Rice paddy (flooded fields), 1996

composition became more complex as those from further locations came to the archipelago. With an advanced knowledge of navigation, people living on the islands traded and interacted with China, India, and Ceylon from as early as the second century A.D.

At more than eighty square kilometers (nearly fifty square miles), or comparable to the size of England, Java is the most populous of the islands, with 141 million people and nearly sixty percent of the country's population. In early times, the forests in Java provided resources such as teak to build palaces for kings and monasteries for priests. It also supplied rattan, bamboo, and palm leaves for huts in which farmers and other village people lived. The great empires were predominantly inland states with agriculture as their basis—primarily wet-field rice cultivation. The wealth from this feudal system

248

was distributed to priests, architects, and builders who created temples honoring the Buddha or Hindu Gods, such as Siva, Vishnu and Brahma.[106]

The outer coastal areas focused on trade, in which ivory, spices, and cotton cloth were exchanged. Waves of influences passed through the islands with exotic ideas, innovations, culture, and religions. While they readily absorbed the foreign ideas or customs, these were subtly molded to fit into the cultural ecology of the island people.

Those living in coastal regions had more contact with other coastal communities than with the semi-nomad farmers of the rain forests and upland valleys. The *orang lauts* (people of the sea) "were traders, pirates, mercenaries, slavers . . . (and) recorders and suppliers for land-bound communities." [107] The separation between those living in port cities and inland continued through Indonesia's colonial history. The sea people became expert boat builders making ships that could sail against the wind and powered by up to 200 rowers (slaves or men who owed taxes). These ships could "maneuver among shoals, sandbanks, reefs, and islands and against currents and whirlpools. They were able to outperform European ships until the introduction in Indonesian waters of the flat-bottomed, steam-powered ships in the 1850s." [108]

A former career counselor, I sometimes wonder about vocations of earlier times. Jean Gilman Taylor offers a list from tax levy inscriptions in the ninth century showing that the population made: cloth and dyes and dyed cloth; made clay pots, bamboo screens and mats; processed sugar and coconut oil; snared birds and animals, or bred animals. There were smiths and those who made items from gold, iron, and copper. Some worked in trade as boatmen, porters, ferry operators, or were traders themselves. Others were carpenters, water carriers, and cooks. Still others mentioned were washers of corpses, medical specialists, canters of songs, musicians, drummers, organizers of cockfights, cooks, elephant riders, and prostitutes.[109] This extensive list, I believe, helps convey some of the lifestyle of the early people.

---

[106] Jean Gelman Taylor. (2003). "Communities and Kingdoms: Histories Through Writing and Temples," *Indonesia: Peoples and histories*, p. 35.
[107] IBID., p. 9.
[108] IBID., p. 53.
[109] IBID., p. 34.

In addition, inscriptions on tablets show that vendors linked port with village markets that bought and sold buffaloes, cows goats, pigs and rice, cotton, clothing, metals, salt and salted fish and cooking oils.[110] The people grew bananas, cucumbers, onions, garlic, and ginger and raised ducks, geese, and chickens.

Religion

> Java, …which over a period of more than fifteen hundred years has seen Indians, Arabs, Chinese, Portuguese, and Dutch come and go; and which today has one of the world's densest populations, highest development of the arts, and most intensive agriculture, is not easily characterized under a single label…. [111]

The first known influence on the archipelago occurred with the Dong-Son civilization from what is now North Vietnam and Southern China. A gradual process of Indianization occurred from the third century through the thirteenth century. Hinduism was brought to the islands around the second century and Buddhism in the fourth century. The Buddhist Empire of Srivijaya was established at Palembang in South Sumatra in the seventh century. The last Javanese-Hindu Empire of Majapahit, during the thirteenth century, was in Eastern Java.

> Mountain temple complexes, individual small shrines, and the numerous large-scale plains temples crowding this region of Java are products of extraordinary labor, building resources, management, and vision. Dominating the picture of Javanese pasts is the Borobudur, an enormous temple dedicated to worship the Buddha and designed by its architects to represent Buddhist doctrines through its form, the carvings on its walls, and its scriptures. [112]

---

[110] IBID., 34.
[111] Clifford Geertz. (1976). *The religion of Java*, p. 57.

[112] Jean Gelman Taylor. (2003). "Communities and Kingdoms: Histories Through Writing and Temples," *Indonesia: Peoples and histories*, p. 37.

250

The Borobudur is a stone square building on a hill with seven levels that make a type of dome about thirty meters (hundred feet) high. Going up, you pass through gateways to five successive terraces. It has parapets containing nearly 400 larger-than-life sitting Buddhas. The walls have bas-reliefs depicting mythological scenes.[113]

Borobudur, the world's largest Buddhist temple was built in the ninth century during the Sailendra Dynasty.

Astounding sites, I visited both the **Borobudur** and the Hindu monument **Prambanan**. The Hindu-Javanese culture peaked in the fourteenth century when Islamic influences arrived. The Islam that came to Indonesia in the fifteenth century was of a Sufi (mystical) variety that was readily received within Javanese syncretism and **melded Indian and Persian Sufism with the existing Hindu-Buddhist animist beliefs.** A form of mysticism and magic, mystical practices had always been the essence of the Javanese culture.

> Whatever of their more ancient faith may remain in the institutions, habits, and affections of the Javans, the island abounds in less perishable memorials of it. The antiquities of Java consist of ruins and edifices, and in particular to temples sacred to the former worship; images of deities found within them scattered throughout the country, either sculptured in stone or cast in metal; inscriptions on stone and copper in ancient characters, and ancient coins.[114]

Magical and mystical practices have always been part of the Javanese culture. According to Mulder, who researched Javanese mystical practices in the 1970s:

---

113 James A. Rush. (1996). "Thomas Stamford Raffles Discovers Java's Antiquities, 1815," *Java: A traveller's anthology*, Oxford University Press, p. 35.
114 IBID., p. 36.

...five to ten percent ...adhere to a rather purist form of Islam, some thirty percent to a strongly syncretist and Javanized version of Islam, while most of the remainder reckon themselves to be nominal Muslims, that is, ...(with) practices closest to the old Javanese and Indic-Javanese traditions.[115]

Prijaji has its roots in Hindu-Javanese courts with intricately expressed dance, drama, music, and poetry, along with Hindu-Buddhist mysticism.[116] Remnants of these practices are laced within the stories of my ancestors. While part Javanese, my father's family's religion was Christian. But like the indigenous (Islamic) Javanese, those of mixed heritage also had syncretic beliefs and practices.

Wajang – Puppet Theater

Artist painting wajang puppets.

Much of the major classical literature of Malay and Java, shaped by Hinduism, was preserved and was not extensively influenced by Islam. Dramatization of this literature was performed through shadow-puppet theater called wajang (wayang). The dance, drama, music, and shadow-puppet theater blends lavish narrative of Hindu epics and Islamic tales with religious ritual. This was a form of expression in which the indigenous Indonesian culture remained and the indigenous legends and sagas of the islands were originally told. The *delang* (dalang, puppeteer) maneuvers the puppets and recites the lines.

In 1996, I wiatched wayang performances on Java and Bali, where stories based on the Hindu epics *Ramayana and Bharatayuddha* were enacted. The Javanese form I saw is called *wayang kulit*, in which flat parchment puppets are used. *Wayang golek* (round wooden puppets with moveable heads

---

[115] Niels Mulder. (1980). *Mysticism & everyday life in contemporary Java* (2nd ed), p. 1. Note: I did not research twenty-first century religion in Indonesia.
[116] IBID.

and arms) are usually used for *Menak* stories, which are highly elaborate romances inspired by Islamic legend. These performances are sacred; the objects used, such as *batik* cloth, *kris* (Indonesian dagger), and puppets "had spiritual personalities and released supernatural energies...." [117] There is a lingering association of wayang with ancestors and life cycles and with the boundary between the seen and unseen world. Javanese figures were originally more naturalistic until the fifteenth century when, with the rise of Islam, realistic representations of people were forbidden.

I had purchased two leather wayang-kulit puppets, which I had mounted on the wall facing each other. An Indisch acquaintance later told me that I must be careful with how I position and display the puppets—they could bring bad luck. A wayang image can have different forms and different forces. If one has brought a wrong image into the home, it is said that it can result in consequences. These symbolic puppets are used for storytelling not for decoration. (I took them down.)

VOC coins

The structure of a Javanese shadow play parallels the four stages of human life: infancy, childhood, middle age, and old age. When performed in their entirety, these plays run from dusk to dawn in which the hours correspond to cycles of life and the cosmos. At around midnight, the clowns come out, signaling disruption that must be restored through humor. Usually free, wayang is popular and offers a shared cultural experience. The plays include action, philosophy, romance, magic, mythology, and lewd humor. They are historically thought provoking and technically incredible. Like Shakespeare, they possess high drama and low comedy.

The VOC and Colonization

The Portuguese, the first Europeans to come to the islands, were never able to monopolize the Asian spice market or have much influence on the Indonesians. However, their activity disrupted the Asian trade system by

---

[117] M.C. Ricklefs. (1993). *A History of modern Indonesia since c. 1300 (2nd ed.)*. Stanford University Press, p. 57.

dispersing the trading communities.[118] The Dutch, by establishing the VOC (Dutch East India Company) were able to control much of Indonesia. The Dutch used various strategies to gain power, such as acquiring the loyalty of lesser nobles who used their connections with the supernatural to influence the peasants. They also used a network of spies and strategic marriages. The initial European settlers were adventurers and interested in trade. Ricklefs makes an interesting note:

> The personnel of the VOC in Asia were…not always of the highest caliber, especially in its later years. Honourable men of vision who wished to undertake hazardous careers in Asia were hard to find. Although the VOC as an organization was Dutch, many of its personnel were not. Adventurers, vagabonds, criminals and the unfortunate from throughout Europe took its oath of allegiance. [119]

The Indies was an unstable region, and the Dutch used that as an advantage. They discouraged European competition with naval forces. Early on, the VOC was only interested in trade. The Dutch East Indies was not like other settler colonies that originated by emigration and displacing indigenous peoples. Instead, the military force that supported the VOC controlled the large indigenous populations.[120] While the original VOC policy was to focus on trading posts and not territorial conquest, they became involved in the internal politics of Java due to European competition and resistance from Indonesians.

The few thousand Dutch colonials controlled thirty million Javanese by appeasing Javanese aristocracy with exorbitant fees and by using the feudal system already in place. In this system, Dutch Residents and Assistant Residents guided local prijaji (local aristocracy) called Regents. The Dutch Residents were considered 'elder brothers' to the Regents and offered recommendations, which were actually obeyed as orders. The Javanese farmers carried out corvées for their Regents and provided them goods without payment. Under the Regent were various chiefs who managed the

---

[118] IBID. p. 23-24.
[119] IBID., p. 27.
[120] "Indos in Colonial History," *Wikipedia.*
Retrieved April 23, 2019 from: https://en.wikipedia.org/wiki/Indos_in_colonial_history

254

indigenous population of an area the size of a small county. Under the Dutch Assistant Residents were Controllers that would manage and keep a check on the lower native rulers. His duties were to visit the various districts and hear complaints. There were twenty-two residencies on Java. Educated at universities in Holland, they also received additional education that included "Malay language, the economic botany of the Indies, Dutch law, and Mohammedan justice, since, in their capacity as local magistrates they must make their decisions conform with the tenets of the Koran..." [121]

Eliza Ruhamah Scidmore continues with:

The governor general, who's salary is twice that of the president of the United States, lives in a palace in Buitenzorg, forty miles away in the hills, with a second palace still higher up in the mountains, and comes to the Batavia palace only on state occasions. This ruler of 24 million souls, who rules as a viceroy instructed from The Hague, with the aid of a secretary general and a council of the Indies, has, in addition to his salary of $100,000, an allowance of $60,000 a year for entertaining and it is expected that he will maintain a considerable state and splendor. [122]

Through expansion and "indolent bureaucracy...that was tolerant of graft and extortion," by the eighteenth century it had become unwieldy. [123] E. M. Beekman, translator of Dutch colonial literature, tells, "In 1799, after nearly two centuries, the Company ceased to exist. Its debt of 140 million guilders was assumed by the state, and the commercial enterprise became a colonial empire." [124] Just prior, in 1795, the Dutch were under the rule of the French, which put them into conflict with Britain. During that time (1811to 1816), the British ruled the archipelago.

In 1830, centralized authority instituted the *Cultuurstelsel* (Cultivation System) intending to increase revenues and improve the lifestyle of the Javanese peasant. In theory, twenty to thirty percent of their rice fields were

[121] Eliza Ruhamah Scidmore. (1899). *Java, the garden of the East*, New York: The Century Company, p. 32.
[122] Eliza Ruhamah Scidmore. (1899). *Java, the garden of the East*, pp. 31-32.
[123] E. M. Beekman. (1996). *Troubled pleasures: Dutch colonial literature from the East Indies 1600-1950*. Oxford: Clarendon Press, p.12.
[124] IBID., p.12.

to be used as export crops, such as sugar cane, tea, coffee, rubber, and tobacco. Between 1830 and 1870, this provided the state treasury in Holland with revenues of 823 million guilders. Javanese coffee and sugar yielded thirty-two percent of the entire Dutch state income between the years 1851 and 1860.[125].

The Cultivation System was designed, by way of the chiefs or prijaji, to persuade local farmers to give a portion of their time to the cultivation of coffee, sugar, tea, and other profitable products. A fixed wage was given to

help clear the grounds and form plantations. The Indonesian elite derived their wealth through the labor of peasants, and the products were sold to the Dutch Government at a low, fixed price. The prijaji chiefs and Regents would get a percentage of the profit and some went to the farmers.[126] These two strategies resulted in abject poverty and widespread starvation of the farmers along with distrust of

The regent of Soerabaja, Raden Tumenggung Musono, in gala dress for his installation

colonial authority that eventually led to uprisings. Between 1845 and 1950, hundreds of thousands of Javanese died. The Cultivation System was replaced with the plantation system that reduced some of the burden that the peasants had by bypassing local rulers. Nevertheless, the prijaji and the peasants grew upset with the Dutch domination, which developed into a nationalist movement.

---

[125] "Dossier Indië," Wereld Museum, Rotterdam (November 2019). https://www.wereldmuseum.nl/nl/zien-en-doen-in-het-wereldmuseum/tentoonstellingen
[126] James A. Rush. (1996). "Thomas Stamford Raffles Discovers Java's Antiquities, 1815," *Java: A traveller's anthology*, Oxford University Press, p. 69.

Multatuli, the pen name of Eduard Douwes Dekker, wrote *Max Havelaar*, which was based on his experiences of a government employee in the Indies. It was a protest against these policies and raised the awareness of the Dutch (in Holland), as well as other Europeans, showing that the wealth they enjoyed was the result of suffering in other parts of the world. This awareness eventually formed the motivation for the new Ethical Policy by which the Dutch colonial government attempted to 'repay' their debt to their colonial subjects by providing education to some classes of natives, generally members of the elite loyal to the colonial government. While a small consolation, this education was, a half a century later, a major factor leading to the nationalist movement that ended Dutch colonialism in Indonesia. At first it was mainly the Indonesian aristocracy who became interested in learning Dutch and who sent their sons (and sometimes daughters) to be educated as Europeans in Dutch schools.

Schools for the noble sons of the country included high schools, normal schools, and the Foktor-DJAWA school. For the regular population, children learned Javanese, reading, writing, and a little arithmetic. No Malay was taught. According to Kartini—a young woman of Javanese aristocracy who had received Dutch education—the Dutch government believed that if the people were educated, they would no longer be willing to work the land. In 1895, it was decreed that, without the special permission of his Excellency the Governor General, no native child from six to seven years old who could not speak Dutch would be admitted to the free grammar school for Europeans. This was interesting, because many of those with Dutch nationality, raised by inlandse baboes, could also not speak Dutch.[127] The more liberal reform that came by the end of the nineteenth century set out to improve agriculture, public hygiene, and expand transportation networks.

---

[127] Raden Adjeng Kartini. (n.d.) *Letters of a Javanese Princess.* Agnes Louise Symmers (Trans.), p. 18.

Afterword

128

The story began with the family legend of a duel in Dietz, Germany. Decades before I had any interest in exploring my roots, my father took me on a trip to a village near Solingen, Germany to see the Berg castle (*Schloss Burg*). Johan Jacob, the son of the duelist, informed his sons Noetie and Fritz, as he showed them the Berg coat of arms, that the early inhabitants of this castle were their ancestors. My father discovered the same coat of arms painted on the castle walls of Schloss Burg. However, according to the genealogy on those castle walls, the last male Berg died in the fifteenth century. As romantic and intriguing as this story of a Berg castle and ancestors is, my curiosity took me elsewhere. With only Dutch, German, and French last names in our genealogy, I veered towards the veiled Indonesian ancestors.

Research sources in the Netherlands included the *Nationaal Archief* (National Archives) for military history, and the *Indisch Familie Archief* (Indisch Family Archive) for genealogy. I give special thanks to Linda van Wijk, the secretary of that volunteer organization, who turns out to be the niece of a

---

128 Painting at Schloss Burg, Germany, 204.

friend of my father. A cousin, Maureen, the daughter of Bob Butteweg, contributed the family tree of the Buttewegs.

There have been many personal, informal contributions, including five hours of mini-cassettes containing interviews with my father. He was eighty-six at the time. His sister, Tante Maggie, sent me several hand-written letters (about thirty pages worth) in late 1999 and early 2000. Contributions came from cousins Johanna and Maarten (children of Tante Maggie), Carl and Raoul (sons of Oom Os), and my sister, Vivi. My brother Danny passed away in 2011 before I had thought of interviewing my generation. My younger brother, Carl, very close to my paternal grandparents, had many incidentals to contribute regarding their lives.

The stories and letters about my father, his siblings, and his parent's family life up through World War II and beyond the Bersiap period that include descriptions of their parents, grandparents, aunts, uncles, and cousins, has helped me to form a more coherent story about my father's and his parent's generations. This was enhanced and verified by reading about life in the Indies (see References) and filled in by way of the imaginal. I have very little information on my great-grandparents and none on the great great-grandparents, except for names, dates, and places of birth, marriages, children, and deaths. I was able to find the military records of Fransz Joseph and Johan Jacob.

To inspire this story, I did a family constellation[129] with Louise Arnold Bik, an Indisch woman living in the Netherlands who has performed many family constellations for those of Dutch-Indonesian heritage. My request was unique—less to enlighten and heal a particular personal issue than to gain some insight into far-away ancestors. In the end, I think it comes out the same. My questions were: Who was this Fransz Joseph Berg? What happened at and after the duel? Who was Helena Falck? Why did the two wait until she

---

[129] A family constellation is based on the idea that trauma sifts down through generations to cause stress in the each ensuing generation. One can learn about the traumas of one's parents and ancestors through the morphogenic field of energy that surrounds their family. "History And Methods Of Family Constellation Therapy," better help. Retrieved October 22, 2019 from: https://www.betterhelp.com/advice/therapy/history-and-methods-of-family-constellation-therapy/

was eight months pregnant to marry? And finally, who is the mother of Johan Jacob? I used the intuitive-feeling content that came forth for both Louise and me to seed Fransz and Helena's stories. In the constellation of Fransz's first family—Joseph Carl, Johan Jacob, and Helena—we felt on the perimeter the presence of a very young mother, who became Lintang, Johan's mother. During the family constellations, we could sense into an unknown inlandse woman, as well as characteristics, emotions, and motivations, which I then used to unfold their stories. Once I began, the characters took over and the story unfolded. Adele, Adriaan, and Suus —from other ancestral lines and based on the few stories I had—guided me as well in writing their tales. I had less interest in some ancestors, which troubled me at first. However, perhaps they just don't want more of their stories to be told.

Much of the earlier part of family history is not literally true. My intention was to tell a saga that *could* have happened, that was commonplace in the culture, and that entailed customs, practices, and history I wanted readers to, and that I needed to, understand. I wanted to express the experiences of 'being Indisch' (and to a lesser extent, being an inlandse) in Indonesia between 1830 and 1950.

In 2007, I attended the Pasar Malam Basar, which means Great Night Market. To be more inclusive of the offspring from other Dutch colonies, it is now called the Tong Tong Festival. Held in The Hague, it has food courts, performances, workshops, lectures, and interviews, and, as the former name implies, a bizarre for selling merchandise. Here I saw an exhibit showcasing the story of the njais. Upon reading the book by Reggie Baay, I understood the reason I could not find the Indonesian bloodline through ancestral research and genealogy charts. Most often inlandse mothers were njais, hidden and/or discarded. Both Sarina and Lintang are creations of possible njai ancestors. The descriptions of their inlandse life are sparse. I attribute that to how they were hidden and barely acknowledged even by those who lived with them and shared their homes and beds. I made concerted efforts using 'rasa' as well as western 'ratio' methods to understand their lives.

As far as I know, Helena Falck was not a Dutch woman living in the Netherlands who went to Indonesia to be married *met de witte handschoen* (with the white glove). She could have been raised in the Indies from birth. I took the liberty to invent her story so as to show the Dutch East Indies from the eyes of a relatively open-minded and adventure-seeking *baru* (newcomer). If

261

not Helena, it is very likely that a pair of ancestors were married with the white glove. In addition, names of and characters not in the official genealogy chart nor mentioned by my father and aunt were invented. I added the fictional Sarina and Lintang to the chart for the readers. In any official chart, these unmarried njais would not be added.

The episodes describing the use of guna for healing were imagined. I did not research Indonesian dukun-healing practices. The story about Oma Sok, however, is a replica of what my father and aunt told me. As stated earlier, there were many stories about the use of magic told in the Indies family community. I used those to seed my imagination.

Not knowing much about the life of a military man in the Indies in the 1800s, I visited the Museum Bronbeek and research library in Arnhem. The museum focuses on the role of the KNIL in the Netherland's colonial history. Other Internet and book resources are cited and in the reference section. In addition, unless otherwise cited, photos are from my own collection or from Wikimedia Commons and the Tropenmuseum Commons.

I have read dozens of books about Indisch culture and Indonesian history. The two by Jean Gelman Taylor, *The Social World of Batavia* and *Indonesia: Peoples and History* as well as *Being "Dutch" in the Indies* by Ulbe Bosma and Remco Raben delineated the early development of Indisch culture and history that occurred before the lives of my father and his immediate family. It was somewhat difficult to find books in Dutch or English from the perspective of an Indonesian village person living in the nineteenth century. The writings of Augusta de Wit, Kartini's letters, and the enjoyable *Java: A Travellers Anthology* by James Rush and *Java, the Garden of the East* by Eliza Ruhamah Scidmore, all written during that time period, helped spark my imagination. I also liberally used the Internet to research terms, historical incidents, geography, and the like.

Since 2017, I have been following the teachings of Thomas Hübl, a modern mystic and contemporary spiritual teacher who works with intergenerational trauma. This psycho-spiritual work has furthered the process of unleashing my Indo family's story at a deeper and more visceral level the trauma of my ancestors as the result of colonization and of war. While not explicitly described, effects of this work may have influenced my writing.

262

My experiences of family life are written from my perspective and wounding. I purposely did not offer details or stories about the adult lives of aunts and uncles and of the family members from my generation. I understand that memory is subjective. My siblings and cousins may have their own and different stories to tell and may not have experienced or remembered growing up with the same type of relationships to their parents and grandparents as I have had.

Astrid Berg
astridberg4@gmail.com
July 2021

Glossary

To be faithful to the culture of Dutch and Dutch-Indonesians (Indisch) during the colonial times, I used the spelling they used at that time. For instance, the Dutch would use an 'oe.' In present time, Indisch or Indonesian words with the former 'oe' are spelled with a 'u.'

Aap – monkey (Dutch)

Achter hun glimlach –behind their smile (Dutch)

Adat – teachings, rules to follow (Indonesian)

Akar bahar – Akar means root, whereas bahar is Arabic for 'sea.' (Indonesian)

Alang alang – reed (instrument) (Indonesian)

Alun alun – town square, plaza (Indonesian)

Alus or Halus – Alus means pure, refined, polished, polite, exquisite, ethereal, subtle, civilized, smooth. (Indonesian)

Anak Kompanie – child of the battalion (Javanese)

Arjuna Wiwaha – Arjuna's Wedding (Indonesian)

Asam gelugar – dried tamarind (Indonesian)

Aurau – a prayer house and community center (Indonesian)

Baboe, babu – maid, nanny (Javanese)

Banjo – jacket (Indonesian)

Balanganjar – type of gamelan (Indonesian)

Bani mati – dares to face death (Javanese)

Baru – person living in the Indies born in the Netherlands (Javanese)

Batik cloth – made with wax-resist dyeing process using a spouted tool called a tjanting, or by printing the resist with a copper stamp called a cap. (Indonesian)

Batin – the inner aspect of one's existence; the secret place where one meets God. (Indonesian)

Becap – rickshaw (Indonesian)

Bersiap period – the Indonesian independence movement from the Dutch that occurred after World War II (1945-1949) (Javanese)

Beschaafd or Beschaafdheid – culture, being civilized, manners (Dutch)

Bescheiden – humble but is also used to mean civilized.

Betel – tobacco, often chewed (Indonesian)

Binta – hard slap (Japanese)

Blanda – of European ancestry (Javanese)

Blank, blanke – light, referring to skin color (Dutch)

Blonde Indo – literal blonde, Caucasian-looking person of mixed blood (Dutch)

Boerong – the spirit of a woman who lost her child (Javanese)

Bonang – horizontal gong

Borobudur – the 1200-year-old Buddhist temple (Indonesian)

Broertje – diminutive for brother, younger brother (Dutch)

Bromo – crater of an active volcano Tengger Massif (Indonesian)

Bukit berkabut – misty hill (Indonesian)

Cengkih – cloves (Indonesian)

Cultuurstelsel – Cultivation System (Dutch)

Cukup – enough (Indonesian)

Dekat – close (Indonesian)

De Groote Postweg – Great Post Road (Dutch)

Delang or dalang – puppeteer (Javanese)

Dendeng – beef jerky (Javanese)

Djongo – house boy (Javanese)

Dodok – drop to heels and walk (Javanese)

Duku – fruit that looks like grape (Javanese)

Dukun – healer, medicine man or woman (Indonesian)

Eigenwijs – willful, obstinate (Dutch)

Erkent – recognized, legitimized, referring to whether a child was legitimate (Dutch)

Gambang kajoe – xylophone (Javanese)

Gado Gado – parched vegetable salad with peanut sauce (Indonesian)

Gajong – metal dipping cup with a long handle (Javanese)

Getientjanged – cut into pieces. Note: this is an Indonesian word (tientjanged) conjugated in Dutch (ge). In growing up speaking Dutch and English, we would use verbs from one language and conjugate in another.

Gladakker – scoundrel (Dutch)

Goeleh toendjang – meat with young bamboo shoots (Indonesian)

Groot Hertoginnelaan – Grand Duchess Lane (Dutch)

Guna – white magic (Indonesian)

Guna guna – black magic (Indonesian)

Hadjas – those who have performed the pilgrimage to Mecca (Indonesian)

Haole – Hawaiian for white, newcomer

Hogere Burgerschool (HBS) – Higher Commoner's School (Dutch)

Holland, the Netherlands – My father and grandparents used Holland rather than the Netherlands. When I refer to present-day the Netherlands or descriptions that are not part of the story, I use the term the Netherlands. The term 'Holland' actually refers to the two provinces, North and South Holland. These two provinces were in power in the earlier part of Dutch history.

Indisch – Indo-European, person of European and Indonesian blood.

Indische jongen – familiar term for Dutch-Indonesian man (Dutch)

Indische meisje – familiar term for Dutch-Indonesian woman (Dutch)

Indische na-oorlogse generatie – Post war Dutch-Indonesian generation (Dutch)

Inlands, inlandse or inlander – literal, inlander. One indigenous to any of the islands in the Indonesia archipelago. (Dutch)

Indo – person of European and Indonesian blood (Dutch)

Jeruk – pomelo (Indonesian)

Jongen – boy (Dutch)

Kabaja – lace blouse for a woman (Javanese)

Kale kak – literal translation, bald shit; snobby, uppity (Dutch)

Kali – river (Indonesian)

Kasian – sorry, poor thing (Indonesia)

Kebatinan – the culture of inner-man, the essence of Javaneseness; Javanese mystical practice (Javanese)

Kebayar – a fast-paced sound in gamelan (Indonesian)

Kebon – gardener (Javanese)

Kedang – drum

Kedongdong – ambarella fruit (Indonesian)

Kelapa – coconut (Indonesian)

Kenari – shady nutmeg trees that also produce a large, variety of almonds.

Kendhang – hand played drums (Indonesian)

Ketipoeng – drum (Indonesian)

Klamboe – canopy for bed against mosquitoes (Javanese)

Klapperbomen – klapper – coconut (Indonesian); bomen – trees (Dutch)

Koffie tubruk – Indonesian style in which ground coffee is put in a cup, hot water is poured in, and one waits for the grinds to float down; Koffie - Dutch; tubruk - Javanese

Kokkie – cook (Javanese)

Koninklijk Nederlands-Indies Leger (KNIL – Royal East Indies Army (Dutch)

Koelie – indentured worker (Dutch)

Kraton – palace (Indonesian)

268

Kris – Indonesian dagger (Indonesian)

Lepel – shoehorn, spoon (Dutch)

Lieve – Dutch for dear, dear one, kind (Dutch)

Luchtbeschermingsdienst LBD – Air Protection Service (Dutch)

Mam, Mama, Moes – Mom (Dutch)

Mandy – tub of water used for bathing (Javanese)

Manga – mango (Indonesian)

Manggis – mangosteen (Indonesian)

Meisje – girl (Dutch)

Menak stories – Javanese version of highly elaborate romances inspired by legend in Islamic stories

Mestizo – term used in 17th and part of 18th century referring to those with European and Indonesian and/or Asian heritage.

Mevrouw – Mrs. (Dutch)

Mokkataart – yellow cake with butter-mocha icing (Dutch)

Nakinderen – literally, after children; children born from a European woman after father had sired children from an njai (Dutch)

Narima – to accept life as it comes (Indonesian)

Nasi goreng – fried rice (Indonesian)

Nederlands-Indië – Dutch East Indies; Indonesian archipelago between 1600-1949 (Dutch)

(The) Netherlands, Holland – My father and grandparents used Holland rather than the Netherlands. When I refer to present-day the Netherlands or descriptions that are not part of the story, I use the term the Netherlands. Holland actually refers to the two provinces, North and South Holland. These two provinces were in power in the earlier part of Dutch history.

Njai or Nyai – translated as concubine, a housekeeper who also shared sexual relations with her employer. (Javanese)

Oom – uncle (Dutch)

Oma – grandma (Dutch)

Opa – grandpa (Dutch)

Orang lauts - people of the sea (Indonesian)

Paatje - Pops (Dutch)

Pak - Javanese used for an elder, or out of respect (Javanese)

Paleb – viol (Indonesian)

Pamrih – self interest (Indonesian)

Pap, Papa – dad (Dutch)

Pasar, passer – bizarre, market-place (Javanese)

Pantuns – poetry or love songs (Indonesian)

Pencak silat – an Indonesian version of marshal arts (Indonesian)

Pepaya – papaya (Indonesian)

Pijiting – massaging (Javanese)

Pisang – banana (Indonesian)

Poeaja – someone of lower class (Javanese)

Poesat Keibodan (PK) – Vigilance Corps (Javanese)

Politieke Inlichting Dienst (PID) – Political Intelligence Service (Dutch)

Prambanan – 1100-year-old Hindu temple (Indonesian)

Prijaji – A complex term tha refers to an elite class. In the mystical sense, prijaji refers to a behavior one takes on for sake of social harmony. It also relates to an inner refinement developed from spiritual practice, as in meditation and meditative prayer.

Puputan – mass-suicide (Indonesian)

Rasa – intuitive inner feeling, the way to essential knowledge (Indonesian)

Rebabs – a bowed instrument (Indonesian)

Ria – non-attachment (Indonesian)

Rijsttafel – literal, rice table, an assortment of small dishes, such as, fish, meat, a variety of curries, sauces, preserved fruit, pickles. (Dutch)

Romusha – forced laborer (Japanese)

Rukun – to live in harmony (Indonesian)

Rumah gadan – long house (Indonesian)

Sabar – trustful patience (Indonesian)

Sambal – pepper paste seasoning (Indonesian)

Sarapan – breakfast (Indonesian)

Sarong – supple cloth wrapped around the waste with a fold in front and about ankle length that ties at one side of the waste (Indonesian)

Saté – satay, marinated pork, chicken or lamb on skewers cooked on a fire (Javanese)

Saté padang – skewered beef with yellow curry sauce (Javanese)

Sembah – put both hands together with their thumbs under the nose, as a way of showing reverence (Indonesian)

Sepi ing pamrih – to sacrifice your self interest (Indonesian)

Sering – Syringa or Common Lilac (Dutch)

Setan – spirit (Javanese)

Skola djonkok – literally, crouching school. Perhaps it meant crouching like for those of lesser value.

Slamatan or selametan, selamatan – communal Javanese feast symbolizing social unity (Indonesian)

Slendang – cloth wrapped around mother as well as child to carry the child, like the baby carriers of today (Javanese)

Smoel – mug, face (Dutch)

Soeling – bamboo flute

SOS – a social club or fraternity for the colonials (Dutch)

Stichting INGO or Indische Na-Oorlogse Generatie – Dutch-Indonesian Post War Generation Foundation (Dutch)

Tafelmeisje – literally, girl table; female guest at one's table (Dutch)

Tamba – seconds during a meal (Javanese)

Tapa – asceticism (Indonesian)

Tante – aunt (Dutch)

TAVENU – Abbreviation for Tot Algemene Verpozing en Nuttige Uitspanning – Towards A General Rest and Useful Relaxation (Dutch)

Tempo doeloe – time of old, good old days (Javanese)

Terima kasih – thank you (Indonesian)

Tjelem poeng – zither

Tjeritas – stories or historical tales (Indonesian)

Toewan, tuan – used in from of a man's name out of respect (Javanese)

Totok – Dutch born in Indonesia or European who has lived in the Indies numerous years and considered it home (Javanese)

Terima kasih – thank you (Indonesian)

Trassi – for cooking made of fermented fish (Indonesian)

Tulambens – musicians (Indonesian)

Voorkinderen – literal, children before, or those from a njai (Dutch)

Vereenigde Oostindische Compagnie, VOC – Dutch East India Company (Dutch)

Vreemde Oosterlingen – literal, other Easterners, like Chinese and Arabs (Dutch)

Wadjans – woks (Indonesian)

Wapen – coat of arms (Dutch)

Waringin – banyan (Javanese)

Warung – food stand (Javanese)

Wayang golek – puppet show using round wooden puppets with moveable heads and arms, or the puppets themselves (Indonesian)

Wewe gombel – scary supernatural creature (Javanese)

Zwart, zwartje – black, black one (Dutch)

Zonderling – eccentric loner (Dutch)

Berg Genealogy

Fifth Generation
Pieter Joseph + Gertruida Kortschillsch
    Fransz Joseph, April 26, 1812 –Dietz, Germany
    ! January 25, 1884 – Ambarawa, Indonesia
    (Unknown whether there were other children)

Fourth Generation
Fransz Joseph + Sarina (Fictionalized mother of Joseph Carl Leonard*)*,
        Yogyakarta, 1820
        Joseph Carl Leonard, July 8, 1841, Padang Panjang ,
        Sumatra
        ! August 25, 1908 Ngawi (Madioen)

        + Lintang, (fictionalized mother of Johan Jacob),
    Soerabaja, 1832
        Johan Jacob, November 18, 1849, Grissee, Soerabaja
        ! January 18,1928 Malang

        + Helena (Augusta?) Falck, no birthdate or place
    (May 27, 1853 Soerabaja)
    ! July 2, 1853, Ambarawa
        Helena Augusta (Berg), June 24, 1853,
        Ambarawa, Java
        ! 1895

        + Christina Cornelia Corver – Lobrij, June 6, 1833
    Soerakarta
    (November 30, 1853, Semarang)
    ! February 12, 1908, Malang
        Josephina Christina, September 12, 1857
        ! April 16, 1917 Soerabaja
        Johanna Christina, December 10, 1859

Children of Fransz Joseph and Christina Cornelia, continued

Rosina Augustina, August 14, 1866
! Malang December 1, 1918

Third Generation
Johan Jacob + Johanna Catharina Pichel, September 13, 1873
(May 26, 1856, Semarang)
! April 22, 1894, Modjosarie
Franz Joseph Eduard, May 30, 1874, Batavia
! September 24, 1875
Eugenie Emelie Rosalie, October 14, 1875
+ Carl Hendrik Padberg, October 13, 1905
Djombang
Joseph Carel Leonardo, July 7, 1876, Soerabaja
(Unclear who mother is)
+ Carolina Wilhelmina Krijgsman, February 6, 1902,
Madioen
+ Antje Moll. May, 15, 1907, Djokja
(second marriage of Joseph Carel Leonardo)
August Johan Jacob, December 20, 1876, Semarang
(Unclear who mother is)
Catharina Christina Beerman, May 22, 1913
Johanna Catharina Wilhelmina, March 1, 1878,
Bojolali
Theodoor Alex Ferdinand, July 6, 1884, Ambarawa
+ Adella Celine Pielaat, January 16, 1911, Bangil
Johanna Frederika Constantina, no birthdate
+ Nettekoven, Keboemen, March, 30, 1892
Marinus Arnold Hendrik, February 16, 1893,
Poerbolinggo
+ Jeanne Julie Carolina d'Hamecourt, Soerakarta
Josephine Ernestine Louise, no birthdate
+ Klaten, October 8, 1881

,

Johan Jacob + Josephine Susana Paulina Abels,
>January 5, 1863, Madioen
>(February 27, 1895, Malang)
>! 1954 or 1955, The Hague

>>**Frederik Willem Karel,** December 21, 1895
>>! March 28, 1985, Den Haag, Nederland
>>Johanna Catherina Susanna, March 13, 1898,
>>Djombang
>>! (?)1954, Den Haag, Nederland

Second Generation
Frederik Willem Karel + Johanna Wilhelmina Butteweg,
>January 6, 1898, Malang
>December 16, 1916, Soerabaja)
>! May 16, 1987, Den Haag
>>**Anton Berg, November 18, 1917, Soerabaja**
>>! June 29, 2006, Las Vegas
>>**Oscar, June 14, 1919, Soerabaja**
>>! 30 January 1994
>>**Mildred, September 6, 1922, Malang**
>>! September 2008, Seal Beach, CA

First Generation
Anton Berg + Louise Adelaide De Haas, June 6, 1919
>(October 24, 1941 Soerabaja)
>! December 11, 1951, Den Haag, Nederland
>>Danny, January 14, 1947, Batavia
>>! September 17, 2011, Camarillo, CA
>>Virginia, January 9, 1948, Batavia

>**+ Anna Speet, November 1, 1928**
>(October 29, 1953)
>>Astrid Miranda Henriette, April 26, 1955, 's
>>Hertogenbosch, Nederland
>>Carl Frederick, April 4, 1960, Glendale, CA

Oscar Berg	+ Fernanda Maria Paulus, 24 October 1946
	Cyril, October 29, 1947 Soerabaja
	Raoul, December 15, 1948, Batavia
	Carl Lubertus, July 11, 1956, Den Haag
	Yvette Melanie, July 30 1957, Den Haag
	! July 29 2004. The Hague

Mildred Berg	+ Charles Geul (divorced)
	+ Willem Couwenberg, 2 June, 1948
	Inge Marie, April 16, 1949
	Maarten Luther, March 25, 1951
	Johanna Clemence, November 29, 1955
	Esther Mirjam, January 10, 1959

Legend:

Name, birthdate, and place
+ Wed to: name
(Date & place married)
! Date and place of demise

References

Aniba, Ton. (n.d.). *Kroniek van een koloniaal: Het leven van Johannes Slüsser.*

Baay, Reggie. (2008). *De Njai: Het concubinaat in Nederlands-Indië.* Amsterdam: Athenaeum-Polak &Van Gennep.

Beattie, Rod. (2007). *The Thai-Burma Railway: The true story of the Bridge on the River Kwai.* Kanchanaburi, Thailand: T. B. R. C. Co. Ltd.

Beck, Sanderson, *Indonesia and the Dutch 1800-1950.* Retrieved November 18, 2018 from: http://www.san.beck.org/20-11-Indonesia1800-1950.html

Beekman, E. M. (1996). *Troubled pleasures: Dutch colonial literature from the East Indies 1600-1950.* Oxford: Clarendon Press.

Begeman, F. A. (n.d.). *De oorlog van mijn ouders: Interviews met kinderen van oorlogsslachoffers.* Utrecht, Nederland: Stichting ICODO.

Boomgaard, Peter & van Dijk, Janneke. (n.d.). *Het Indië boek.* Zwolle, Nederland: Waanders Uitgevers.

Bosma, Ulbe & Raben, Remco. (2008). *Being "Dutch" in the Indies: A history of Creolisation and empire, 1500-1920.* (W. Shaffer, Trans.). Athens, OH: Ohio University Press.

Bosma, Ulbe & Raben, Remco. (2003). *De oude Indische wereld 1500-1920.* Amsterdam: Uitgeverij Bert Bakker.

BridgeRiverKwai.com.
Retrieved April 14, 2019 from http://www.bridgeriverkwai.com/

Buiter, Hans. (1993). *Nederlands-Indië (1930-1849): Een kolonie in ontwikkeling.* Utrecht/Arnhem, Nederland: Kosmos – Z & K Uitgevers.

Da Costa, Celinne. (Nov. 27, 2017). "Words Beyond Translation: Rasa," *Being Human.* Retrieved July 18, 2019 from: https://celinnedacosta.com/2017/11/27/words-beyond-translation-rasa/

De Wit, Augusta. (1920). *De drie vrouwen in het Heilige Woud.* Amsterdam: Meulenhoff.

De Wit, Augusta (1905). *Java: Facts and fancies.* London: Chapman & Hall, Ltd.

"East Indies Camp Archives." Retrieved April 14, 2019 from: https://www.indischekamparchieven.nl/en/general-information/about-de-camps/daily-life-in-the-camps

Fragmenten uit: Djangan Loepah! Huishoudelijke wenken voor gerepatrieerden. (Jan. 1960 - Dec.1961). Den Haag, The Netherlands: Comité van Kerkelijk en Particulier initiatief voor Sociale Zorg t.b.v. gerepatrieerden (C.C.K.P).

Geertz, Clifford. (1976). *The religion of Java.* Chicago and London: University of Chicago Press.

Geertz, Clifford. (1960). *The religion of Java.* London: Collier-MacMillan Ltd. The Free Press of Glencoe.

Hagen, Piet. (2018). *Koloniale oorlogen in Indonesië: Vijf eeuwen verzet tegen vreemde overheersing.* Amsterdam: De Arbeiderspers.

Harpe, T. & Dolman, W. (2002). *Achter mijn glimlach: Vannuit het donker naar het licht.* Dieman, Nederland: Uitgeverij KJB '40-'49.

Hellwig, Tineke & Tagliacozzo, Eric (Eds.). (2009). *The Indonesia reader: History, culture, politics.* Durham, NC: Duke University Press.

Hollander, Inez. (2008). *Silenced voices: Uncovering a family's colonial history in Indonesia.* Athens, OH: Ohio University Press.

Holmes, L. G. (2002, February). "Dutch civilian compensation from Japan and the American dilemma," *JPRI Working Paper No. 84.* Retrieved from http://www.jpri.org/publications/workingpapers/wp84.html

Hübl, Thomas. (2020). *Healing collective trauma: A process for healing intergenerational and cultural wounds.* Boulder, CO: Sounds True.

Hübl, Thomas. https://thomashuebl.com/

Immerzeel, B .R. & van Esch, F. (Eds.). (1993). *Verzet in Nederlands-Indië tijdens de Japanse bezetting 1942-1945.* Den Haag, Nederland: SDU Uitgeverij Koninginnegracht.

"Indische Kamparchieven." Retrieved 5/6/19 from: https://www.indischekamparchieven.nl/nl/bezetting-en-bersiap/bevrijding-en-evacuatie

"The Japanese Occupation" *Indonesia: World War II and the struggle for independence, 1942–50,* Retrieved July 15, 2019 from http://www.country-data.com/cgi-bin/query/r-6196.html

Jung, Carl. (1989). *Memories, dreams and reflections.* New York: Vintage Books.

Kartini, **Raden Adjeng.** (n.d.). *Letters of a Javanese princess.* (Agnes Louise Symmers, Trans.).

Kruseman, Mina. (2009). *Een huwelijk in Indië.* Amsterdam: KIT Publishers.

Lulofs, Madelon. (1990). *Coolie* (3rd ed.). (G. J. Renier and I. Clepahane, Trans). New York: Oxford University Press.

Mulder, N. (1980). *Mysticism & everyday life in Java* (2nd ed.). Singapore: Singapore University Press.

Multatuli. (2018). *Max Havelaar: Op de koffieveilingen van Nederlandse handelmaatschappij* (14th ed.). Amsterdam: NCR Boeken.

"Redelijk inzetbaar: Overlevenden van de Jappenkampen moesten meteen weer vechten," *ncr.nl.* Retrieved May 6, 2019 from: https://www.nrc.nl/nieuws/1998/10/03/redelijk-inzetbaar-overlevenden-van-de-jappenkampen-7417255-a174354

Richter, A. (1994). *Arts and crafts of Indonesia.* San Francisco: Chronicle Books.

Ricklefs, M. C. (1994). *A history of modern Indonesia since c. 1300* (2nd ed.). Stanford, CA: Stanford University Press.

Rowley, T. (2015, January). "Burma railway: British POWs break silence over horrors," *The Telegraph*. Retrieved from http://www.telegraph.co.uk/history/world-war-two/10382906/Burma-Railway-British-POW-breaks-silence-over-horrors.html

Rush, James. (Ed.). (1996). *Java: A travellers' anthology*. New York: Oxford University Press.

Scidmore, Eliza Ruhamah. (1899). *Java, the garden of the East*. New York: The Century Company.

Soechting, Dirk. (2004). *Die Reihe archivbilder Schloss Burg an der Wupper*. Erfurt, Deutschland: Sutton Verlag.

Solomon, Marion F. & Daniel J. Siegal, Eds. (2003). *Healing trauma: Attachment, mind, body and brain*. NY: W. W. Norton & Company.

Stellingwerff, J. (1980). *Fat man in Nagasaki: Nederlandse krijgsgevangenen overleefden de atoombom*. Amsterdam: T. Wever B.V. Franeker

"Stichting Oorlogsgetroffenen in de Oost: Met Japanse archieven en contacten (SOO)." Retrieved August 4, 2019 from http://pow.s-o-o.nl/Camp/

Taylor, Jean Gelman. (2009). *The social world of Batavia*. Madison, WI: The University of Wisconsin Press.

Taylor, Jean Gelman. (2003). *Indonesia: Peoples and histories*. New Haven: Yale University Press.

Tolle, Eckhart. (2005). *A new earth: Awakening to your life's purpose*. New York: Penguin Books.

van den Doel, H. W. (1996). *Het rijk van insulinde: Opkomst en ondergang van een Nederlandse kolonie*. Amsterdam: Prometheus.

van der Molen, Ella. (Ed.). (2002). *De mooiste Indonesische mythen en sagen*. Ede, Nederland: Uitgeverij Verba.

"Vijf eeuwen migratie." Retrieved October 25, 2018 from: http://www.vijfeeuwenmigratie.nl/term/Europese%20 Koninklijk Nederlands-Indisch Leger (KNIL) Koninklijk Nederlands Indisch Leger-soldaten/volledige-tekst/

Wasing, René & Wasing-Visser, Rita. (1992). *Adoeh Indië! Het beste van Hein Buitenweg*. Noordwijkerhout, Nederland: Atrium.

Watson, Lyall. (1991). *Gifts of unknown things: A true story of nature, healing, and initiation from Indonesia's "Dancing Island."* Rochester, VT: Destiny Books.

Wikipedia. "Indos in Colonial History." Retrieved April 23, 2019 from: https://en.wikipedia.org/wiki/Indos_in_colonial_history

Wikipedia. "Diponegoro." Retrieved March 20, 2019 from: https://en.wikipedia.org/wiki/Diponegoro

Wikipedia. "Dutch Empire." Retrieved March 13, 2019 from https://en.wikipedia.org/wiki/Dutch_Empire

Wikipedia. "Dutch Intervention in Bali (1849)." Retrieved March 13, 2019: https://en.wikipedia.org/wiki/Dutch_intervention_in_Bali_(1849)

Williams, Wim. (2001). De uittocht uit *Indië: De geschiedenis van Indische Nederlanders.* Amsterdam: Uitgeverij Bert Bakker.

Wils, Esther (composition), Timmer, Rugier (photographer), & Hoeks, Henk (essay). (2005). *Wonen in Indië: House and home in the Dutch East Indies.* (Paul Regeer & Janey Tucker, Trans.) Den Haag, Nederland: Stichting Tong Tong.

Worldometers. Retrieved April 2, 2019 from: http://www.worldometers.info/world-population/indonesia-population/

Images

p. 1
https://commons.wikimedia.org/wiki/File:The_shadow_puppet.JPG
PL 05 SIGIT, CC BY-SA 3.0 <https://creativecommons.org/licenses/by-sa/3.0>, via Wikimedia Commons

p. 29
https://commons.wikimedia.org/wiki/File:COLLECTIE_TROPENMUSE
UM_Wandschildering_%27La_r%C3%A9ception_de_Cornelis_de_Houtman
_a_Java_en_1595%27_door_Paulides_in_het_Nederlandse_paviljoen_op_de
_Koloniale_Wereldtentoonstelling_in_Parijs_TMnr_60011222.jpg

p. 33
https://commons.wikimedia.org/wiki/File:COLLECTIE_TROPENMUSE
UM_Een_Chinees_die_stof_ter_verkoop_aanbied_TMnr_3728-774.jpg

p. 34
Early Batavia, Copper plate printed on paper
https://commons.wikimedia.org/wiki/File:AMH-5643-
KB_View_of_the_Tijgersgracht_on_Batavia.jpg
Koninklijke Bibliotheek, Public domain, via Wikimedia Commons

p. 41
https://commons.wikimedia.org/wiki/File:COLLECTIE_TROPENMUSE
UM_De_stad_Batavia_TMnr_3728-537.jpg

p. 42
https://commons.wikimedia.org/wiki/File:Nicolaas_Pieneman_-
_The_Submission_of_Prince_Dipo_Negoro_to_General_De_Kock.jpg

p. 53
https://commons.wikimedia.org/wiki/File:Dewi_Sri_Java_Bronze.jpg
Gunawan Kartapranata, CC BY-SA 3.0
<https://creativecommons.org/licenses/by-sa/3.0>, via Wikimedia
Commons

p. 56

https://commons.wikimedia.org/wiki/File:COLLECTIE_TROPENMUSE
UM_Minangkabau_raadhuis_in_Matoer_TMnr_60043198.jpg

p. 57

https://commons.wikimedia.org/wiki/File:COLLECTIE_TROPENMUSE
UM_Huis_van_Europeanen_op_een_plantage_Nederlands-
Indi%C3%AB_TMnr_60022661.jpg

p. 59

https://commons.wikimedia.org/wiki/File:COLLECTIE_TROPENMUSE
UM_Galerij_van_het_huis_van_Europeanen_op_een_plantage_Nederlands-
Indi%C3%AB_TMnr_60022724.jpg

p. 62

COLLECTIE_TROPENMUSEUM_De_vrucht_de_bloemen_en_het_blad_
van_de_Durio_zibethinus_L._TMnr_3401-1688 (1).jpg

p. 66

https://commons.wikimedia.org/wiki/File:COLLECTIE_TROPENMUSE
UM_Een_eetstalletje_(warung)_met_o.a._bananen_in_Midden-
Java_TMnr_10002636.jpg

p. 72

https://commons.wikimedia.org/wiki/File:COLLECTIE_TROPENMUSE
UM_Het_huis_van_de_resident_in_Surabaya_TMnr_3728-839.jpg

p. 86

https://commons.wikimedia.org/wiki/File:Puputan_of_the_Raja_of_Boelele
ng.jpg

p. 89

https://commons.wikimedia.org/wiki/File:COLLECTIE_TROPENMUSE
UM_Een_paardenwisselstation_langs_de_Grote_Postweg_TMnr_60022693.j
pg

p. 95
https://commons.wikimedia.org/wiki/File:COLLECTIE_TROPENMUSE
UM_Het_met_watergieters_besproeien_van_de_weg_Nederlands-
Indi%C3%AB_TMnr_60040110.jpg

p. 96
https://commons.wikimedia.org/wiki/File:COLLECTIE_TROPENMUSE
UM_Aanlegplaats_voor_sloepen_bij_Fort_Speelwijk_Bantam_TMnr_100020
74.jpg

p. 102
https://commons.wikimedia.org/wiki/File:Tropenmuseum_Royal_Tropical_
Institute_Objectnumber_60006336_Portret_van_een_Javaanse_vrouw_met_
ee.jpg

p. 113
https://commons.wikimedia.org/wiki/File:COLLECTIE_TROPENMUSE
UM_Portret_van_de_familie_Ponse_met_visite_in_de_tuin_TMnr_60028997
.jpg

p. 133
https://commons.wikimedia.org/wiki/File:Mata_Hari_13.jpg

p. 149
https://commons.wikimedia.org/wiki/File:COLLECTIE_TROPENMUSE
UM_Een_dukun_tijdens_de_bereiding_van_zijn_geneesmiddelen_TMnr_600
27035.jpg

p. 159
https://commons.wikimedia.org/wiki/File:COLLECTIE_TROPENMUSE
UM_Bedoyo_danseressen_aan_het_hof_van_de_sultan_van_Yogyakarta_TM
nr_3728-444.jpg

p. 160
https://commons.wikimedia.org/wiki/File:COLLECTIE_TROPENMUSE
UM_Legong_danseressen_Saba_TMnr_60030392.jpg

p. 169
https://commons.wikimedia.org/wiki/File:COLLECTIE_TROPENMUSE
UM_Een_Europese_vrouw_in_sarong_en_kebaya_bekijkt_op_de_stoep_van
_haar_huis_te_Buitenzorg_de_vruchten_van_een_fruitverkoper_TMnr_1000
3029.jpg

p. 223
https://commons.wikimedia.org/wiki/File:Meersburg_old.jpg

Mike Chapman, Public domain, via Wikimedia Commons

P. 229
https://commons.wikimedia.org/wiki/File:Bali_0713a.jpg
Yves Picq http://veton.picq.fr, CC BY-SA 3.0
<https://creativecommons.org/licenses/by-sa/3.0>, via Wikimedia
Commons

p. 251
https://commons.wikimedia.org/wiki/File:COLLECTIE_TROPENMUSE
UM_De_Borobudur_TMnr_10015649.jpg

p. 252
https://commons.wikimedia.org/wiki/File:COLLECTIE_TROPENMUSE
UM_Beschilderen_van_wajangpoppen_TMnr_4925-2.jpg

p. 253
https://commons.wikimedia.org/wiki/File:VOC_duit.jpg

p. 256
https://commons.wikimedia.org/wiki/File:COLLECTIE_TROPENMUSE
UM_De_regent_van_Surabaya_Raden_Tumenggung_Musono_loopt_opweg
_naar_zijn_installatie_het_gouverneurserf_op_en_wordt_vergezeld_door_pat
ih_en_wedono%27s_in_gala-tenue_TMnr_10003356.jpg

Made in the USA
Las Vegas, NV
15 June 2022

50234824R10164